THE NU[...]

Section of homestead and kraal (Eastern Gaajok)

THE NUER

A DESCRIPTION OF
THE MODES OF LIVELIHOOD AND
POLITICAL INSTITUTIONS OF
A NILOTIC PEOPLE

BY

E. E. EVANS-PRITCHARD

M.A. (OXON.), PH.D. (LONDON)

RESEARCH LECTURER IN AFRICAN SOCIOLOGY AT THE
UNIVERSITY OF OXFORD
SOMETIME PROFESSOR OF SOCIOLOGY AT THE
EGYPTIAN UNIVERSITY, CAIRO

OXFORD UNIVERSITY PRESS

NEW YORK AND OXFORD

First published 1940
First American printing 1969
30 29 28 27 26 25 24
Printed in the United States of America

TO
THE STAFF OF THE
AMERICAN MISSION
AT NASSER

'Ah, the land of the rustling of wings, which is beyond the rivers of Ethiopia: that sendeth ambassadors by the sea, even in vessels of papyrus upon the waters, (saying) Go ye swift messengers, to a nation tall and smooth, to a people terrible from their beginning onward; a nation that meteth out and treadeth down, whose land the rivers divide.'

(*The Holy Bible* (Revised Version), Isaiah xviii. 1-2.)

PREFACE

MY study of the Nuer was undertaken at the request of, and was mainly financed by, the Government of the Anglo-Egyptian Sudan, which also contributed generously towards the publication of its results. Part of the inquiry was carried out as a Leverhulme Research Fellow. To the Sudan Government and to the Leverhulme Research Fellowships Committee I make grateful acknowledgements.

I owe Professor and Mrs. C. G. Seligman a great debt for their friendship during the last fifteen years. Without their backing and encouragement this book might not have been written. Moreover, although they made no investigations among the Nuer, their brilliant researches among other Nilotic peoples, particularly the Shilluk and Dinka, laid the foundations of all future studies in these regions.[1]

I thank all those in the Sudan, at Khartoum and in Nuerland, who have given me hospitality and assistance; Sir John Maffey, then Governor-General; Sir Harold MacMichael, then Civil Secretary; Mr. and Mrs. S. Hillelson; Mr. C. A. Willis, Mr. A. G. Pawson, Mr. M. W. Parr, and Mr. E. G. Coryton, who were in turn Governors of the Upper Nile Province; Mr. P. Coriat, Capt. A. H. A. Alban, Capt. H. A. Romilly, Mr. J. F. Tierney, the late Mr. L. F. Hamer, Mr. B. J. Chatterton, Mr. B. A. Lewis, and Mr. F. D. Corfield, all of whom were at one time Commissioners of Nuer Districts. To Mr. F. D. Corfield, *amico et condiscipulo meo*, I am especially grateful for the interest he has shown in my work and for his generosity in allowing me to use many of his fine photographs.

I thank also the staff of the American Mission at Nasser, of the Congregation of Verona at Yoahnyang, and of the Church Missionary Society at Ler. I wish to make particular acknowledgement to the staff of the American Mission, especially to Miss B. Soule, who unreservedly placed their home, their time, and their knowledge at my disposal. I dedicate this book to them not only as an expression of personal gratitude, but also as a tribute to their devoted service to the Nuer.

[1] *Pagan Tribes of the Nilotic Sudan*, by C. G. and B. Z. Seligman, 1932.

My warmest thanks are further rendered to the many Nuer who made me their guest and befriended me. Rather than speak of individuals, I express my general respect for this brave and gentle people.

The following friends and colleagues have read this book and have given me valuable criticism and advice: Professor C. G. Seligman, Professor A. R. Radcliffe-Brown, whose influence on the theoretical side of my work will be obvious to any student of anthropology, Dr. M. Fortes, and Dr. H. M. Gluckman. I owe a special debt to Dr. Fortes. My ideas about the aims and methods of Social Anthropology have been influenced by the many talks we have had on the subject during several years of comradeship and, since in such a relationship it is not easy to state what one has taken and given, I acknowledge unreservedly that I have been greatly stimulated by our discussions.

Professor Seligman has pointed out to me, in reading the proofs, that my use of 'horticulture' and 'horticultural' is unusual. I did not intend to depart from conventional usage. However, I did not feel justified in altering these words to 'agriculture' and 'agricultural' throughout the book in the present difficulties of publication. Readers who prefer 'agriculture' and 'agricultural' can make the substitution for themselves.

A considerable part of the facts related in this book have been previously recorded, chiefly in *Sudan Notes and Records* and *Africa*, and I thank the editors of these journals and the editor of *Custom is King* for permission to republish them. I am indebted also to the editors and printers of both journals, to George Routledge & Sons, Ltd., and to Messrs. Hutchinson & Co., for the use of photographic blocks.

Several friends have lent me photographs, sketch-maps, and diagrams. These are acknowledged in the list of plates and figures, but I desire to record expressly my gratitude to Mr. F. D. Corfield, Dr. H. E. Hurst, Director of the Physical Department of the Egyptian Government, Mr. B. A. Lewis, Mr. C. L. Armstrong, the staff of the American Mission, Nasser, the late Mr. L. F. Hamer, Dr. E. S. Crispin, and Yuzbashi Talib Ismail.

My thanks are due to Mr. W. R. Key for his many secretarial services in the preparation of this volume.

E. E. E.-P.

January 1940

CONTENTS

LIST OF PLATES

PLATES VII, VIII, XV, XXI, and XXVI are from blocks in *Sudan Notes and Records*; Plates XXV and XXVIII from C. G. and B. Z. Seligman, *Pagan Tribes of the Nilotic Sudan* (George Routledge & Sons, Ltd.); and Plate XXIII from *Custom is King* (Messrs. Hutchinson & Co.). Plate XVI is from a print supplied by the Physical Department of the Egyptian Government.

MAPS AND TEXT-FIGURES

Figs. 1, 5, 6, 7, 10, and 15 are from drawings of specimens which form part of the author's collection in the Pitt-Rivers Museum, Oxford, and Figs. 2, 3, 4, 11, 12, 13, and 14 are from drawings which form part of the author's collection in the University Museum of Archaeology and Ethnology, Cambridge.

THE NUER

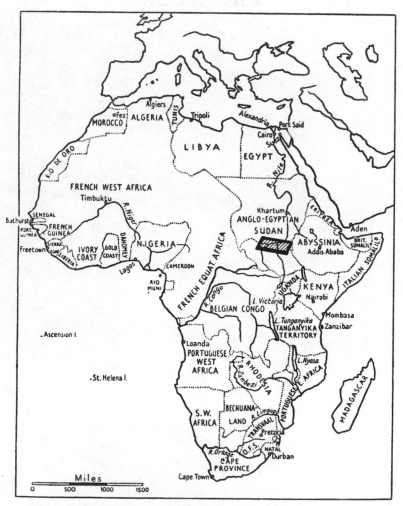

Map showing approximate area (*shaded*) occupied by the Nuer.

INTRODUCTORY

I

FROM 1840, when Werne, Arnaud, and Thibaut made their ill-assorted voyage, to 1881, when the successful revolt of the Mahdi Muhammad Ahmed closed the Sudan to further exploration, several travellers penetrated Nuerland by one or other of the three great rivers that traverse it: the Bahr el Jebel (with the Bahr el Zeraf), the Bahr el Ghazal, and the Sobat. I have not been able to make much use of their writings, however, for their contact with the Nuer was slight and the impressions they recorded were superficial, and sometimes spurious. The most accurate and the least pretentious account is by the Savoyard elephant-hunter Jules Poncet, who spent several years on the borders of Nuerland.[1]

A later source of information about the Nuer are the *Sudan Intelligence Reports* which run from the reconquest of the Sudan in 1899 to the present day, their ethnological value decreasing in recent years. In the first two decades after the reconquest there are a few reports by military officers which contain interesting, and often shrewd, observations.[2] The publication of *Sudan Notes and Records*, commencing in 1918, provided a new medium for recording observations on the customs of the peoples of the Anglo-Egyptian Sudan, and several political officers contributed papers on the Nuer. Two of these officers were killed in the performance of their duty, Major C. H. Stigand by the Aliab Dinka in 1919 and Captain V. H. Fergusson by the Nuong Nuer in 1927. In the same journal appeared the

---

[1] Some of the writings from which I have derived information are Ferdinand Werne, *Expedition zur Entdeckung der Quellen des Weissen Nil* (1840-1), 1848; Hadji-Abd-el-Hamid Bey (C. L. du Couret), *Voyage au Pays des Niam-Niams ou Hommes à Queue*, 1854; Brun-Rollet, *Le Nil Blanc et le Soudan*, 1855; G. Lejean, *Bulletin de la Société de Géographie*, Paris, 1860; Jules Poncet, *Le Fleuve Blanc (Extrait des Nouvelles Annales de Voyages*, 1863-4); Mr. and Mrs. J. Petherick, *Travels in Central Africa*, 1869; Ernst Marno, *Reisen im Gebiete des blauen und weissen Nil, im egyptischen Sudan und den angrenzenden Negerländern, in den Jahren 1869 bis 1873, 1874*. Others are mentioned later, particularly on pp. 126-7 and 134.

[2] These reports were used by Lieut.-Colonel Count Gleichen in his compilation: *The Anglo-Egyptian Sudan*, 2 vols., 1905.

first attempt, by Mr. H. C. Jackson, to write a comprehensive account of the Nuer, and great credit is due to him for the manner in which, in spite of serious obstacles, he carried it out.[1] After I had begun my researches a book by Miss Ray Huffman, of the American Mission, and some papers by Father J. P. Crazzolara, of the Congregation of Verona, were published.[2] Although my own contributions to various journals are reprinted, in a condensed form, in this book, or will be reprinted in a subsequent volume, I allude to them here so that the reader may have a complete bibliography. I have omitted much detail that appeared in these articles.[3] Lists of a few Nuer words were compiled by Brun-Rollet and Marno. More detailed vocabularies have been written by Major Stigand and Miss Huffman, and grammars by Professor Westermann and Father Crazzolara. Professor Westermann's paper contains also some ethnological material.[4]

---

[1] Major C. H. Stigand, 'Warrior Classes of the Nuers', *S. N. & R.*, 1918, pp. 116–18, and 'The Story of Kir and the White Spear', ibid., 1919, pp. 224–6; Capt. V. H. Fergusson, 'The Nuong Nuer', ibid., 1921, pp. 146–55, and 'Nuer Beast Tales', ibid., 1924, pp. 105–12; H. C. Jackson, 'The Nuer of the Upper Nile Province', ibid., 1923, pp. 59–107 and 123–89 (this paper was reprinted as a book under the same title by El Hadara Printing Press, Khartoum, no date, and contained a terminal essay of 23 pages by P. Coriat on 'The Gaweir Nuers').

[2] Ray Huffman, *Nuer Customs and Folk-lore*, 1931, 105 pp.; Father J. P. Crazzolara, 'Die Gar-Zeremonie bei den Nuer', *Africa*, 1932, pp. 28–39, and 'Die Bedeutung des Rindes bei den Nuer', ibid., 1934, pp. 300–20.

[3] E. E. Evans-Pritchard, 'The Nuer, Tribe and Clan', *S. N. & R.*, 1933, pp. 1–53, 1934, pp. 1–57, and 1935, pp. 37–87; 'The Nuer, Age-Sets', ibid., 1936, pp. 233–69; 'Economic Life of the Nuer', ibid., 1937, pp. 209–45, and 1938, pp. 31–77; 'Customs Relating to Twins among the Nilotic Nuer', *Uganda Journal*, 1936, pp. 230–8; 'Daily Life of the Nuer in Dry Season Camps', *Custom is King, A Collection of Essays in Honour of R. R. Marett*, 1936, pp. 291–9; 'Some Aspects of Marriage and the Family among the Nuer', *Zeitschrift für vergleichende Rechtswissenschaft*, 1938, pp. 306–92; 'Nuer Time-Reckoning', *Africa*, 1939, pp. 189–216. The chapter on the Nuer (Chap. VI) in *Pagan Tribes of the Nilotic Sudan*, by Prof. C. G. and Mrs. B. Z. Seligman, 1932, was compiled from my notebooks.

[4] Brun-Rollet, 'Vokabularien der Dinka-, Nuehr- und Schilluk-Sprachen', *Petermann's Mittheilungen, Erg. II.* 1862–3, pp. 25–30; Marno, 'Kleine Vocabularien der Fungi-, Tabi-, Bertat- und Nuehr-Sprache', *Reisen im Gebiete des blauen und weissen Nil*, 1874, pp. 481–95; Professor Diedrich Westermann, 'The Nuer Language', *Mitteilungen des Seminars für Orientalische Sprachen*, 1912, pp. 84–141; Major C. H. Stigand, *A Nuer-English Vocabulary*, 1923, 33 pp.; Ray Huffman, *Nuer-English Dictionary*, 1929, 63 pp., and *English-Nuer Dictionary*, 1931, 80 pp.; Father J. P. Crazzolara, *Outlines of a Nuer Grammar*, 1933, 218 pp.

II

I describe in this volume the ways in which a Nilotic people obtain their livelihood, and their political institutions. The information I collected about their domestic life will be published in a second volume.

The Nuer,[1] who call themselves Nath (sing. *ran*), are round about 200,000 souls and live in the swamps and open savannah that stretch on both sides of the Nile south of its junction with the Sobat and Bahr el Ghazal, and on both banks of these two tributaries. They are tall, long-limbed, and narrow-headed, as may be seen in the illustrations. Culturally they are similar to the Dinka, and the two peoples together form a subdivision of the Nilotic group, which occupies part of an East-African culture-area the characteristics and extent of which are at present ill-defined. A second Nilotic subdivision comprises the Shilluk and various peoples who speak languages similar to Shilluk (Luo, Anuak, Lango, &c.). Probably these Shilluk-speaking peoples are all more alike to one another than any one of them is to the Shilluk, though little is yet known about most of them. A tentative classification may be thus presented:

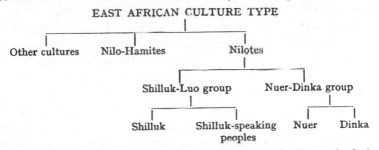

Nuer and Dinka are too much alike physically and their languages and customs are too similar for any doubt to arise about their common origin, though the history of their divergence is unknown. The problem is complicated: for example, the Atwot, to the west of the Nile, appear to be a Nuer tribe who have adopted many Dinka habits,[2] while the Jikany tribes of

[1] The word 'Nuer' is sanctioned by a century of usage. It is probably of Dinka origin. I use it in singular and plural, speaking of 'a Nuer man' and of 'the Nuer people'.

[2] Poncet, op. cit., p. 54. They appear as Atot in the map on p. 129.

Nuerland are said to be of Dinka origin. Moreover, there has been continuous contact between the two peoples that has resulted in much miscegenation and cultural borrowing. Both peoples recognize their common origin.

When we possess more information about some of the Shilluk-speaking peoples it will be possible to state what are the defining characters of Nilotic culture and social structure. At present such a classification is exceedingly difficult and I postpone the attempt, devoting this book to a plain account of the Nuer and neglecting the many obvious comparisons that might be made with other Nilotic peoples.

Political institutions are its main theme, but they cannot be understood without taking into account environment and modes of livelihood. I therefore devote the earlier part of the book to a description of the country in which the Nuer live and of how they obtain the necessities of life. It will be seen that the Nuer political system is consistent with their oecology.

The groups chiefly dealt with in the later part of the book are the people, the tribe and its segments, the clan and its lineages, and the age-sets. Each of these groups is, or forms part of, a segmentary system, by reference to which it is defined, and, consequently the status of its members, when acting as such towards one another and to outsiders, is undifferentiated. These statements will be elucidated in the course of our inquiry. We first describe the interrelation of territorial segments within a territorial, or political, system and then the relation of other social systems to this system. What we understand by political structure will be evident as we proceed, but we may state as an initial definition that we refer to relations within a territorial system between groups of persons who live in spatially well-defined areas and are conscious of their identity and exclusiveness. Only in the smallest of these communities are their members in constant contact with one another. We distinguish these political groups from local groups of a different kind, namely domestic groups, the family, the household, and the joint family, which are not, and do not form part of, segmentary systems, and in which the status of members in respect to each other and to outsiders is differentiated. Social ties in domestic groups are primarily of a kinship order, and corporate life is normal.

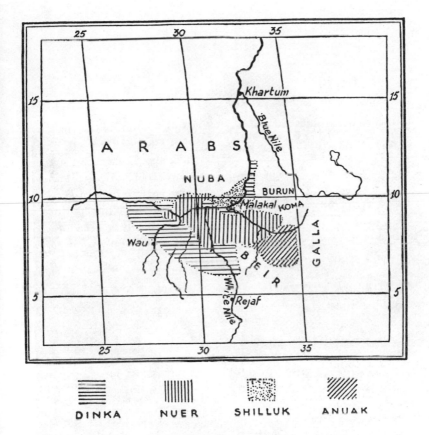

DINKA   NUER   SHILLUK   ANUAK

The Nuer and neighbouring peoples

PLATE I

Youth (Eastern Gaajok) fastening giraffe-hair necklace on friend

The Nuer political system includes all the peoples with whom they come into contact. By 'people' we mean all persons who speak the same language and have, in other respects, the same culture, and consider themselves to be distinct from like aggregates. The Nuer, the Shilluk, and the Anuak each occupy a continuous territory, but a people may be distributed in widely separate areas, e.g. the Dinka. When a people is, like the Shilluk, politically centralized, we may speak of a 'nation'. The Nuer and Dinka, on the other hand, are divided into a number of tribes which have no common organization or central administration and these peoples may be said to be, politically, a congeries of tribes, which sometimes form loose federations. The Nuer differentiate those tribes which live in the homeland to the west of the Nile from those which have migrated to the east of it. We find it convenient to make the same distinction and to speak of the Western Nuer and the Eastern Nuer. The Eastern Nuer may be further divided, for descriptive purposes, into those tribes which live near the Zeraf river and those which live to north and south of the Sobat river.

The largest political segment among the Nuer is the tribe. There is no larger group who, besides recognizing themselves as a distinct local community, affirm their obligation to combine in warfare against outsiders and acknowledge the rights of their members to compensation for injury. A tribe is divided into a number of territorial segments and these are more than mere geographical divisions, for the members of each consider themselves to be distinct communities and sometimes act as such. We call the largest tribal segments 'primary sections', the segments of a primary section 'secondary sections', and the segments of a secondary section 'tertiary sections'. A tertiary tribal section consists of a number of villages which are the smallest political units of Nuerland. A village is made up of domestic groups, occupying hamlets, homesteads, and huts.

We discuss the institution of the feud and the part played in it by the leopard-skin chief in relation to the political system. The word 'chief' may be a misleading designation, but it is sufficiently vague to be retained in the absence of a more suitable English word. He is a sacred person without political authority. Indeed, the Nuer have no government, and their state might be described as an ordered anarchy. Likewise they lack law, if we understand by this term judgements delivered by an independent and impartial authority which has, also, power to enforce its decisions. There are signs that certain changes were taking place in this respect, and at the end of the chapter on the political system we describe the emergence of prophets, persons in whom dwell the spirits of Sky-gods, and we suggest that in them we may perceive the beginnings of political development. Leopard-skin chiefs and prophets are the only ritual specialists who, in our opinion, have any political importance.

After an examination of the political structure we describe the lineage system and discuss the relation between the two. Nuer lineages are agnatic, i.e. they consist of persons who trace their descent exclusively through males to a common ancestor. The clan is the largest group of lineages which is definable by reference to rules of exogamy, though agnatic relationship is recognized between several clans. A clan is segmented into lineages, which are diverging branches of descent from a common ancestor. We call the largest segments into which a clan is divided its 'maximal lineages', the segments of a maximal lineage its 'major lineages', the segments of a major lineage its 'minor lineages', and the segments of a minor lineage its 'minimal lineages'. The minimal lineage is the one to which a man usually refers when asked what is his lineage. A lineage is thus a group of agnates, dead or alive, between whom kinship can be traced genealogically, and a clan is an exogamous system of lineages. These lineage groups differ from political groups in that the relationship of their members to one another is based on descent and not on residence, for lineages are dispersed and do not compose exclusive local communities, and, also, in that lineage values often operate in a different range of situations from political values.

After discussing the lineage system in its relation to territorial segmentation we describe briefly the age-set system. The adult male population falls into stratified groups based on age, and we call these groups 'age-sets'. The members of each set become such by initiation and they remain in it till death. The sets do not form a cycle, but a progressive system, the junior set passing through positions of relative seniority till it becomes the senior set, after which its members die and the set becomes a memory, since its name does not recur. The only significant age-grades are those of boyhood and manhood, so that once a lad has been initiated into a set he remains in the same age-grade for the rest of his life. There are no grades of warriors and elders such as are found in other parts of East Africa. Though the sets are conscious of their social identity they have no corporate functions. The members of a set may act jointly in a small locality, but the whole group never co-operates exclusively in any activity. Nevertheless, the system is organized tribally and each tribe is stratified according to age independently of other tribes, though adjacent tribes may co-ordinate their age-sets.

The Nuer, like all other peoples, are also socially differentiated according to sex. This dichotomy has a very limited, and negative, significance for the structural relations which form the subject of this book. Its importance is domestic rather than political and little attention is paid to it. The Nuer cannot be said to be stratified into classes. Within a tribe there is slight differentiation of status between members of a dominant clan, Nuer of other clans, and Dinka who have been incorporated into the tribe, but, except perhaps on the periphery of Nuer expansion eastwards, this constitutes distinction of categories rather than of ranks.

Such, briefly, is the plan of this book and such are the meanings we attach to the words most frequently used to describe the groups discussed in it. We hope in the course of our inquiry to refine these definitions. The inquiry is directed to two ends: to describe the life of the Nuer, and to lay bare some of the principles of their social structure. We have endeavoured to give as concise an account of their life as possible, believing that a short book is of greater value to the student and administrator than a long one, and, omitting much material, we have recorded only what is significant for the limited subject of discussion.

III

When the Government of the Anglo-Egyptian Sudan asked me to make a study of the Nuer I accepted after hesitation and with misgivings. I was anxious to complete my study of the

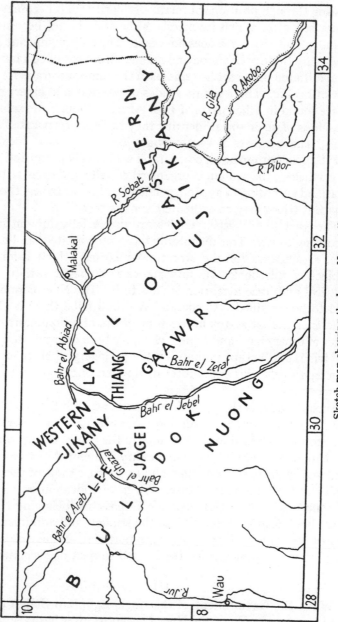

Sketch-map showing the larger Nuer tribes.

Azande before embarking on a new task. I also knew that a study of the Nuer would be extremely difficult. Their country and character are alike intractable and what little I had previously seen of them convinced me that I would fail to establish friendly relations with them.

I have always considered, and still consider, that an adequate sociological study of the Nuer was impossible in the circumstances in which most of my work was done. The reader must judge what I have accomplished. I would ask him not to judge too harshly, for if my account is sometimes scanty and uneven I would urge that the investigation was carried out in adverse circumstances; that Nuer social organization is simple and their culture bare; and that what I describe is almost entirely based on direct observation and is not augmented by copious notes taken down from regular informants, of whom, indeed, I had none. I, unlike most readers, know the Nuer, and must judge my work more severely than they, and I can say that if this book reveals many insufficiencies I am amazed that it has ever appeared at all. A man must judge his labours by the obstacles he has overcome and the hardships he has endured, and by these standards I am not ashamed of the results.

It may interest readers if I give them a short description of the conditions in which I pursued my studies, for they will then be better able to decide which statements are likely to be based on sound observation and which to be less well-grounded.

I arrived in Nuerland early in 1930. Stormy weather prevented my luggage from joining me at Marseilles, and owing to errors, for which I was not responsible, my food stores were not forwarded from Malakal and my Zande servants were not instructed to meet me. I proceeded to Nuerland (Leek country) with my tent, some equipment, and a few stores bought at Malakal, and two servants, an Atwot and a Bellanda, picked up hastily at the same place.

When I landed at Yoahnyang[1] on the Bahr el Ghazal the Catholic missionaries there showed me much kindness. I waited

---

[1] I take this early opportunity to inform readers that I have not spelt Nuer names and other words with phonetic consistency. I raise no objection, therefore, to any one spelling them differently. Generally I have given the nominative form, but an occasional genitive has crept into the text, diagrams, and maps.

for nine days on the river bank for the carriers I had been promised. By the tenth day only four of them had arrived and if it had not been for the assistance of an Arab merchant, who recruited some local women, I might have been delayed for an indefinite period.

On the following morning I set out for the neighbouring village of Pakur, where my carriers dropped tent and stores in the centre of a treeless plain, near some homesteads, and refused to bear them to the shade about half a mile further. Next day was devoted to erecting my tent and trying to persuade the Nuer, through my Atwot servant who spoke Nuer and some Arabic, to remove my abode to the vicinity of shade and water, which they refused to do. Fortunately a youth, Nhial, who has since been my constant companion in Nuerland, attached himself to me and after twelve days persuaded his kinsmen to carry my goods to the edge of the forest where they lived.

My servants, who, like most natives of the Southern Sudan, were terrified of the Nuer, had by this time become so scared that after several sleepless and apprehensive nights they bolted to the river to await the next steamer to Malakal, and I was left alone with Nhial. During this time the local Nuer would not lend a hand to assist me in anything and they only visited me to ask for tobacco, expressing displeasure when it was denied them. When I shot game to feed myself and my Zande servants, who had at last arrived, they took the animals and ate them in the bush, answering my remonstrances with the rejoinder that since the beasts had been killed on their land they had a right to them.

My main difficulty at this early stage was inability to converse freely with the Nuer. I had no interpreter. None of the Nuer spoke Arabic. There was no adequate grammar of the language and, apart from three short Nuer–English vocabularies, no dictionary. Consequently the whole of my first and a large part of my second expedition were taken up with trying to master the language sufficiently to make inquiries through it, and only those who have tried to learn a very difficult tongue without the aid of an interpreter and adequate literary guidance will fully appreciate the magnitude of the task.

After leaving Leek country I went with Nhial and my two

Zande servants to Lou country. We motored to Muot dit with the intention of residing by the side of its lake, but found it entirely deserted, for it was too early for the annual concentration there. When some Nuer were found they refused to divulge the whereabouts of nearby camps and it was with considerable difficulty that we located one. We pitched our tents there and when the campers retired on Muot dit we accompanied them. My days at Muot dit were happy and remunerative. I made friends with many Nuer youths who endeavoured to teach me their language and to show me that if I was a stranger they did not regard me as an obnoxious one. Every day I spent hours fishing with these lads in the lake and conversing with them in my tent. I began to feel my confidence returning and would have remained at Muot dit had the political situation been more favourable. A Government force surrounded our camp one morning at sunrise, searched for two prophets who had been leaders in a recent revolt, took hostages, and threatened to take many more if the prophets were not handed over. I felt that I was in an equivocal position, since such incidents might recur, and shortly afterwards returned to my home in Zandeland, having accomplished only three and a half months' work among the Nuer.

It would at any time have been difficult to do research among the Nuer, and at the period of my visit they were unusually hostile, for their recent defeat by Government forces and the measures taken to ensure their final submission had occasioned deep resentment. Nuer have often remarked to me, 'You raid us, yet you say we cannot raid the Dinka'; 'You overcame us with firearms and we had only spears. If we had had firearms we would have routed you'; and so forth. When I entered a cattle camp it was not only as a stranger but as an enemy, and they seldom tried to conceal their disgust at my presence, refusing to answer my greetings and even turning away when I addressed them.

At the end of my 1930 visit to Nuerland I had learnt a little of the language but had the scantiest notes of their customs. In the dry season of 1931 I returned to make a fresh attempt, going first for a fortnight to the American Mission at Nasser, where I was generously assisted by the American and Nuer staff, and then to cattle camps on the Nyanding river—an unfortunate choice, for the Nuer there were more hostile than those I had hitherto encountered and the conditions were harsher than any I had previously experienced. The water was scanty and foul, the cattle were dying of rinderpest, and the camps swarmed with flies. The Nuer would not carry my stores and equipment, and as I had only two donkeys, one of them lame, it was impossible to move. Eventually I managed to obtain a lorry and extricate myself, but not before experiencing the Nuer in his most paralysing mood. As every effort was made to prevent me from entering the cattle camps and it was seldom that I had visitors I was almost entirely cut off from communication with the people. My attempts to prosecute inquiries were persistently obstructed.

Nuer are expert at sabotaging an inquiry and until one has resided with them for some weeks they steadfastly stultify all efforts to elicit the simplest facts and to elucidate the most innocent practices. I have obtained in Zandeland more information in a few days than I obtained in Nuerland in as many weeks. After a while the people were prepared to visit me in my tent, to smoke my tobacco, and even to joke and make small talk, but they were unwilling either to receive me in their windscreens or to discuss serious matters. Questions about customs were blocked by a technique I can commend to natives who are inconvenienced by the curiosity of ethnologists. The following specimen of Nuer methods is the commencement of a conversation on the Nyanding river, on a subject which admits of some obscurity but, with willingness to co-operate, can soon be elucidated.

I: Who are you?
Cuol: A man.
I: What is your name?
Cuol: Do you want to know my *name*?
I: Yes.
Cuol: You want to know *my* name?
I: Yes, you have come to visit me in my tent and I would like to know who you are.
Cuol: All right. I am Cuol. What is your name?
I: My name is Pritchard.
Cuol: What is your father's name?

I: My father's name is also Pritchard.

Cuol: No, that cannot be true. You cannot have the same name as your father.

I: It is the name of my lineage. What is the name of your lineage?

Cuol: Do you want to know the name of my lineage?

I: Yes.

Cuol: What will you do with it if I tell you? Will you take it to your country?

I: I don't want to do anything with it. I just want to know it since I am living at your camp.

Cuol: Oh well, we are Lou.

I: I did not ask you the name of your tribe. I know that. I am asking you the name of your lineage.

Cuol: Why do you want to know the name of my lineage?

I: I don't want to know it.

Cuol: Then why do you ask me for it? Give me some tobacco.

I defy the most patient ethnologist to make headway against this kind of opposition. One is just driven crazy by it. Indeed, after a few weeks of associating solely with Nuer one displays, if the pun be allowed, the most evident symptoms of 'Nuerosis'.

From the Nyanding I moved, still without having made any real progress, to a cattle camp at Yakwac on the Sobat river where I pitched my tent a few yards from the windscreens. Here I remained, save for a short interval spent at the American Mission, for over three months—till the commencement of the rains. After the usual initial difficulties I at last began to feel myself a member of a community and to be accepted as such, especially when I had acquired a few cattle. When the campers at Yakwac returned to their inland village I had no means of accompanying them and intended to visit Leek country again. A severe attack of malaria sent me to Malakal hospital, and thence to England, instead. Five and a half months' work was accomplished on this second expedition.

During the tenure of a subsequent appointment in Egypt I published in *Sudan Notes and Records* essays which form the basis of this book, for I had not expected to have a further opportunity to visit the Nuer. However, in 1935 I was granted a two years' research fellowship by the Leverhulme trustees to make an intensive study of the Pagan Galla of Ethiopia. As delay was caused by diplomatic chicanery I spent two and a half

months on the Sudan–Ethiopian frontier making a survey of
the Eastern Anuak, and when, at last, I entered Ethiopia the im-
minence of Italian invasion compelled me to jettison my Galla
studies and enabled me to advance my investigation of the Nuer,
during a further seven weeks' residence in their country, by
revising earlier notes and by collecting more material. I visited
the Nuer who live on the Pibor river, renewed my acquaintance
with friends of the Nasser Mission and at Yakwac, and spent
about a month among the Eastern Jikany at the mouth of the
Nyanding.

In 1936, after making a survey of the Nilotic Luo of Kenya,
I spent a final seven weeks in Nuerland, visiting that part of it
which lies to the west of the Nile, especially the Karlual section
of the Leek tribe. My total residence among the Nuer was thus
about a year. I do not consider a year adequate time in which
to make a sociological study of a people, especially of a difficult
people in adverse circumstances, but serious sickness on both
the 1935 and 1936 expeditions closed investigations prematurely.

Besides physical discomfort at all times, suspicion and obstinate resistance encountered in the early stages of research,
absence of interpreter, lack of adequate grammar and dictionary,
and failure to procure the usual informants, there developed a
further difficulty as the inquiry proceeded. As I became more
friendly with the Nuer and more at home in their language they
visited me from early morning till late at night, and hardly a
moment of the day passed without men, women, or boys in my
tent. As soon as I began to discuss a custom with one man
another would interrupt the conversation in pursuance of some
affair of his own or by an exchange of pleasantries and jokes. The
men came at milking-time and some of them remained till midday. Then the girls, who had just finished dairy-work, arrived
and insisted on attention. Married women were less frequent
visitors, but boys were generally under the awning of my tent if
grown-ups were not present to drive them away. These endless
visits entailed constant badinage and interruption and, although
they offered opportunity for improving my knowledge of the
Nuer language, imposed a severe strain. Nevertheless, if one
chooses to reside in a Nuer camp one must submit to Nuer
custom, and they are persistent and tireless visitors. The chief

privation was the publicity to which all my actions were exposed, and it was long before I became hardened, though never entirely insensitive, to performing the most intimate operations before an audience or in full view of the camp.

Since my tent was always in the midst of homesteads or windscreens and my inquiries had to be conducted in public, I was seldom able to hold confidential conversations and never succeeded in training informants capable of dictating texts and giving detailed descriptions and commentaries. This failure was compensated for by the intimacy I was compelled to establish with the Nuer. As I could not use the easier and shorter method of working through regular informants I had to fall back on direct observation of, and participation in, the everyday life of the people. From the door of my tent I could see what was happening in camp or village and every moment was spent in Nuer company. Information was thus gathered in particles, each Nuer I met being used as a source of knowledge, and not, as it were, in chunks supplied by selected and trained informants. Because I had to live in such close contact with the Nuer I knew them more intimately than the Azande, about whom I am able to write a much more detailed account. Azande would not allow me to live as one of themselves; Nuer would not allow me to live otherwise. Among Azande I was compelled to live outside the community; among Nuer I was compelled to be a member of it. Azande treated me as a superior; Nuer as an equal.

I do not make far-reaching claims. I believe that I have understood the chief values of the Nuer and am able to present a true outline of their social structure, but I regard, and have designed, this volume as a contribution to the ethnology of a particular area rather than as a detailed sociological study, and I shall be content if it is accepted as such. There is much that I did not see or inquire into and therefore plenty of opportunity for others to make investigations in the same field and among neighbouring peoples. I hope they will do so and that one day we may have a fairly complete record of Nilotic social systems.

CHAPTER I

INTEREST IN CATTLE

I

A PEOPLE whose material culture is as simple as that of the Nuer are highly dependent on their environment. They are pre-eminently pastoral, though they grow more millet and maize than is commonly supposed. Some tribes cultivate more and some less, according to conditions of soil and surface water and their wealth in cattle, but all alike regard horticulture as toil forced on them by poverty of stock, for at heart they are herdsmen, and the only labour in which they delight is care of cattle. They not only depend on cattle for many of life's necessities but they have the herdsman's outlook on the world. Cattle are their dearest possession and they gladly risk their lives to defend their herds or to pillage those of their neighbours. Most of their social activities concern cattle and *cherchez la vache* is the best advice that can be given to those who desire to understand Nuer behaviour.[1]

The attitude of Nuer towards, and their relations with, neighbouring peoples are influenced by their love of cattle and their desire to acquire them. They have profound contempt for peoples with few or no cattle, like the Anuak, while their wars against Dinka tribes have been directed to seizure of cattle and control of pastures. Each Nuer tribe and tribal section has its own pastures and water-supplies, and political fission is closely related to distribution of these natural resources, ownership of which is generally expressed in terms of clans and lineages. Disputes between tribal sections are very often about cattle, and cattle are the compensation for loss of life and limb that is so frequently their outcome. Leopard-skin chiefs and prophets are arbiters in questions in which cattle are the issue, or ritual agents in situations demanding sacrifice of ox or ram. Another ritual specialist is the *wut ghok*, the Man of the Cattle. Likewise, in speaking of age-sets and age-grades we find ourselves des-

[1] Nuer interest in their cattle has been emphasized by early travellers in their country. *Vide* Marno, op. cit., p. 343; Werne, op. cit., p. 439; du Couret, op. cit., p. 82.

PLATE II

Girl in kraal (Eastern Gaajok)

PLATE III

Milking a restless cow (Lou)

cribing the relations of men to their cattle, for the change from boyhood to manhood is most clearly marked by a corresponding change in those relations at initiation.

Small local groups pasture their cattle in common and jointly defend their homes and herds. Their solidarity is most evident in the dry season when they live in a circle of windscreens around a common kraal, but it can also be seen in their wet season isolation. A single family or household cannot protect and herd their cattle alone and the cohesion of territorial groups must be considered in the light of this fact.

The network of kinship ties which links members of local communities is brought about by the operation of exogamous rules, often stated in terms of cattle. The union of marriage is brought about by payment of cattle and every phase of the ritual is marked by their transference or slaughter. The legal status of the partners and of their children is defined by cattle-rights and obligations.

Cattle are owned by families. While the head of the household is alive he has full rights of disposal over the herd, though his wives have rights of use in the cows and his sons own some of the oxen. As each son, in order of seniority, reaches the age of marriage he marries with cows from the herd. The next son will have to wait till the herd has reached its earlier strength before he can marry in his turn. When the head of the household dies the herd still remains the centre of family life and Nuer strongly deprecate breaking it up, at any rate till all the sons have married, for it is a common herd in which all have equal rights. When the sons are married they and their wives and children generally live in adjacent homesteads. In the early part of the dry season one sees a joint family of this kind living in a circle of windscreens around a common kraal, and in the big camps formed later in the year one finds them occupying a distinct section in the lines of windscreens. The bond of cattle between brothers is continued long after each has a home and children of his own, for when a daughter of any one of them is married the others receive a large portion of her bride-wealth. Her grandparents, maternal uncles, paternal and maternal aunts, and even more distant relatives, also receive a portion. Kinship is customarily defined by reference to these payments, being most clearly pointed at marriage, when movements of cattle from kraal to kraal are equivalent to lines on a genealogical chart. It is also emphasized by division of sacrificial meat among agnatic and cognatic relatives. The importance of cattle in Nuer life and thought is further exemplified in personal names. Men are frequently addressed by names that refer to the form and colour of their favourite oxen, and women take names from oxen and from the cows they milk. Even small boys call one another by ox-names when playing together in the pastures, a child usually taking his name from the bull-calf of the cow he and his mother milk. Often a man receives an ox-name or cow-name at birth. Sometimes the name of a man which is handed down to posterity is his ox-name and not his birth-name. Hence a Nuer genealogy may sound like an inventory of a kraal. The linguistic identification of a man with his favourite ox cannot fail to affect his attitude to the beast, and to Europeans the custom is the most striking evidence of the pastoral mentality of the Nuer.

Since cattle are a Nuer's most cherished possession, being an essential food-supply and the most important social asset, it is easy to understand why they play a foremost part in ritual. A man establishes contact with the ghosts and spirits through his cattle. If one is able to obtain the history of each cow in a kraal, one obtains at the same time not only an account of all the kinship links and affinities of the owners but also of all their mystical connexions. Cows are dedicated to the spirits of the lineages of the owner and of his wife and to any personal spirit that has at some time possessed either of them. Other beasts are dedicated to ghosts of the dead. By rubbing ashes along the back of a cow or ox one may get into touch with the spirit or ghost associated with it and ask it for assistance. Another way of communicating with the dead and with spirits is by sacrifice, and no Nuer ceremony is complete without the sacrifice of a ram, he-goat, or ox.

We have seen in a brief survey of some Nuer institutions and customs that most of their social behaviour directly concerns their cattle. A fuller study of their culture would show everywhere the same dominant interest in cattle, e.g. in their folklore. They are always talking about their beasts. I used sometimes to despair that I never discussed anything with the young men but live stock and girls, and even the subject of girls led inevitably to that of cattle. Start on whatever subject I would, and approach it from whatever angle, we would soon be speaking of cows and oxen, heifers and steers, rams and sheep, he-goats and she-goats, calves and lambs and kids. I have already indicated that this obsession—for such it seems to an outsider—is due not only to the great economic value of cattle but also to the fact that they are links in numerous social relationships. Nuer tend to define all social processes and relationships in terms of cattle. Their social idiom is a bovine idiom.

Consequently he who lives among Nuer and wishes to understand their social life must first master a vocabulary referring to cattle and to the life of the herds. Such complicated discussions as those which take place in negotiations of marriage, in ritual situations, and in legal disputes can only be followed when one understands the difficult cattle-terminology of colours, ages, sexes, and so forth.

Important though horticultural and piscatorial pursuits are in Nuer economy, pastoral pursuits take precedence because cattle not only have nutritive utility but have a general social value in other respects. I have mentioned a few situations in which this value is manifested, but have not recorded every role of cattle in Nuer culture, for they are significant in many social processes, including some I have mentioned, which lie outside the limited scope of this book. It seemed necessary to give an introductory sketch on these lines in order that the reader might understand that Nuer devotion to the herdsman's art is inspired by a range of interests far wider than simple need for food, and why cattle are a dominant value in their lives. We shall ask later how this value is related to environmental conditions and how far the two, taken together, help us to explain some characteristics of Nuer political structure.

II

Before the present century Nuer were far richer in cattle than they are now and it is probable that they cultivated less millet. Their stock has been impaired by repeated outbreaks of rinderpest, which still decimate the herds. It was probably more destructive in the past than now, though the attacks I witnessed were severe; but in the past the warlike Nuer could always restore their losses by raiding Dinka. All Nuer agree that in the last generation their herds were more considerable and that the payments of bride-wealth and blood-wealth were forty, and sometimes fifty to sixty, head of cattle, whereas to-day the kinsmen of a bride do not expect to receive more than twenty to thirty. At the present time I would say, on a general impression, that the Nuer are far richer in stock than the Shilluk, but not so prosperous as the more favoured of the Dinka tribes.

It was difficult to make a census of cattle, even in a small area, and Nuer would certainly have regarded such an attempt with repugnance. On the few estimates made I would reckon an average of ten head of cattle and five goats and sheep to the byre. A byre of the ordinary size cannot hold more than a dozen or so adult kine. As there are some eight persons to a byre the cattle probably do not greatly exceed the human population. Cows predominate and probably compose about two-thirds of the herds. Many plates in this book show the appearance of Nuer cattle. Nuer say that a very large hump shows Beir origin and that very long horns are evidence of Dinka stock.

Some tribes are richer in cattle than others. Lou country is considered especially suitable for raising stock and is renowned for its large herds. The Eastern Jikany were once very rich in cattle, but their herds are still recovering from losses in epidemics that forced the people to cultivate more extensively. Cattle are everywhere evenly distributed. Hardly any one is entirely without them, and no one is very rich. Although cattle are a form of wealth that can be accumulated, a man never possesses many more beasts than his byre will hold, because as soon as his herd is large enough he, or one of his family, marries. The herd is thereby reduced to two or three beasts and the next few years are spent in repairing its losses. Every household goes through these alternating periods of poverty and comparative wealth. Marriages and epidemics prevent accumulation of cattle and no disparity in wealth offends the democratic sentiment of the people.

When we come to examine the Nuer political system we shall keep in mind that till recent years they have probably been more exclusively pastoral, and more nomadic, than at the present time, and that the dwindling of their herds may partly explain their persistent aggressiveness.

III

Although cattle have many uses they are chiefly useful for the milk they provide. Milk and millet (sorghum) are the staple foods of the Nuer. In some parts of their country, especially among the Lou, the millet supply seldom lasts the whole year, and when it is exhausted people are dependent on milk and fish. At such times a family may be sustained by the milk of a single cow. In all parts the millet crop is uncertain and more or less severe famines are frequent, during which people rely on fish, wild roots, fruits, and seeds, but mainly on the milk of their herds. Even when millet is plentiful it is seldom eaten alone, for without milk, whey, or liquid cheese, Nuer find it stodgy, unpalatable, and, especially for children, indigestible. They regard milk as essential for children, believing that they cannot be well and happy without it, and the needs of children are always the first to be satisfied even if, as happens in times of privation, their elders have to deny themselves. In Nuer eyes the happiest state is that in which a family possesses several lactating cows, for then the children are well-nourished and there is a surplus that can be devoted to cheese-making and to assisting kinsmen and entertaining guests. A household can generally obtain milk for its little children because a kinsman will lend them a lactating cow, or give them part of its milk, if they do not possess one. This kinship obligation is acknowledged by all and is generously fulfilled, because it is recognized that the needs of children are the concern of neighbours and relatives, and not of the parents alone. Occasionally, however, after an epidemic or, to a lesser degree, after two or three youths of the group have married, an entire hamlet, or even a whole village may experience scarcity. Sometimes, also, shortage is caused by a tendency for the cows of a village to cease lactating at about the same time.

Nuer value their cows according to the amount of milk they give and they know the merits of each in this respect. The calves of a good milch cow are more highly prized than the calves of a cow that gives little milk. A cow is never to them just a cow, but is always a good cow or a bad cow, and a Nuer who is owed a cow will not accept in payment of his debt one that does not meet with his approval. If you ask a Nuer in a cattle camp which are the best and worst cows in the herd he can tell you at once. In judging their points he pays little attention to those aesthetic qualities which please him in an ox, especially fatness, colour, and shape of horns, but he selects those which indicate a good milch cow: a broad loose back, prominent haunch bones, large milk-veins, and a much-wrinkled milk-bag. In judging the age of a cow he notes the depth of the trenches which run on either side of its rump towards the tail, the number and sharpness of its teeth, the firmness of its gait, and the number of rings on its horns. Nuer cows have the familiar angular and thin-fleshed characteristics of dairy stock.

Milking is performed twice daily by women, girls, and uninitiated boys. Men are forbidden to milk cows unless, as on journeys or war expeditions, there are no women or boys present. The milker squats by the cow and milks a single teat at a time into the narrow mouth of a bottle-necked gourd balanced on her thighs (see Plates III and V). She milks with thumb and first finger but, the other fingers being closed, the teat is to some extent pressed against the whole hand. It is both a squeezing and a pulling motion. The gourd is kept in position by the downward stroke of the hands which press it against the thighs. When a pot, or a gourd with a wider mouth, is used it is held between the knees and the milker squeezes two teats at a time. Occasionally one sees two girls milking a cow, one at either side. If a cow is restless a man may hold it still by putting his hand in its mouth and gripping its muzzle, and if it kicks, a noose is placed round its hind legs and they are pulled together (see Plate III). I was told that sometimes they ring the nose of a cow that is habitually restless during milking.

The process of milking is as follows. The calf is loosened and with its tethering-cord round its neck runs at once to its dam and begins violently butting her udder. This starts the flow of milk, and Nuer hold that if the calf were not first to suck the cow would hold up its milk. They do not pat the udder with the hand unless the calf is dead, for this is considered bad for the cow. When the calf has sucked a little it is dragged away, resisting stubbornly, and tethered to its dam's peg, where it rubs against her forelegs and she licks it. The girl now milks the first milking, known as the *wic*. When the teats become soft and empty the calf is again loosened and the process is repeated. The second milking is called *tip indit*, the greater *tip*. As a rule there are only two milkings, but if it is a very good milch cow at the height of her lactation period the calf may once more be loosened and a third milking, called *tip intot*, the lesser *tip*, be taken. When the girl has finished milking she wipes her thighs and the milk-gourd with the cow's tail and loosens the calf to finish off what milk is left. The first milking takes longer time and produces more milk than the second, and the second more than the third. The morning yield is greater than the evening yield.

A series of measurements suggest that four to five pints a day may be regarded as a general average for Nuer cows during their lactation period, which lasts, on an average, about seven months. It must be remembered, however, that this is an estimate of the yield for human consumption. The calf gets its share before, during, and after the milking. It is possible, moreover, that, as Nuer declare, some cows hold up their milk for their calves, since the calves often suck for several minutes after milking before their dams refuse them by kicking them or moving so that they cannot reach their udders. Sometimes a small boy drags the calf away and milks the udders himself, licking the milk off his hands, or shares the teats with the calf, but as a rule the calf gets the remainder of the milk. The total yield may, therefore, be as high as seven to nine pints a day and it appears to be far richer than milk given by English cows. It is not surprising that the yield is small, because Nuer cows receive no artificial feeding, succulent pasturage is often difficult to obtain, and they have to endure great hardship. It must, moreover, be emphasized that whereas English dairy farmers require only milk, Nuer herdsmen require milk and also wish to preserve every calf. Human needs have to be subordinated to the needs of the calves, which are the first consideration if the herd is to be perpetuated.

Milk is consumed in various ways. Fresh milk is drunk, especially by children, and is also consumed with millet-porridge. Fresh milk is chiefly drunk by adults in the heat of the dry season when a refreshing draught is most appreciated and food is scarce. Some milk is put aside, where it soon, very rapidly in hot weather, sours and thickens, in which condition it is relished. Nuer like to have a gourd of sour milk always at hand in case visitors come. Part of the daily yield is kept for making cheese, and if there are several cows in lactation one may be reserved for this purpose. Milk for churning is drawn into a different gourd to that used for drinking milk. It is then transferred to a churning gourd (see Fig. 1), in which it stands for several hours, and as churning gourds are not cleaned, unless they smell bad, the acids which remain from the previous churning curdle the milk. After standing it is churned

FIG. 1. Churning gourd.

by a woman, or girl, who sits on the ground with her legs stretched in front of her, and, raising the gourd, brings it down with a jerk on her thighs where she rocks it a few times before repeating her actions: a simple but lengthy way of churning. A small quantity of water is poured into the gourd when the curds are beginning to form to make them set well and to increase the quantity of whey, and some ox's urine may be added to give them consistency. When they have formed, the woman pours the milk into a cup-shaped gourd and scoops them out with a mussel shell into another gourd vessel which is hung up in a hut. The whey, mixed with fresh milk, is mainly drunk by women and boys. Every day they add to the supply of curds and now and again stir some ox's urine with them to prevent them from going bad. They may add to the supply for several weeks before the final boiling over a quick fire, which turns the curds, *lieth in bor*, into solid deep yellow cheese, *lieth in car*. After boiling for a time the liquid is poured into a gourd and the oil on top is removed, to be used as a flavouring for porridge. The cheese is suspended in a net from the roof of a hut in a round gourd, a piece of the shell of which has been cut out so that cords run through it and it acts as a sliding lid (see Fig. 2), and, if air is excluded by a coating of cattle dung, it will keep in good condition for months. Milk may thus be stored in the form of cheese. It is eaten with porridge and is also used for anointing the body.

Sheep and goats are also milked in the mornings, but little importance is attached to their yield, which is drunk by small children and not used for dairy work. The woman milks and the kids and lambs finish what is left in the udders. As they run with their dams at pasture an evening milking is not taken ; but during the day hungry herdboys often squeeze the udders and lick the milk off their hands.

Some points that arise from an account of milking and dairy-work deserve emphasis. (1) The present number and distribution of cattle do not permit the Nuer to lead an entirely pastoral life as they would like to do, and possibly did at one time. On a generous estimate the average daily yield to the byre is probably no more than twelve pints, or one and a half pints per person. A mixed economy is, therefore, necessary. (2) Furthermore the fluctuation in household resources, due to epidemics and transmission of bride-wealth, is further accentuated by the organic character of the staple diet, for cows only produce milk for a certain period after calving and the yield is not constant. It follows that a single family is not a self-sufficient unit, as far as milk is concerned, for it cannot always ensure an adequate supply. Therefore, since milk is considered essential, the economic unit must be larger than the simple family group. (3) Environmental conditions, as well as need for cereal food to supplement their milk diet, prevent Nuer from being entirely nomadic, but milk food enables them to lead a roving life for part of the year and gives them mobility and elusiveness, as their history shows and as has been recently demonstrated in the Government campaign against them. Milk requires neither storage nor transport, being daily renewed, but, on the other hand, involves a straight dependence on water and vegetation which not only permits, but compels, a wandering life. Such a life nurtures the qualities of the shepherd—courage, love of fighting, and contempt of hunger and hardship—rather than shapes the industrious character of the peasant.

IV

Nuer are also interested in their cattle for meat, boiled and roasted. They do not raise herds for slaughter, but sheep and oxen are frequently sacrificed at ceremonies. There are always ghosts and spirits in whose honour a sacrifice would at any time be appropriate, and such sacrifices are generally long overdue, so that there does not lack a proper excuse for a feast when people desire one. Fertile cows are sacrificed in mortuary rites, but, otherwise, only barren females are killed. At sacrifices most people are interested more in the festal than the religious character of the rites. Sometimes, as at marriage ceremonies, the people who perform the ritual are different from those who eat the meat, while at other ceremonies there is a general scramble for the carcass. Desire for meat is shown without shame on these occasions, and Nuer recognize that some men sacrifice without due cause. In some years it is a custom in the rains for young men to join together at a homestead with the purpose of slaughtering oxen and gorging themselves with meat. Except on such occasions, however, people ought not to kill an ox solely for food—it being even thought that the ox may curse them—and they only do so in severe famine. The Lou, who are rich in cattle, have a reputation, of which they are rather ashamed, for killing oxen for meat. Nevertheless, nowhere in Nuerland are cattle ordinarily slaughtered for food, and a man would never kill even a sheep or goat merely on the grounds that he desired meat. On occasions of minor importance sheep or goats are sacrificed rather than oxen, as they are less valuable.

Any animal which dies a natural death is eaten. Even when a youth's favourite ox dies he must be persuaded to partake of its flesh, and it is said that were he to refuse his spear might avenge the insult by cutting his foot or hand on some future occasion. Nuer are very fond of meat, and declare that on the death of a cow, 'The eyes and the heart are sad, but the teeth and the stomach are glad.' 'A man's stomach prays to God, independently of his mind, for such gifts.'

Though oxen are sacrificed and eaten they are not valued only for these purposes, but also for display and for the prestige their possession confers. Colour and shape of horns are significant, but the essential qualities are bigness and fatness, it being considered especially important that the haunch bones should not be apparent. Nuer admire a large hump which wobbles when the animal walks, and to exaggerate this character they often manipulate the hump shortly after birth.

Like other pastoral peoples in East Africa the Nuer extract blood from the necks of their cattle, and this is a supplementary article of diet in dry season camps, where one may generally see at least one cow bled each evening. Cows are bled for culinary purposes more frequently than oxen. The operation, called *bar*, consists of tying a cord tightly round a cow's neck so that the veins stand out and one of them can be stabbed, on the head side of the cord, with a small knife bound with cord or grass to prevent it entering too deeply. The blood spurts out, and when a large gourd has been filled they loosen the cord and it ceases to flow. Some dung is smeared over the wound. If one examines the neck of a cow one sees

FIG. 2. Gourd for storing cheese.

a row of small cicatrices. Cows appear to be a little giddy after the operation and may totter slightly, but otherwise seem none the worse for their experience. Indeed, it may well be, as Nuer assert, that they are the better for it, for they lead a sluggish life. The blood is boiled by women till it is fairly consistent and can be used as a meat flavouring with porridge; or the men let it stand till it coagulates into a solid block, and, after roasting it in the embers of a fire, cut it up and eat it.

Nuer do not regard the blood of cows as a staple article of diet and it does not play an important part in their cuisine. Indeed, they say that they do not perform the operation to acquire food, though they confess that roasted blood is delicious, but for the benefit of the cows. Bleeding is designed to cure a cow of any unfitness by letting out the bad blood of the sickness. Also, Nuer say, it makes the cow fat, for next day it will be more lively and graze avidly. Bleeding, moreover, in their opinion, decreases the desire of a cow to be served. Nuer say that if a cow is served too frequently it may eventually become barren, whereas, if it is bled now and again, it will only require to be served once and will be in calf. Cattle are sometimes bled for medical reasons in the rainy season, when people may be so replete that the blood is given to the boys of the kraal and to the dogs. Sometimes they make incisions in the noses of calves and let the blood flow to the ground in order to make them fat. I have seen Nuer scarify their own legs and the small of their backs to induce fleetness and strength.

The following two points seem to us to be significant. (1) Whilst Nuer normally do not kill their stock for food, the end of every beast is, in fact, the pot, so that they obtain sufficient meat to satisfy their craving and have no pressing need to hunt wild animals, an activity in which they engage little. (2) Except when epidemics are rife the usual occasions of eating meat are ritual and it is the festal character of rites which gives them much of their significance in the life of the people.

V

Apart from milk, meat, and blood, cattle furnish Nuer with numerous household necessities, and when we consider how few are their possessions we can appreciate the importance of cattle as raw material. The bodies and bodily products of cattle have the following uses:

Their skins are used for beds, trays, for carrying fuel (Plate XVII), cord for tethering and other purposes, flails (Fig. 15), leather collars for oxen (Fig. 4), and for the tympana of drums. They are employed in the manufacture of pipes, spears, shields,

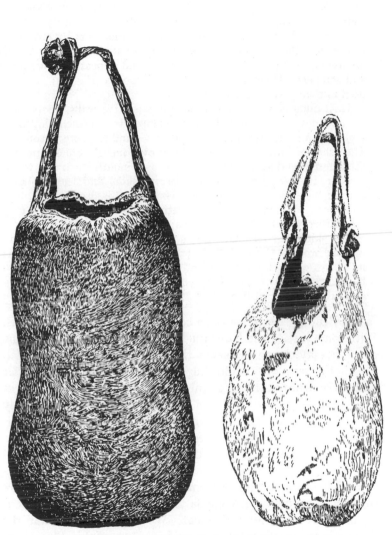

FIG. 3. Bags made from the scrota of a bull and a giraffe.

snuff-containers, &c. The scrota of bulls are made into bags to contain tobacco, spoons, and other small objects (Fig. 3). Tail-hairs are made into tassels used as dance ornaments by girls and to decorate the horns of favourite oxen (Plate IV). Their bones are used for the manufacture of armlets, and as beaters, pounders, and scrapers. Their horns are cut into spoons (Fig. 14) and are used in the construction of harpoons.

Their dung is used for fuel and for plastering walls, floors, and the outsides of straw huts in cattle camps. It is also employed as a plaster in minor technological processes and to protect wounds. The ashes of burnt dung are rubbed over mens' bodies, and are used to dye and straighten the hair, as a mouth wash and tooth powder, in the preparation of sleeping-skins and leather bags, and for various ritual purposes. Their urine is used in churning and cheese-making, in the preparation of gourd-utensils, for tan-ing leather, and for bathing face and hands.

The skins of sheep and goats are worn as loin garments by married women (Plate XXIII (a)), used as rugs to sit on, made into bags for storing tobacco and millet, and are cut into strips to be tied round their ankles by youths when dancing. Their dung and urine are not utilized.

The Bedouin Arab has been called the parasite of the camel. With some justice the Nuer might be called the parasite of the cow. It may, however, seem that the list we have compiled does not cover a very wide range of uses, but so simple is Nuer material culture that it accounts for a very considerable part of their technology and contains items on which they are highly dependent, e.g. the use of dung as fuel in a country where it is difficult to obtain sufficient vegetable fuel for cooking, let alone for the large fires that burn day and night in every byre and windscreen.

We have seen that apart from their many social uses Nuer are directly concerned with cattle as producers of two essential articles of diet, milk and meat. We now perceive that the economic value of cattle is more extensive. Taking into con-sideration also the more general social value of cattle, briefly indicated in Section I, we may already note that there is over-emphasis on a single object, which dominates all other interests and is consistent with those qualities of simplicity, single-mindedness, and conservatism, so characteristic of pastoral peoples.

PLATE IV

Ox with tassels hanging from its horns (Lou)

PLATE V

Girl milking (Lou)

VI

In later chapters we shall describe how the needs of cattle, water, pasturage, protection from carnivorous beasts and biting insects, and so forth, are attended to, and show in what manner they determine human routine and affect social relations. Leaving these broader issues on one side, we ask here whether the Nuer, who are so reliant on their cattle and who value them so highly, are competent herdsmen. It is unnecessary to state that they give their beasts every attention that their knowledge allows, but it is pertinent to inquire whether their knowledge suffices. It was especially noted where Nuer practice is not in accord with the conventions of farming, and the reasons for the divergence were investigated. A few of the more evident difficulties and some general observations on Nuer husbandry are recorded below.

1. Since the cows are not brought back to the kraals at midday the smaller calves must go without nourishment for many hours each day. However, Capt. H. B. Williams, Director of the Sudan Veterinary Department, tells me that Nuer oxen have the reputation of being as good as any in the Sudan, so that their development as young calves cannot be seriously arrested. In the rains the cows are seldom milked before 9 to 10 a.m. and again at about 5 p.m., but in the dry season they may be taken to pasture as early as 8 a.m. and not return till about 5.30 p.m., so that they cannot suckle their calves for about ten hours. However, this long interval is not easily avoided, for in the dry season the grazing grounds are often distant and owing to lack of good pasturage the cattle require longer to feed than in the rains. In the rains it would be a simple matter to pasture the herd at daybreak and bring it home at midday, as many East African peoples do, for the cows to suckle their calves and chew the cud. But Nuer say that when the cattle come out of their hot smoky byres they like to rest a while in the kraal before going to pasture, and their lethargy, which contrasts with their eagerness to graze after a night in the open in dry season camps, seems to justify this statement. Nuer realize that the heat and smoke of byres are bad for the cattle, but they consider mosquitoes worse.

FIG. 4. Ox-bell and collar.

Also by waiting till the dew has evaporated they consider they lessen the risk of digestive troubles, for in the rains the ground is cold and damp till a late hour. A further reason for keeping the cattle late in the kraals is that if they are loosened early they soon graze to repletion and begin to wander in all directions, since they are not usually herded in the rains.

2. It at once strikes a European that the condition of drinking water at periods of the dry season leaves much to be desired, especially if he has to drink it himself. Sometimes the pools have almost dried up and contain foul, even slimy, water which men and cattle drink. I have wondered why they do not move sooner from these small pools, such as that shown on Plate XXI (b), around which they camp in the early drought, to the rivers and lakes where they make their final concentrations, but I do not distrust their judgement, for they are fully aware that dirty water is neither palatable to, nor good for, the cattle, and when circumstances permit they are at pains to ensure that they are supplied with clean water as often as they require it. In moving camp they have to take into account a number of desiderata : pasturage, fishing, the harvest of *Balanites aegyptiaca*, the second millet harvest, &c., besides conditions of water.

3. Unlike some East African peoples Nuer do not keep too many entire animals. If they err at all it is in keeping too few. On the limited observations made it was estimated that there is one adult bull to about thirty or forty adult cows. Nuer try to select as stud bulls the calves of their best milch cows so that they may breed good milch cows from them. They say that if they did not castrate most of the bull calves the cows would get no peace and there would be constant fighting in the kraals and commotion in the byres. A calf is not castrated till it is about eighteen months to two years old: 'When its dam has had another calf and a third is in its womb.' It is thrown, the scrotum is cut with a spear, and the testicles drawn out and severed. There is little loss of blood and the animal soon recovers. A calf may be castrated for sacrificial purposes at any time, but otherwise Nuer prefer to perform the operation in the dry season for there is less chance of inflammation than in the rains. Bulls are not discouraged from fighting unless they belong to the same herd, and fights are often cited in

tradition as the cause of fission and migration of lineages. A very large number of steers and oxen are slaughtered in sacrifices.

4. Heifers are not served till their third year. Nuer know when a cow is on heat by its behaviour in the kraal: it is restless, lows, swishes its tail, sniffs at the vulvas of other cows, and tries to mount them. If a cow has mated in the grazing grounds —for bulls run with the herd—the first signs of pregnancy are said to be vulvar changes. If you ask Nuer when a cow which has been served at a certain time will calve they can at once, and accurately, tell you. They say that if a cow has had no serious illness it will bear about eight calves.

In my experience there is very slight mortality among calves. Nuer give them every attention. When a cow is seen to be about to calve for the first time its owner sits up with it all night, or accompanies it to pasture, to assist delivery. An experienced cow is left to drop its calf itself, but a man is usually present to assist if it is in trouble. He must be present if it calves in the bush, because the calf is too weak to follow its dam, which will stay with it, and they may become separated from the herd and fall a prey to wild beasts. If a calf dies in the womb Nuer try to remove it, and when it is necessary to turn it in the womb they perform this operation. If the afterbirth does not fall, or if the cow does not lick its calf, they administer medicines. When a calf dies they resort to various devices to persuade its dam to give milk. They stuff the head with straw (see Fig. 5), and rub some of the dam's urine on it ; or, especially when a cow aborts, they stuff the whole calf, insert stumps of wood to act as legs, and place it in front of its dam and push its head against her teats, while they gently squeeze and pull them and a boy blows up the vagina.

FIG. 5. Stuffed calf's head.

Nuer say that if a calf is only a day or two old and its dam dies it will also die, but once it knows the *cak tin bor*, 'the white milk' which follows the colostrum, it can be saved. It is fed by hand from a small gourd with a funnel mouth and efforts are made to get another cow in lactation to suckle it. Since Nuer believe, erroneously it seems, that it is dangerous for a calf to drink the discoloured milk at the top of the colostrum, they milk this off before allowing the calf to suck, and if by inadvertence it sucks first they administer a purgative. They regard it as more serious if there is any blood in the milk.

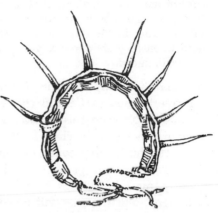

FIG. 6. Calf's weaning ring.

For the first three or four days a calf sucks all its dam's milk except the part drawn off. Then close kinsmen, who live near by, are summoned to eat porridge over which is poured the first milk taken for human consumption. At this ceremony the end hairs of the calf's tail are cut off and its owner spits on them and waves them over the back of the dam, for otherwise the calf will sicken because it resents people stealing its milk. Afterwards, however, they can still say, 'We do not yet share with its calf', for they take very little milk for the first fortnight in order to give it a chance to get strong and for its teeth to harden. When the calf is stronger they take more milk and they then say that the calf shares (*buth*) the milk with men. It continues to suck till its dam is again in calf and refuses it. Weaning devices are not as a rule employed, but if the dam suckles when it is pregnant and it is found impracticable to keep it apart from its calf in the pastures they place a ring of thorns round the calf's muzzle (Fig. 6), which allows it to graze but prevents it from sucking, for the thorns prick the dam's udder and she kicks it aside. It will be seen from this account how Nuer solve the herdsman's problem of making cows provide for their masters without depriving their calves of essential nourishment.

Small calves, after the adult herd has gone to the grazing grounds, are housed till the late afternoon in byres in wet-season villages, and tethered in the shade of a tree in dry-season camps.

They are watered during the afternoon, and boys bring them grasses, especially *poon* (*Oryza Barthii*), which is very fattening. They begin to go to pasture with the older calves, under the care of herdboys, in about their third month and are kept apart from their dams by being driven in the opposite direction to that taken earlier in the day by the adult herd. They run with the herd when they are about a year old, by which time their dams are again in calf.

We shall have opportunities for noting further the attention Nuer give to their cattle and the wisdom of their methods. I have merely given in this section a few examples to illustrate a general conclusion reached in the course of my study: that Nuer cattle husbandry could not in any important particular be improved in their present oecological relations; that, consequently, more knowledge than they possess would in no way assist them; and that, as will be shown, were it not for their unceasing vigilance and care the cattle would not survive the harsh conditions of their environment.

VII

It has been remarked that the Nuer might be called parasites of the cow, but it might be said with equal force that the cow is a parasite of the Nuer, whose lives are spent in ensuring its welfare. They build byres, kindle fires, and clean kraals for its comfort; move from villages to camps, from camp to camp, and from camps back to villages, for its health; defy wild beasts for its protection; and fashion ornaments for its adornment. It lives its gentle, indolent, sluggish life thanks to the Nuer's devotion. In truth the relationship is symbiotic: cattle and men sustain life by their reciprocal services to one another. In this intimate symbiotic relationship men and beasts form a single community of the closest kind. In a few paragraphs I direct attention to this intimacy.

The men wake about dawn at camp in the midst of their cattle and sit contentedly watching them till milking is finished. They then either take them to pasture and spend the day watching them graze, driving them to water, composing songs about them, and bringing them back to camp, or they remain in the kraal to drink their milk, make tethering-cords and ornaments

for them, water and in other ways care for their calves, clean
their kraal, and dry their dung for fuel. Nuer wash their hands
and faces in the urine of the cattle, especially when cows urinate
during milking, drink their milk and blood, and sleep on their
hides by the side of their smouldering dung. They cover their
bodies, dress their hair, and clean their teeth with the ashes of
cattle dung, and eat their food with spoons made from their
horns. When the cattle return in the evening they tether each
beast to its peg with cords made from the skins of their dead
companions and sit in the windscreens to contemplate them and
to watch them being milked. A man knows each animal of his
herd and of the herds of his neighbours and kinsmen: its colour,
the shape of its horns, its peculiarities, the number of its teats,
the amount of milk it gives, its history, its ancestry and its
progeny. Miss Soule tells me that most Nuer know the points
of the dam and grand-dam of a beast and that some know the
points of its forebears up to five generations of ascent. A Nuer
knows the habits of all his oxen, how one bellows in the evenings,
how another likes to lead the herd on its return to camp, and
how another tosses its head more than the rest are wont to do.
He knows which cows are restless during milking, which are
troublesome with their calves, which like to drink on the way
to pasture, and so forth.

If he is a young man he gets a boy to lead his favourite ox,
after which he takes his name, round the camp in the morning
and leaps and sings behind it; and often at night he walks
among the cattle ringing an ox-bell and singing the praises of
his kinsmen, his sweethearts, and his oxen. When his ox comes
home in the evening he pets it, rubs ashes on its back, removes
ticks from its belly and scrotum, and picks adherent dung
from its anus. He tethers it in front of his windscreen so that
he can see it if he wakes, for no sight so fills a Nuer with con-
tentment and pride as his oxen. The more he can display the
happier he is, and to make them more attractive he decorates
their horns with long tassels, which he can admire as they toss
their heads and shake them on their return to camp, and their
necks with bells, which tinkle in the pastures. Even the bull
calves are adorned by their boy-owners with wooden beads and
bells (Fig. 13). The horns of young bulls, destined to be

castrated later, are generally cut so that they will grow in a shape that pleases their masters. The operation, called *ngat*, is probably performed towards the end of their first year and usually takes place in the dry season, as it is said that a steer may die if its horns are cut in the rains. The animal is thrown and held down while its horns are cut through obliquely with a spear. They grow against the cut. The beasts appear to suffer much pain during the operation and I have sometimes heard Nuer compare their ordeal to the initiation of youths into manhood.

When a Nuer mentions an ox his habitual moroseness leaves him and he speaks with enthusiasm, throwing up his arms to show you how its horns are trained. 'I have a fine ox', he says, 'a brindled ox with a large white splash on its back and with one horn trained over its muzzle'—and up go his hands, one above his head and the other bent at the elbow across his face. In singing and dancing they call out the names of their oxen and hold their arms in imitation of their horns.

The attitude towards cattle varies with varying situations in social life and with changes in social development. As soon as children can crawl they are brought into close intimacy with the flocks and herds. The kraal is their playground and they are generally smeared with dung in which they roll and tumble. The calves and sheep and goats are their companions in play and they pull them about and sprawl in the midst of them. Their feelings about the animals are probably dominated by desire for food, for the cows, ewes, and she-goats directly satisfy their hunger, often suckling them. As soon as a baby can drink animal's milk its mother carries it to the sheep and goats and gives it warm milk to drink straight from the udders.

The games of rather older children of both sexes centre round cattle. They build byres of sand in camps and of moistened ashes or mud in villages, and fill the toy kraals with fine mud cows and oxen (Fig. 7), with which they play at herding and marriage. The first tasks of childhood concern cattle. Very small children hold the sheep and goats while their mothers milk them, and when their mothers milk the cows they carry the gourds and pull the calves away from the udders and tether them in front of their dams. They collect urine in gourds and wash themselves in it. When they are a little older and stronger they have to clean the byres and kraals, assist in the milking, and herd the small calves and the sheep and goats at pasture.

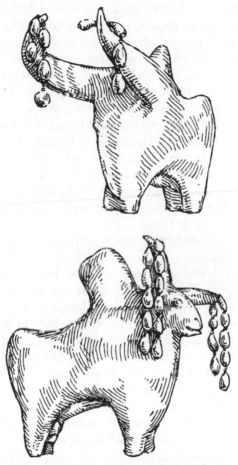

FIG. 7. Mud figures of oxen decorated with tassels.

Food and play contacts with the cattle have changed to labour contacts. At this age the interests of the sexes in cattle begin to diverge and the divergence becomes more apparent as they grow up. The labour of girls and women is restricted to the byres and the kraals and is concerned mostly with the cows, while boys herd the calves at pasture, as well as assisting in the kraal, and after initiation they herd the adult cattle and in the kraal give their attention mainly to the oxen. The women are dairy-maids; the men herdsmen. Moreover, to a girl the cows are essentially providers of milk and cheese and they remain such when she grows up and is married and milks and churns for her husband's people, whereas to a boy they are part of the family herd in which he has property rights. They have entered the herd on the marriage of his kinswomen and one day he will marry with them. A girl is separated from the herd on marriage; a boy remains as its owner. When a boy becomes a youth and is initiated into manhood the cattle become something more than food and the cause of labour. They are also a means of display and marriage. It is only when a man marries and has children and an independent household and herd, when he has become an elder and man of position, that he often uses cattle as sacrifices, invests them with a sacred significance, and employs them in ritual.

The Nuer and his herd form a corporate community with solidarity of interests, to serve which the lives of both are adjusted, and their symbiotic relationship is one of close physical contact. The cattle are docile and readily respond to human care and guidance. No high barriers of culture divide men from beasts in their common home, but the stark nakedness of Nuer amid their cattle and the intimacy of their contact with them present a classic picture of savagery. I ask the reader to look at some of the illustrations, for example the Frontispiece and Plates III, V, and XVII, which will convey to him better than I can do in words the crudity of kraal life.

Cattle are not only an object of absorbing interest to Nuer, having great economic utility and social value, but they live in the closest possible association with them. Moreover, irrespective of use, they are in themselves a cultural end, and the mere possession of, and proximity to, them gives a man his heart's desire. On them are concentrated his immediate interests and his farthest ambitions. More than anything else they determine his daily actions and dominate his attention. We have remarked on the over-emphasis on cattle produced by their wide range of social and economic uses. So many physical, psychological, and social requirements can be satisfied from this one source that Nuer attention, instead of being diffused in a variety of directions, tends, with undue exclusiveness, to be focused on this single object and to be introvertive, since the object has a certain identity with themselves. We will now examine briefly some linguistic material wherein we shall perceive further evidence of this hypertrophy of a single interest and of the identification of men with cattle to which I have alluded.

VIII

Linguistic profusion in particular departments of life is one of the signs by which one quickly judges the direction and strength of a people's interests. It is for that reason, rather than for its intrinsic importance, that we draw the reader's attention to the volume and variety of the Nuer cattle vocabulary. Like all the pastoral Nilotes they use an enormous number of words and phrases about cattle and the tasks of herding and dairy-work, and from this vast assortment we select for comment a single class: the terms by which they describe cattle, chiefly by reference to their colours.[1] These terms are more than a linguistic technique which enables Nuer to speak of cattle with precision in situations of practical husbandry and in the many social contexts in which they figure, for they establish associations on the one hand between wild creatures and cattle and on the other hand between cattle and their masters; they furnish certain ritual categories; and they greatly enrich the language of poetry.

In naming a Nuer cow one has to notice its colours and the way in which they are distributed on its body. When it is not of one colour the distribution of colours is the significant character by which one names it. There are ten principal colour terms: white (*bor*), black (*car*), brown (*lual*), chestnut (*dol*), tawny (*yan*), mouse-grey (*lou*), bay (*thiang*), sandy-grey (*lith*), blue and strawberry roan (*yil*), and chocolate (*gwir*). When a cow is of a single colour it is described by one of these terms. An animal may combine two or more colours, but a combination of more than two, known as *cuany*, is very rare. Normally there is a combination of white with one other colour and twelve common distributions of this com-

---

[1] I have recorded some information on this neglected subject among a neighbouring people in 'Imagery in Ngok Dinka Cattle-Names', *Bulletin of the School of Oriental Studies*, 1934.

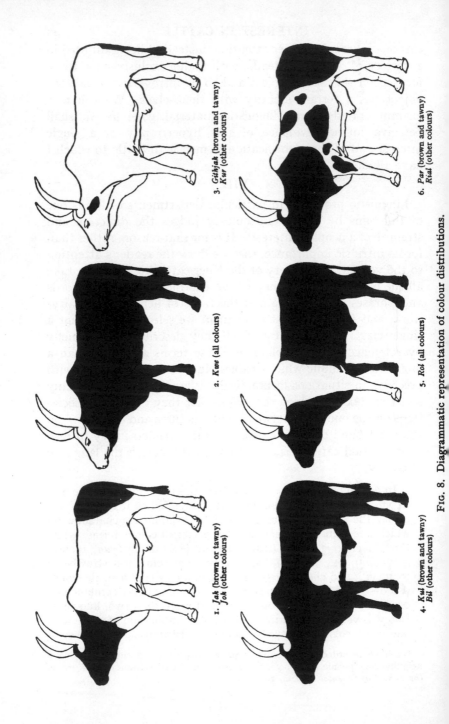

Fig. 8. Diagrammatic representation of colour distributions.

1. *Jak* (brown or tawny) *Jok* (other colours)

2. *Kwe* (all colours)

3. *Gӥthjak* (brown and tawny) *Kwr* (other colours)

4. *Kul* (brown and tawny) *Biel* (other colours)

5. *Rol* (all colours)

6. *Par* (brown and tawny) *Kual* (other colours)

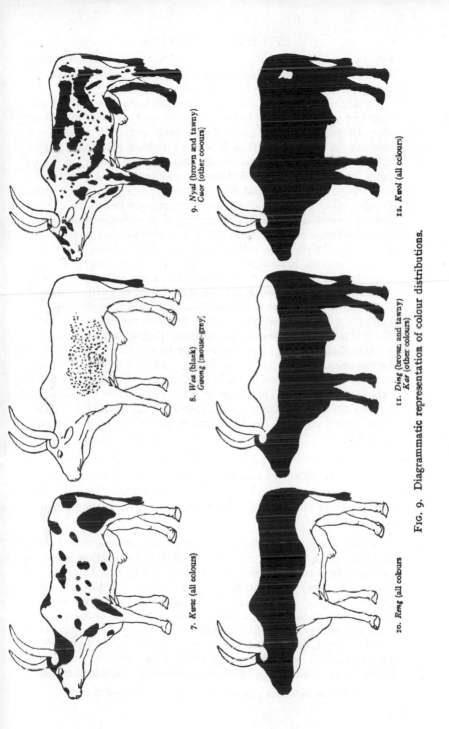

7. *Kwac* (all colours)

8. *Wea* (black)
   Gwong (mouse-grey)

9. *Nyal* (brown and tawny)
   Cuor (other colours)

10. *Reng* (all colours)

11. *Ding* (brown and tawny)
    Kar (other colours)

12. *Kwol* (all colours)

Fig. 9. Diagrammatic representation of colour distributions.

bination are shown in Figs. 8 and 9. There are, however, many more combinations, at least twenty-seven, one of the commonest being varieties of a striped or brindled coat (*nyang*).

In describing a beast one often denotes both the form of distribution and the colour that is combined with white. Thus an ox may be entirely mouse-grey (*lou*); have a mainly mouse-grey colour with a white face (*kwe looka*), white back (*kar looka*), white splash on barrel (*bil looka*), white shoulder (*rol looka*), or white belly (*reng looka*): be brindled mouse-grey (*nyang looka*): be white with large mouse-grey patches (*rial looka*), medium mouse-grey patches (*kwac looka*), or a mouse-grey rump (*jok looka*), &c. There are at least a dozen terms describing different combinations of white and mouse-grey and there are a similar number of terms for a combination of white with each of the other colours. A further example is given to illustrate the wide range of variations: a white shoulder and foreleg (*rol*) may be found on a cow of any colour, e.g. *rol cara, rol yan, rol thiang, rol yili*, &c. There may also be a combination of one form of distribution with another and, in this case, the two combinations constitute the terms of reference and there is no need to denote the colouring that occurs in them, e.g. a white shoulder and foreleg (*rol*) may be combined with a white face (*kwe roal*), black spots (*rol kwac*), speckling (*rol cuor*), brown patches (*rol paara*), white back (*kar roal*), white face and black ears (*kur roal*), &c. There are at least twenty-five terms which include the *rol* distribution, and the other distributions likewise have wide ranges of combinations with colours and with one another.

As I shall elsewhere, and at length, analyse the principles of colour terminology and abstract the rules of nomenclature,[1] I need no more than remark here that it is evident from the few examples cited that there are several hundred colour permutations.

Some colours and combinations of colours are associated with animals, birds, reptiles, and fish, and this association is often indicated by secondary terms of reference and by ritual usages, e.g. *lou* (mouse-grey) is the bustard, *nyang* (striped) is the crocodile, *lith* (sandy-grey) is associated with *manlieth*, the grey kestrel, *thiang* (bay) is the tiang, *dwai* (brown with white stripes) is the female sitatunga, *kwe* (white-faced) is the fish eagle, *kwac* (spotted) is the leopard, *cuor* (speckled) is the vulture, *gwong* (spotted) is the guinea-fowl, *nyal* (brown-spotted) is the python, &c. These linguistic identifications and other colour associations lead to many

---

[1] 'Nuer Cattle Terms', to appear in *Sudan Notes and Records*.

fanciful elaborations of nomenclature, e.g. a black ox may be called *rual mim*, charcoal-burning or *won car*, dark clouds; a brown ox *riem dol*, red blood, or *rir dol*, red tree-cobra; a blue roan ox *bany yiel* after the blue heron; a mouse-grey ox *duk lou*, the shady gloom of forests, &c. These fancy names add greatly to the list of Nuer cattle terms.

Besides the vast vocabulary which refers to colours, distribution of colours, and colour associations, cattle can also be described by the shape of their horns and, as the horns of oxen are trained, there are at least six common designations in use besides several fancy names. Words denoting shape of horns add considerably to the number of permutations, for they can be combined with many of the colour and distribution terms, e.g. a sandy-grey cow with horns which almost meet in a curve above the head is a *duot lieth*, a shorthorn with *rial* markings is a *cot rial*, a brindled ox with one horn trained across its face is a *gut nyang*, &c. The ears of cattle, sheep, and goats are often cut in different shapes and it is permissible, and with sheep and goats usual, to describe them by reference to these incisions. Sheep and goats have very different mixtures of colours from those one finds among cattle, but the same terms can be used to cover all combinations, because they are never exact descriptions of colour dispositions but represent ideal distributions, to one or other of which any actual disposition approximates.

A further range of permutations is created by prefixes which denote the sex or age of an animal, e.g. *tut*, bull, *yang*, cow, *thak*, ox, *nac*, heifer, *ruath*, male calf, *dou*, female calf, *kol*, calf which has not yet begun to graze, and so forth. Thus one may speak of a *tut ma kar looka, dou ma rial, thak ma cuany*, &c. Indeed, if we were to count every possible mode of referring to animals of the flocks and herds they would be found to number several thousand expressions—an imposing and complicated system of ramifications which bears eloquent witness to the social value of cattle.

Furthermore, as we have mentioned, every man takes one of his names from the term by which one of his oxen is described, and these ox-names are the preferred salutations among agemates. A youth generally takes his first ox-name from the beast his father gives him at his initiation, but he may later take further names from any oxen of his herd which delight him. Men salute one another with these names and shower them, with many a fanciful elaboration, on their companions at dances. They also chant them when they display themselves with their oxen in camps, sing them in their poems, and shout them when they spear men, animals, or fish.

A man may be called by the identical name of his ox, e.g. Bi(l)rial, Kwac(c)uor, Werkwac, and so forth, but generally one part of the term is dropped and the other part is prefixed by a new term, usually descriptive of some ornament worn by the ox or some characteristic of it, not employed in defining its own name, e.g. *luth*, a large bell (Fig. 4), *gier*, a small bell, *lue*, a long tassel, *dhuor*, a short tassel (Plate IV), *wak*, the tinkling of an ox-bell, *lang*, a brass ring attached to an ox's collar or tethering-cord (one can be seen on the animal in the foreground of Plate II), *rot*, bellowing of oxen, *cwai*, fatness, *boi*, shining whiteness, &c. Thus a man whose favourite ox has *rial* distribution of colours may be called Luthrial, Gierrial, Luerial, Dhuorrial, Boirial, and so on. When ox-names are used between age-mates at dances they are generally preceded by dance-names which are selected to harmonize with the ox-names, euphony being considered of great importance in all these word formations. Ox-names are voluminous and abstruse, and in describing them, as in describing cattle-colours, I have not only made a meagre selection from the wealth at my disposal, but have also chosen for illustration the simplest examples and neglected the more obscure.

Names of cattle, especially of oxen, and ox-names of men are used profusely in songs. The Nuer, like most pastoral peoples, are poetic and most men and women compose songs which are sung at dances and concerts or are composed for the creator's own pleasure and chanted by him in lonely pastures and amid the cattle in camp kraals. Youths break into song, praising their kinsmen, sweethearts, and cattle, when they feel happy, wherever they may be. I give a free translation of the first verses of two songs, the first sung by girls as they sit together in the evening after the day's work is done, and the second sung by its creator when he is happy.

1. The wind blows *wirawira* ;[1]
   Where does it blow to?

---

[1] Literally 'My wind'. The singer runs against it and seems by so doing to add to its strength. This is the north wind which blows at the time of rich

It blows to the river.
The shorthorn carries its full udder to the pastures;[1]
Let her be milked by Nyagaak;
My belly will be filled with milk.
Thou pride of Nyawal,
Ever-quarrelling Rolnyang.[2]
This country is overrun by strangers;
They throw our ornaments into the river;
They draw their water from the bank.[3]
Blackhair my sister,
I am bewildered.
Blackhair my sister,
I am bewildered.
We are perplexed;
We gaze at the stars of God.[4]

2. White ox good is my mother
And we the people of my sister,
The people of Nyariau Bul.
As my black-rumped white ox,
When I went to court the winsome lassie,
I am not a man whom girls refuse.
We court girls by stealth in the night,
I and Kwejok
Nyadeang.[5]
We brought the ox across the river,
I and Kirjoak
And the son of my mother's sister
Buth Gutjaak.
Friend, great ox of the spreading horns,
Which ever bellows amid the herd,
Ox of the son of Bul
Maloa.[6]

It is not necessary to add more examples of cattle-terms and

pasture when the cows give plenty of milk: hence the connexion between
the first three lines and those which follow them.

[1] The cow has refused to suckle its calf or to be milked before going to graze.
[2] Nyagaak is the sister of the poet. Pride (*gweth*) is the dance-name of a
girl, Nyawal. Rolnyang is a youth's ox-name.
[3] The strangers are Government forces. The reference to drawing water
from the bank is obscure.
[4] Blackhair is a girl's name. The Nuer are perplexed by foreign invasion
and the last line is a prayer to God to help them in their adversity.
[5] The ox referred to in the first and fourth lines is the poet's ox. Kwejok
is a friend, whose mother is Nyadeang.
[6] Buth is the birth-name of a friend whose ox-name is Gutjaak. The poet,
who is a son of Bul Maloa, addresses his ox as his friend in the final lines.

their uses to demonstrate that we are dealing with a galaxy of words in the arrangement of which a thesaurus of some magnitude might be compiled. I need only emphasize that this intricate and voluminous vocabulary is not technical and departmental but is employed by every one and in manifold situations of ordinary social life. I have only treated a fragment of a fragment of the linguistic field relating to cattle. I could enter into further detail, but, at best, I have only surveyed, and in an amateur way, that field, which invites broader and more specialist research. My purpose has been to draw attention to it and to show how a study of the dominant interest of Nuer might be approached from this angle. The subject is necessarily vast, because, as we have seen, it is not possible to discuss with Nuer their daily affairs, social connexions, ritual acts, or, indeed, any subject, without reference to cattle which are the core round which daily life is organized and the medium through which social and mystical relations are expressed. Nor is Nuer interest in cattle confined to their practical uses and social functions, but is displayed in their plastic and poetic arts, in which they are the chief theme. The over-emphasis on cattle is thus strikingly shown in language, which, moreover, by compelling reference to cattle, whatever be the subject of speech, continually focuses attention on them and makes them the superlative value of Nuer life.

IX

Another way in which Nuer engrossment in cattle can be illustrated—our last exemplification thereof—is by noting how readily and frequently they fight about them, for people risk their lives for what they greatly value and in terms of those values.

At the present time cattle are the main cause of hostility towards, and suspicion of, the Government, not so much on account of present taxation as of earlier tax-gathering patrols which were little more than cattle raids and of the avowedly plundering expeditions of the Egyptian Government era that preceded them. Nuer war with the Dinka has been almost entirely offensive and directed towards appropriation of herds and annexation of grazing grounds. Cattle have also been the chief occasion of strife among Nuer themselves. Indeed, after a successful raid on Dinka stock there is often further fighting over the booty. Moreover, Nuer tribes raid one another for cattle. Thus the Leek raid the Jikany, Rengyan, and other western tribes, and cattle raids are of common occurrence along tribal boundaries elsewhere, for to 'steal' (*kwal*) cattle from another tribe is regarded as laudable. Within a tribe, also, fighting frequently results from disputes about cattle between its sections and between individuals of the same section, even of the same village or homestead. Nuer fight on slight provocation and most willingly and frequently when a cow is at stake. On such an issue close kinsmen fight and homes are broken up. When ownership of cattle is in dispute Nuer throw over caution and propriety, showing themselves careless of odds, contemptuous of danger, and full of guile. As my Nuer servant once said to me: 'You can trust a Nuer with any amount of money, pounds and pounds and pounds, and go away for years and return and he will not have stolen it; but a single cow— that is a different matter.'

Nuer say that it is cattle that destroy people, for 'more people have died for the sake of a cow than for any other cause'. They have a story which tells how, when the beasts broke up their community and each went its own way and lived its own life, Man slew the mother of Cow and Buffalo. Buffalo said she would avenge her mother by attacking men in the bush, but Cow said that she would remain in the habitations of men and avenge her mother by causing endless disputes about debts, bride-wealth, and adultery, which would lead to fighting and deaths among the people. So this feud between Cow and Man has gone on from time immemorial, and day by day Cow avenges the death of her mother by occasioning the death of men. Hence Nuer say of their cattle, 'They will be finished together with mankind', for men will all die on account of cattle and they and cattle will cease together.

It must not, however, be supposed that Nuer live in continuous turmoil: the very fact that they are prepared to resist any infringement of their rights in cattle induces prudence in the relations between persons who regard themselves as members of the same group. It may be said, furthermore, that the great vulnerability of cattle coupled with the extensive living-space required for them are compatible only with a far recognition of conventions in the settlement of disputes, or, in other words, the existence of a tribal organization embracing a large territory, and of some feeling of community over yet larger areas.

Fighting about ownership of cattle and seizing cattle for what are claimed as debts and compensation for losses are of a somewhat different order to raiding for cattle over which no rights, other than the power of the strong, are asserted. War against foreign peoples, as distinct from warfare within a tribe, is almost entirely for plunder. Nuer war against the Dinka, therefore, differs from most primitive warfare in that its primary object is acquisition of wealth, for cattle are a form of wealth that not only lasts a long time and reproduces itself, but is, also, easily seized and transported. Furthermore, it enables invaders to live on the country without commissariat. Crops and dwellings can be destroyed, but cattle can be confiscated and taken home. This quality, which has given pastoral peoples a bias in favour of the arts of war rather than the arts of peace, has meant that the Nuer are not entirely dependent on their own cattle, but can augment their herds and restore the ravages of rinderpest, and have, in fact, for a long time increased their stock, and hence supplemented their food-supply, by raiding; a condition that has shaped their character, economy, and political structure. Skill and courage in fighting are reckoned the highest virtues, raiding the most noble, as well as the most profitable, occupation, and some measure of political agreement and unity a necessity.

We hasten to add that an explanation of warfare between Nuer and Dinka by reference to cattle and pastures alone is too simple a reduction. Hostility is expressed in terms of cattle, and desire for cattle accounts for some peculiarities of the struggle and some characteristics of the political organizations involved in it, but the struggle itself can only be fully understood as a structural process and we present it as such later.

We now pass to a brief examination of the oecological system of which Nuer and their cattle form part to discover the conditions in which cattle-husbandry is practised and how far its practice in a certain environment influences political structure.

CHAPTER II

OECOLOGY

I

FROM a European's point of view Nuerland has no favourable qualities, unless its severity be counted as such, for its endless marshes and wide savannah plains have an austere, monotonous charm. It is throughout hard on man and beast, being for most of the year either parched or a swamp. But Nuer think that they live in the finest country on earth and, it must be admitted, for herdsmen their country has many admirable features. I soon gave up trying to convince Nuer that there is any country more suited for cattle husbandry than their own, an attempt rendered more useless since a few of them have been taken to Khartoum, which they consider to be the home of all white men, and, having seen the desert scrub of that latitude, have been confirmed in their opinion that their land is superior to ours.

The grasses necessary for the welfare of the herds depend for existence on suitable conditions of soil and water. The soils of Nuerland are heavy clays, broken by the sun into deep cracks in the drought and sodden in the rains. They hold up water and consequently enable certain species of grasses to survive the dry months and provide pasture for the cattle. Nuer and their cattle would not, however, be able to live if it were not that there are more sandy elevated spots on which they can take refuge in flood-time and where they can practise horticulture.

Surface water comes partly from rainfall and partly from the flooding of the rivers which traverse Nuerland and is more than adequate to make grass. In an average year the rains commence in April, when a few showers fall and the sky is overclouded, but it is not till the end of May that they set in with a will. At their maximum, in July and August, the weather is cool, even cold in the mornings and evenings, the sun is overcast during most of the day, and a south-westerly wind prevails. Showers become lighter and less frequent in October and usually have ceased altogether by the middle of November when the north wind begins to blow. It blows consistently down the valley of the Nile till March. In March and April the heat is intense. The rainfall, which is fairly even over all parts of Nuerland, is not so heavy as farther east, on the Ethiopian Plateau, or south, in the basin of the Victoria Nile and along the Nile-Congo divide, though the effects are more felt, because clay beds hold up the water,

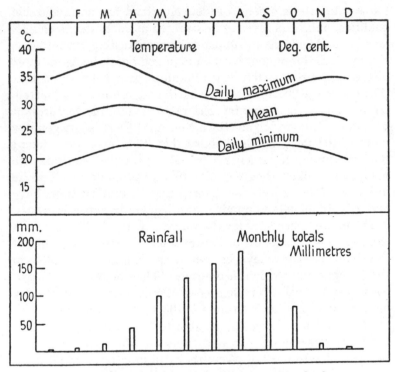

Temperature and Rainfall estimates for Nuerland.
(*Physical Department of the Egyptian Government.*)

the flatness of the country prevents surface drainage, and the annual flooding of the rivers occurs simultaneously.

The main rivers which so greatly influence Nuer life are shown on the map on p. 8. They are the Nile itself, known in these regions as the Bahr el Jebel, which derives its water from the Plateau of the Great Lakes; its western tributaries the Bahr el Ghazal and the Bahr el Arab, which are fed by streams flowing from the Nile-Congo divide; the Baro, the lower reaches of which are known as the Sobat, coming from the Ethiopian

Highlands; and the Pibor which flows from the same direction
and also drains to a lesser extent the northern slopes of the
Plateau of the Great Lakes and the Sudan Plains. The Bahr el
Zeraf is another channel of the Bahr el Jebel.[1] All these rivers
flood at the time of the rains and, owing to its flatness, the
country is turned into a vast morass.

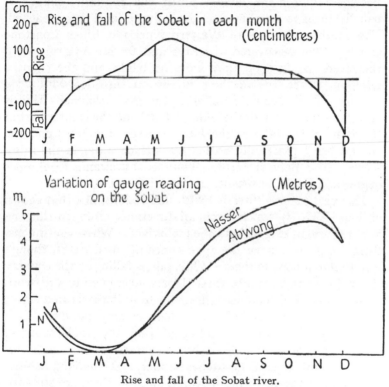

Rise and fall of the Sobat river.
(*Physical Department of the Egyptian Government.*)

The whole of Nuerland is an almost dead level plain, covered
during the rains with high grasses reaching to the waists, and
near streams, where they are higher and coarser, to the shoulders
of the tall Nuer. It approximately coincides with the extension
of true savannah in the Sudan. Here and there are patches of
thornwood forest, but often no tree is visible in any direction

[1] For an excellent description of these rivers see H. E. Hurst and P. Phillips,
The Nile Basin, vol. i, 1931.

and a desolate waste stretches everywhere to the horizon (Plates VI and XI (*a*) and (*b*)). A belt of forest sometimes lines a river where its banks are high, but never extends far inland. North of the Sobat, on its lower reaches, true savannah gives way to thorny savannah and beyond the southern extremities of Eastern Nuerland one enters park-like savannah forest which becomes thicker the farther south one proceeds, though it usually turns to marshland as the Bahr el Jebel is approached. The southern borders of Western Nuerland fringe ironstone country, likewise covered with savannah forest. As a rule when the rivers are in flood they have no banks and the country lying on either side of them is swamp threaded with wide lagoons, often running parallel to the main channel. This is especially the case with the Bahr el Jebel and the greater part of the Bahr el Ghazal and the Bahr el Arab, the Jebel and the Ghazal being practically united by surface water in the rainy season. The Bahr el Zeraf is bounded by swamp to a lesser degree and the lower reaches of the Sobat not at all.

This vast plain is threaded with depressions, like that shown on Plate XIX (*b*), which run in all directions, often crossing one another, and linking up with the main rivers. Where continuous, these depressions have the appearance of small rivers, though water seldom flows in them. While rain is falling on the country the main rivers flood into these depressions, making a network of waterways which prevents drainage from the saturated earth, so that the rainwater lies everywhere in deep puddles which slowly extend till by the middle of June the whole country, except for occasional higher land, is inundated. The water remains several inches deep till September, and Nuerland has the appearance of a great grass-covered swamp; there are streams, lagoons, and pools wherever there are slight depressions, and islands,. on which are perched villages, wherever there are ridges and knolls. The rivers begin to fall about the same time as the rains decline, the fall being most rapid on the Sobat (diagram on p. 53). The blazing sun then quickly evaporates the surface water, while the streams, instead of being channels of overflow from the rivers, now feed them, and by the middle of November the grasses are dry enough to be fired. By the end of December a great part of the country has been burnt

PLATE VI

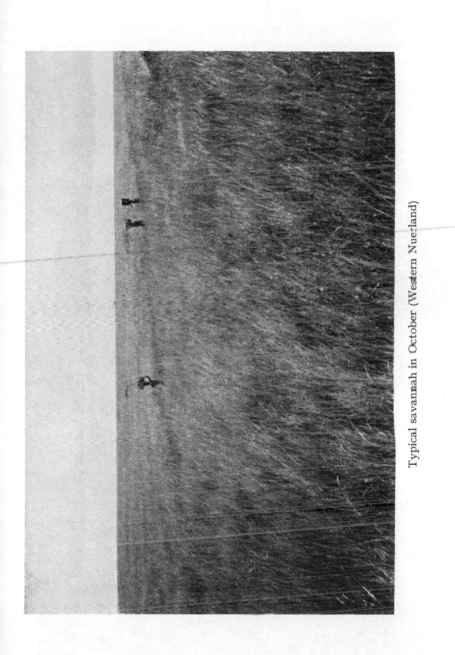

Typical savannah in October (Western Nuerland)

PLATE VII

a. Homesteads on mound (Lou)

b. Homesteads on mound (Lou)

and is cracked into deep fissures. The wet and dry seasons are therefore very pronounced and the transition from one to the other sudden.

Scarcity of rain is probably more serious than low river water, but both may inconvenience Nuer to the point of famine, because sufficient water may not be held up in the clay beds to enable the grasses to recover from firing; inland watercourses may quickly dry up and compel movement to lakes and rivers earlier than is desirable; and there may be a shortage of the marsh pasturage which is usually the mainstay of the cattle at the end of the dry season. Insufficient rain may also destroy the millet. Moreover, it is probable that low rainfall over the whole of North-East Africa causes insufficiency of rain and low rivers to occur in Nuerland simultaneously. Western Nuerland is less subject to drought than Eastern Nuerland, and to the west of the Nile there is always water within easy reach of villages. This seems largely due to the fact that the Bahr el Jebel and the Bahr el Ghazal do not sink in their beds to any extent, since they are fed by perennial streams and have enormous marsh and lake reservoirs. High rainfall and high river water probably also go together and in such years of flood it is difficult for the cattle to find enough grazing to maintain life.

The main characteristics of Nuerland are: (1) It is dead flat. (2) It has clay soils. (3) It is very thinly and sporadically wooded. (4) It is covered with high grasses in the rains. (5) It is subject to heavy rainfall. (6) It is traversed by large rivers which flood annually. (7) When the rains cease and the rivers fall it is subject to severe drought.

These characteristics interact with one another and compose an environmental system which directly conditions Nuer life and influences their social structure. The determination is of so varied and complex a nature that we do not attempt to summarize its full significance at this stage of our description, but shall ask ourselves a simpler question: to what extent are the Nuer controlled by their environment as herdsmen, fishermen, and gardeners? We have demonstrated that their chief interest is in their herds and shall first discuss how this interest, combined with physical conditions, necessitates a certain mode of life.

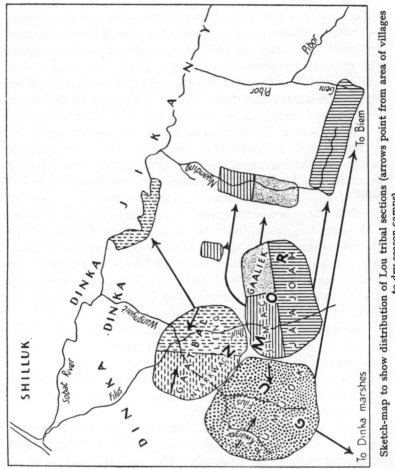

Sketch-map to show distribution of Lou tribal sections (arrows point from area of villages to dry season camps).

Here we make only two observations of a more general order. (1) Although the Nuer have a mixed pastoral-horticultural economy their country is more suitable for cattle husbandry than for horticulture, so that the environmental bias coincides with the bias of their interest and does not encourage a change in the balance in favour of horticulture. If it were not for rinderpest—a recent introduction it might be possible to live a purely pastoral life, but, as we shall see later, a purely horticultural life would be precarious. (2) Nuer cannot, except in a few favoured spots, live in one place throughout the year. The floods drive them and their herds to seek the protection of higher ground. Absence of water and pasture on this higher ground compels them to move during the drought. Hence their life is of necessity migratory, or, more strictly, transhumant. A further reason that urges them to change their abode according to the seasons is their inability at the present time to subsist solely on the products of their cattle. A milk and meat diet has to be supplemented by grain and fish; and whereas the most suitable place for cultivation of millet is inland, on the edge of slightly elevated ground, fish are found in rivers which are generally distant from these elevated stretches.

II

Excess or insufficiency of water is the first problem that faces Nuer. It is essential that cattle should be protected from the water that covers the country in the rains, for they quickly get diseases of the hoof if they have to stand in water for long periods. Village sites are selected on the only spots affording such protection to man and beast: patches of slightly higher ground. When the rains have ceased water supplies near villages are soon exhausted, because, naturally, the highest and driest sites have been selected for building, and it becomes necessary to move to pools, lakes, lagoons, marshes, and rivers. Owing to the vast rivers that traverse Nuerland and the thorough irrigation they give to the country through a network of channels there is seldom difficulty about finding surface water, though people may have to go far to obtain it. Only in parts of Lou, Gaawar, and Eastern Jikany, as far as is known, are they regularly forced to dig wells in the beds of streams at the height of the

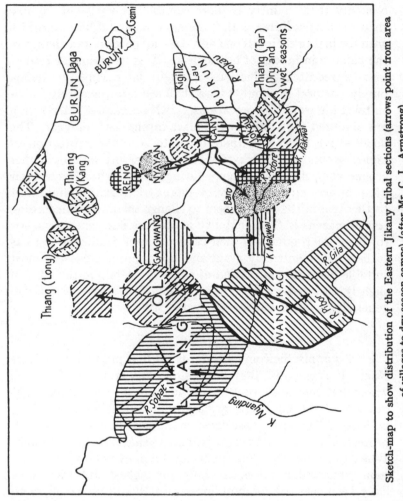

Sketch-map to show distribution of the Eastern Jikany tribal sections (arrows point from area of villages to dry season camps) (after Mr. C. L. Armstrong).

drought. Twenty years ago this was probably more customary among the Lou than to-day, for they had not then the undisputed access to open water that most sections now enjoy. The wells, which have to be redug each year, are two to three feet in diameter and twenty to thirty feet in depth, and their excavation takes two or three days of hard labour. The water, about a foot deep, is clean and fresh and the wells are frequently cleaned out, steps being cut in the walls for this purpose (Plate XV (b)). Each household has its own well which is surrounded by shallow mud troughs where the cattle are watered three times daily. Considerable labour is required to draw water for them and much attention is devoted to prevent it from being fouled by sheep and goats, which have their special troughs. Fights sometimes break out over these troughs.

The problem of water is closely related to that of vegetation. In their seasonal movements Nuer seek pasturage as well as drinking-water and they take the cattle to where they know that both can be obtained. When herdsmen drive the cattle from camp to grazing grounds they do not guide them haphazardly across the plain, but with purpose towards stretches of succulent grasses. It is probable, too, that not only are daily and seasonal movements influenced by distribution of grasses, but also that the direction of Nuer expansion has been controlled by their habitat. Nuer claim that they have not overrun the country of the Ngok Dinka because it is poor pasture land and that they are little interested in the Shilluk kingdom for the same reason.

The early rains are the season of fatness, for then the grasses germinate, or renew their growth after the long drought, and the cattle can graze on the young shoots to their content. As the rains advance, grazing becomes more difficult, the ground being flooded and the vegetation rank, and in years of high water may be a serious problem. The cattle have to rely on the short grasses that prevail on village ridges: a further reason that compels Nuer to occupy these sites in the rains. When rain ceases, the overcropped grasses on these ridges soon wither, while the rank grasses of the plains impede the movements of the herds and no longer provide good grazing. Therefore Nuer hasten to burn them as soon as they are dry, since some species

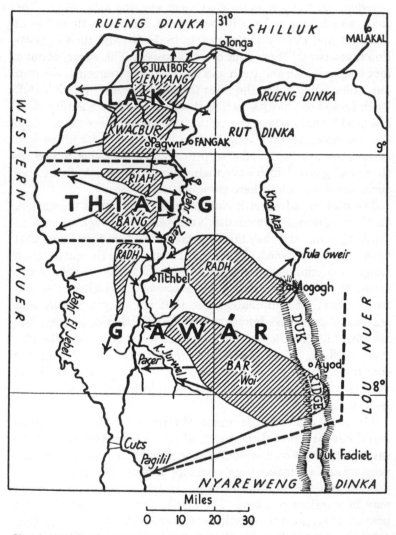

Sketch-map showing the direction (indicated by arrows) of movement in the
dry season of the Zeraf tribes (after Mr. B. A. Lewis).

send up new shoots a few days after being fired—probably those that have roots long enough to tap water held up in the clay beds and a clump formation that protects the core of the plants from the flames. If it were not for this habit cattle could not survive, at any rate inland, during a dry year. When the grasses have been fired cattle can wander as they please, being no longer frustrated by surface water and rank growth, and satisfy their appetites on the new shoots. As water becomes scarcer and grazing poorer Nuer fall back on permanent water where they make large camps and the cattle can graze on marsh plants that abound in numberless depressions and make good milk. In May, when the new rains set in, they are able to return to their villages. The few cattle Nuer possess, the vast spaces they can exploit, and their nomadic existence ensure that there is nowhere serious overgrazing.

Variation of water-supplies and vegetation thus forces Nuer to move and determines the direction of their movements. In a later section we shall see that fishing is another important consideration in these movements. In late November or early December the youths and some of the girls take the cattle from the villages to camps, generally some miles away, leaving the older people to harvest the second millet crop and repair huts and byres. Usually a few lactating cows are left behind to provide milk for the small children. These early camps (*wec jiom*) are made near pools in a place where the grasses have previously been fired. In Lou country they are often made in thornwood forest, where *Balanites aegyptiaca* is abundant, but in many parts of Nuerland, especially to the west of the Nile, they are formed on stream banks for fishing. When the second harvest has been reaped the cattle are brought back to the villages to eat the millet stalks, if they are near enough. As pools dry up, pasturage is exhausted, or fishing becomes poor, the youths make new camps, where they are joined by the married people, and they may move camp several times before settling in their final camping grounds (*wec mai*) at the side of lakes or rivers in January and February. The early camps are small, being manned by a few kinsmen, but they tend to get larger as the season advances and water becomes scarcer, and the final camps may contain several hundred persons.

The dry season movements of the Lou, the Eastern Jikany, and the Zeraf River tribes are shown on the sketch-maps accompanying this section. Of the Sobat tribes, the Lou stay inland as long as they can and in a wet year may remain inland throughout the dry season, falling back on the deeper pools, some large enough to be called lakes, e.g. Muot tot, Muot dit, Fading, Fadoi, Gwonggwong, Yollei, Tepjor, and Nyerol. If forced to leave them the Gun primary section moves north to the Sobat and south-west to the flooded plains of the Bahr el Zeraf in the country of the Twic Dinka, and the Mor primary section moves north-east to the Nyanding river and east to the Geni and Pibor. In the old days fighting frequently occurred if the Lou moved to these camping sites, because the banks of the Sobat were in the hands of the Balak Dinka while their occupation of the Geni and Pibor was disputed by the Anuak and Beir and their move to the south-west was trespass on Dinka grazing grounds. Even the lower reaches of the Nyanding do not belong to the Lou, but to the Gaajok. Therefore they probably only moved to these sites when absolutely necessary.

The Eastern Jikany have not so much need to move as have the Lou. Nevertheless they all fall back on rivers or marshes before the drought is far advanced. The three primary sections of the Gaajok move as follows: the Laang concentrate on the Sobat, the Wangkac move south-east to the banks of the Pibor and Gila, and the Yol either camp near the junction of the Wokau and Sobat or northwards along the edges of the Machar swamp. The Gaagwang move to the western end of Khor Makwai. The Gaajak primary sections move as follows: the northern Thiang sections (Kang and Lony) go to the Daga river while the southern Thiang section (Tar) and the Reng, Nyayan, Wau, and Cany sections camp on the banks of the Baro, Jokau, Adura, and Makwei, mainly in Ethiopia.

The three Zeraf river tribes fall back on the Bahr el Jebel and the Bahr el Zeraf and streams flowing into these two rivers, as shown in Mr. Lewis's sketch. The Gaawar who live on the left bank of the Zeraf can build their villages on high ground near that river and do not have to move far in the drought.

The Western Nuer mainly camp on inland streams which are no great distance from their villages. The Karlual primary section of the Leek tribe mostly concentrate first on the Loogh stream and afterwards on the Cal and Wangtac, all of which link up with the Bahr el Ghazal. The Dok camp near pools in the beds of inland streams. The Western Jikany move to the Jikany marshes at the edge of the Bahr el Ghazal. Without giving further details, which, indeed, I could not furnish, about the disposition of the Western Nuer in the dry season, it may be said that they travel very much less than most of the Eastern Nuer tribes, especially the Lou.

Different villages and sections tend to move about the same time and to visit the same pools each year, though time and place and, to some extent, degree of concentration vary according to climatic conditions. Usually, however, the main dry season camps are formed yearly at the same spots. When the rains commence in May the older people return to the villages to prepare the ground for sowing and they are joined there in June by the youths and girls, who bring the cattle with them. When the younger people return the whole camp is broken up on the same day, and the cattle are driven to their village with as few halts as possible. The move from villages to camps, on the contrary, is less concerted and abrupt. The younger members of two or three families form a small camp, after the firing of the grasses in November, when and where they please. Several days later they may be joined by other people from the same village, or these may form a separate camp. There is still water and some grazing on the village sites and there is still work to be accomplished in gardens and homesteads. Thus, while camps change into villages overnight, villages change into camps more slowly. By the height of the drought every one is in camp and the villages are silent and deserted.

The year thus consists of a period in villages and a period in camps, and the camp period is divided into the early part of the dry season when the younger people move from small camp to small camp and the latter part of the dry season when every one is concentrated in large camps round permanent water which they do not leave till they return to their villages.

III

Nuer are forced into villages for protection against floods and mosquitoes and to engage in horticulture, and are forced out of villages into camps by drought and barrenness of vegetation and to engage in fishing. I describe these villages and camps very shortly.

Some tribes are better off for sites than others. The Lou

and the Eastern Jikany are especially fortunate in this respect, but in Western Nuerland, though there are many suitable ridges, the country is more inundated and there are few elevated stretches of any size, except, as far as my observations go, among sections of the Leek and Dok tribes, which are better off than those tribes which lie in between.

What is needed for a village site is not only room for building but also for grazing and cultivations. Many villages are perched on mounds (Plates VII and XVI), the surfaces of which are accumulations of debris, at the edge of those rivers that have banks in flood, and the cattle graze on the slopes or in near-by thornwood forest, where also gardens are cultivated. More usually homesteads are strung out along sandy ridges (Plate VIII), a mile or two in length and a few hundred yards in breadth, sites which allow greater spacial division between them, and the gardens run at their backs and the grazing-grounds to their fronts. In some parts of Nuerland, especially in the favoured tribes I have mentioned, stretches of higher ground, sometimes several miles in extent, enable the people to build anywhere, except near the narrow depressions that thread them, and little groups of homesteads are dotted here and there, surrounded, and separated, by their gardens and grazing grounds. Nuer prefer to dwell in this greater privacy and show no inclination for true village life.

By making their villages on elevated ground Nuer keep themselves and their cattle above the flood that lies everywhere on the vast plain beneath and gain some protection from the swarms of mosquitoes which breed in the standing water. In Western Nuerland I have seen low mud dykes at the foot of occupied ridges to keep back the water in years of heavy flood. As they build always on the highest spots the torrential rains that fall daily after June run off the slope so that the hard floors of kraals soon dry. How terrific are these rains may be judged from Plate XIV, taken from under the awning of my tent during a moderate shower in August, and how considerably they flood all but village sites may be seen in Plate XII, which shows a millet garden, on a higher level than the plain, in October. On a tour of Western Nuerland in October of 1936, a fairly dry year, we walked almost continuously in several inches of water for seventeen days, apart from having to cross numerous deep depressions. In some parts of Lou and Eastern Jikany, particularly in Gaajak, people build in open thornwood forest, but generally Nuer prefer to make their villages in open country, even where there is forest near-by, because their cattle are better protected from wild beasts, insect pests, and damp, and also, apparently, because millet does not do so well in wooded country. Building in the open seems also to give freedom from termites.

A Nuer homestead consists of a cattle byre and huts. Their byres are of size and workmanship that have evoked the admiration of all travellers. Their form, and the appearance of huts, may be seen in several plates, and their mode of construction is excellently portrayed in Mr. Corfield's photograph (Plate XVIII). It is only necessary to explain that the roofs are supported by trunks of trees erected inside the barns. Both byres and huts are of wattle and daub, though in Western Nuerland, where there is less forest, bundles of millet stalks are employed as rafters. Building and repairs generally take place early in the dry season when there is plenty of straw for thatching and enough millet to provide beer for those who assist in the work. During the rains fences are erected from the byres along two sides of the kraal and around huts to control the movements of cattle and to prevent them messing the homesteads and damaging the crops (Plate XVII). Grazing and the use of grass, trees, &c., is the common right of all members of a village community.

Families often change their place of residence from one part of a village to another and from village to village, and, in the case of small villages, if there have been many deaths, the cattle are poorly, there have been fights within the village, or pastures and cultivations are exhausted, the whole village community may move to a new site. After about ten years both pastures and gardens show evident signs of exhaustion on the smaller ridges, and huts and byres need rebuilding after some five years.

In dry-season camps men sleep in windscreens and women in beehive-huts, or both sexes in beehive-huts. These flimsy shelters are erected a few yards from water, generally in a semi-circle or in lines with their backs to the prevailing wind, and are simply constructed, the roots of grasses, or occasionally stems of millet, being tightly packed in a narrow trench to make windscreens, and the tops of the grasses being bound together and plastered with dung on the outside to make huts (Plates XV (*a*), XIX (*a*), and XXI (*b*)). The whole space within a windscreen is occupied by a hearth of ashes on which the men sleep around a fire, and the openings face the kraal. If people do not intend to spend more than a few days at a site they often sleep in the open and do not trouble to erect windscreens and huts. These light dwellings can be erected in a few hours.

IV

Another circumstance that determines Nuer movements is the abundance of insect life, which is an ever-present menace, for the cattle get little rest from stinging flies and ticks from morn till nightfall and would be worried to death if their masters did not give them some protection.

Mosquitoes swarm in the rains, their ravages being terrible from July to September, when, as soon as the sun sets, men and beasts have to take refuge in huts and byres. The doors of the huts are tightly closed, the air-holes blocked, and fires lit. In the centre of the byres, which house the cattle, burn large dung fires which fill them with smoke so dense that one cannot even see the cattle. Young men sleep on platforms above the fires, and if the smoke clears—the doors are shut, but it escapes through the thatched roof—they descend to pile on more fuel. By this means the beasts are enabled to obtain some rest at night. At the end of the rains while the cattle are still in the villages they are left in the kraals till their masters go to bed, when they are shut in the byres to protect them from lions. Fires are not made up so high at this season, for mosquitoes are less troublesome, since there is no surface water, the millet has been cut, and the grasses are close-cropped. Later those men who remain in the villages, while the others go into camps, often erect windscreens in the kraals and spend the night outside with any cows which have been left behind. In the dry season mosquitoes are absent except near pools and marshes, and even in the vicinity of water they are not troublesome from January to May, so that the herds can sleep in the open. Nevertheless, they are surrounded by windscreens in which their masters sleep at the side of dung fires from which smoke rises on every side to envelop the camp.

Another unpleasant pest is the seroot fly. It appears to be seasonal, flourishing on cloudy days from May to July, though it sometimes appears at other times of the year. The seroot attack the cattle in the mornings and accompany them to pastures, where they bite them so effectively that they are often driven, stained with blood, back to camp, where dung fires are lit to give them protection. On such days the cattle are unable to graze, fitfully, for more than two or three hours. Another biting fly, the *stomoxys*, is prevalent throughout the year, being especially conspicuous in the dry season and early rains. It is probably this fly which is responsible for the presence of trypanosomiasis in parts of Nuerland, especially among the Eastern Jikany, by transmitting the trypanosomes directly on its proboscis from beast to beast, for the tsetse does not occur in Nuerland, except, perhaps, on its eastern extremities, though its lethal character is well known to Nuer. There are other insects which annoy the cattle, but it is not known whether any of them carry disease in this latitude. Of these may be mentioned the eight-legged cattle tick, which Nuer remove from the bodies of their animals when they return to camp in the evenings—though not frequently or systematically enough; an insect called *tharkwac* which is said to live on the bodies of cattle, though its bites do not cause bleeding; a fly called *miek*; and the common black fly, like our house fly in appearance, which worries the herds a good deal in hot weather—damp and cold seem to kill it off. Red soldier ants occasionally infest the byres so that the cattle have to be removed while the floors are sprinkled with ashes, but they are rare in Nuerland. Nuer are helpless against most of these insects, though, no doubt, smoke keeps them away to some extent.

Speaking from personal experience I may say that one is continuously tormented by insects in Nuerland, especially by the common black fly and the mosquito. It is evident that the cattle suffer considerably from their attentions and there can be little doubt that this constant irritation lowers their vitality and affects their milk yield, for they seldom have any real rest. In the circumstances their hardiness and endurance are remarkable.

Since several species of tsetse in the Southern Sudan carry trypanosomes pathogenic to cattle it is fortunate for the Nuer that they do not occur in his country. This immunity is undoubtedly due to the absence of shady forest which, in its turn, is probably due in the main to flooding and partly to firing. The prevalence of tsetse in the forest belt that stretches along the foot-hills of the Ethiopian escarpment has prevented the Nuer from expanding as far eastwards as they might have done, for it is clear that one of the reasons for their evacuation of Anuakland was the loss of stock. In relation to tsetse the Nuer, in their present territory, occupy a more favourable position than most Southern Sudan peoples.

A further consideration of great importance is the presence of many microscopic organisms that cause disease in men and cattle. This is not a subject about which we can say much. With regard to stock it may, however, be said that it suffers from many different diseases and that Nuer usually have some treatment for them, though it may be doubted whether it has much, if any, therapeutic value. The two most serious contagious diseases are bovine pleuro-pneumonia, which in some years causes heavy mortality among the herds, and rinderpest. Rinderpest entered the Sudan not more than fifty years ago and Nuer refer to the period before it came, along with Arab invaders, at the time the Boiloc age-set was being initiated, as 'the life of the cattle'. They have no way of combating the scourge once it has attacked a herd, but they are aware that an infected herd ought to be isolated. They are so used to it now that they generally take the precaution of splitting up their herd in the dry season, when it is prevalent, and placing beasts in widely separated camps, so that if it breaks out in any part of the country the cattle placed in another part may escape. An animal which recovers from the disease is known to be immune from further attacks and its value is thereby enhanced, though Nuer are aware that its calves will not enjoy the same immunity. Miss Soule tells me that Nuer claim to be able to tell if an animal has had rinderpest by scraping the tip of the horns and noting the colour beneath the surface. If it is white the animal is immune. Though threatened with starvation in the years of its visitation Nuer face the scourge with resignation and detachment.

Rinderpest has caused and continues to cause terrible havoc in the herds. It cannot exactly be estimated what, and how

PLATE VIII

Sandy ridge with cattle byres on the horizon (Dok)

PLATE IX

Harpoon-fishing from canoe (Sobat river)

extensive, have been the social changes which have resulted from this disturbance of the oecological equilibrium. Since bride-wealth consists of cattle there must have been for a time considerable dislocation of marriage arrangements, but stability has been reached to-day by lowering the number of cattle which have to be paid. A like assessment on a new footing does not seem to have been achieved in homicide negotiations, in which there is not the same goodwill between the parties as in marriage, and blood-wealth appears to have been claimed up to the present time at the old rate of payment, though Nuer recognize that bride-wealth and blood-wealth should rise and fall together. One cannot make any precise statement on the matter, but it is likely that feuds were less easily concluded than before and that consequently tribal relations were affected. It may also be supposed that decrease in stock has led to a general deterioration of the standard of living, for climatic conditions do not allow adequate compensation by expending further labour on horticulture. No doubt Nuer grew more millet than before, but they must have suffered a decrease in their total food-supply and, above all, in security. It will be seen in a later section that Nuer can no more exist on a purely horti- cultural economy than they can, at any rate since the introduc- tion of rinderpest, exist on a purely pastoral economy. They must have a mixed economy and can compensate on one side or the other only to a very limited degree. Nuer sought to repair their losses rather by extensive raiding of their Dinka neigh- bours, passing on to them their own losses in stock. We know that Nuer raided Dinka before rinderpest entered the country, but it is likely that their foreign relations have been affected by the greater stimulus to aggression. Other probable effects could be noted, especially in kinship relations, but one can only guess their importance, so we confine our speculations to a few of those that may be supposed to have occurred in Nuer economy and political life.

V

It was noted in Chapter I that to exist Nuer have to make use of a mixed economy, since their herds do not supply them with adequate nourishment. It will be seen in a later section that their millet harvest is often meagre and uncertain. Fish, therefore, are an indispensable article of food, and the pursuit of them influences seasonal movements.

The rivers teem with fish of many edible species which greatly supplement the diet of the Nuer in the dry season and enable them to survive years in which the crops fail or there are epidemics among the herds. In choosing camp sites opportunities for fishing are considered no less than water and pasturage. Nevertheless, Nuer do not regard themselves as a water-people, and despise people like the Shilluk who, they say, live mainly by fishing and hunting hippopotami. In spite of this suggestion of superiority Nuer enjoy fishing and the feeling of well-being a full fish diet gives them. One may judge how great their catch must be at the height of the dry season from the fact that one can see along the Baro and Sobat cattleless fishing camps (*kal*) in which, except for a little grain, goat's milk, and an occasional wild beast, people live on fish alone for several weeks. These are poor people who either have no cattle or have one or two cows which they have placed in the care of richer relatives, for no Nuer would live without his cattle if he could help it, and they are despised as persons of Anuak or Balak Dinka descent. Some Nuer tribes fish more than others, according to their opportunities. Thus Lou country has poor fishing compared with Eastern Jikany which has a network of waterways. Tribes and tribal sections jealously guard their fishing rights, and people who want to fish extensively in a pool must first obtain permission from its owners if they do not want to provoke fighting.

It is the seasonal flooding, due to the rise and fall of the rivers and the flatness of the country, that allows Nuer to kill fish in such large numbers, for they are carried out of the rivers, where they are little accessible to the simple methods of Nuer fishing, into streams and lagoons where they are more vulnerable. The best months are November and December, when the rivers begin to fall and to drain streams and lagoons, which can be dammed at suitable points and the fish speared in their efforts to break downstream. Fishing from dams is conducted mainly at night, fires being lighted behind the fishers, who fix their attention on a line of withies placed upstream from the dam and hurl their spears at whatever point of the line fish reveal their presence by striking the withies. My friend the late Mr. L. F. Hamer, who took the photograph reproduced in Plate XXII(*a*), about sunrise, reckoned that quite a hundred fish are caught from a dam in a single night. The dams are lowered as the water falls.

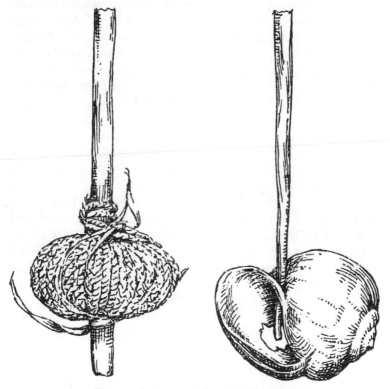

FIG. 10. Instruments for attracting fish.

As the dry season advances a great number of fish are imprisoned in lakes and lagoons from which there is no outlet, and as these dry up they are confined to a smaller and smaller expanse of water and are killed by individual fishers using barbed spears and long harpoons (Plates X and XXII (*b*)), and, at the end of the season, by battues in which gaffs and basket traps may also be employed. Fishing is fairly consistently productive throughout the drought, its yield increasing somewhat in the battue period and rising to a second peak at the commencement of the rains, in April and May, when the rivers begin to rise again and bring the fish into the shallows where they are easily speared among the reeds and weeds. There is very little fishing—by spear in occasional lagoons—after the Nuer have returned to their villages, for these are mainly inland, away from open water, and the streams are too deep and too infested with crocodiles to encourage fishing. Also, the fish are widely distributed by flood water and protected by rank marsh vegetation. Those Nuer whose villages are on the banks of large rivers sometimes fish from dug-out canoes (Plate IX) with long harpoons, but the Nuer possess very few good canoes —and these they have exchanged or stolen from the Anuak— for they have neither the wood nor the skill to make more than crudely burnt-out vessels of palm and sycamore.

Nuer are fine spearsmen but, otherwise, not very ingenious fishermen. Except for occasional fish spitted with amazing rapidity from the bows of canoes by harpoons and spears as they jump or rise to the surface, Nuer never see their prey, but either hurl their spears at random into likely spots amid weeds and reeds or set up grasses and withies to indicate the presence of fish. A myth recounts that once upon a time all fish were visible to the human eye but that God later made them invisible in the water. The chief Nuer weapon is the barbed spear, though the harpoon is considerably used. When fishing in shallows with spears they sometimes strike the water with a ball of twine or the shell of a giant snail attached to a stick (Fig. 10) to attract the fish. Fish are eaten roasted or boiled.

VI

Nuerland is also very rich in game, though Nuer do not exploit this source of food extensively. There are vast herds of tiang and cob; other antelopes are plentiful; and buffalo, elephant, and hippopotami abound. Nuer eat all animals except carnivora, monkeys, some of the smaller rodents, and zebra, and they kill the last for its skin and tail in the south of Lou country, where it roams in the dry season. Lions abound, especially to the west of the Nile, and are a serious menace to the herds, but Nuer only kill them and leopards, the skins of which are worn by chiefs, if they attack cattle in kraals or grazing grounds, as frequently happens, especially in the early dry season. They seldom go out to hunt game animals, except gazelle and giraffe, and only pursue those that approach their camps. Indeed, they cannot be considered keen hunters and may even be said to treat the sport with a measure of condescension, holding that only absence of cattle makes a man engage in it other than casually. Their flocks and herds provide them with meat, and this fact probably accounts in part for their lack of interest in hunting, which is, however, also to be related to the nature of their country, for its open plains offer little opportunity for successful hunting with the spear.

Nuer refuse all reptiles, except the crocodile and the turtle. Ostriches, bustards, francolin and guinea-fowl, geese, duck, teal, and other waterfowl, abound, but Nuer consider it shameful for adults to eat them and, except in very severe famines it is probable that only children, poor cattleless men, and an occasional elderly person, eat them, and then rarely and secretly in the bush. They do not keep domesticated fowls and show particular repugnance to the idea of eating them. Likewise eggs are not eaten. No insects are eaten, but the honey of wild bees is collected after the firing of the grasses in December and January and is either eaten in the bush or with porridge at home.

The only tribe who possess more than an odd gun or two are the Eastern Gaajak, who obtain them from Ethiopia. Nuer hunt with dogs and the spear, and rely on their fleetness, endurance, and courage. Hunting in the rains is therefore impossible, because not only does rank vegetation impede pursuit but also animals can choose their ground, there being everywhere sufficient water and grazing. At the height of the dry season they are forced to drink at the same pools, lagoons, and river inlets as men, and the dry bare country allows open chase, for except in tracking giraffe, Nuer hunt by sight and not by spoor. It is only gazelles, which are worried by dogs, and buffaloes, which prefer attack to flight, that can be tackled by one or two men. Other animals, such as tiang, cob, and buck, are only killed when they approach a camp and can be cut off by a large number of young men. I saw several animals killed on the Sobat by being surrounded on the landward side and driven into the reeds, where their only escape was by swimming the river. In this district, and perhaps elsewhere, Nuer, spurred by hunger, leave camp after the first heavy showers to look for giraffe tracks and pursue these animals relentlessly till they overtake them. This is only possible at the time of the first rains when the animals still have to approach camps to drink while their large hooves stick in the moist earth and slow down their movements. The Nuer, particularly those of the Zeraf river, have a reputation for their courage and skill in hunting elephants, which are surrounded and speared by large parties.

Nuer hunting has thus the same character of simplicity as their fishing. They use little cunning and, except for the spiked-wheel trap, no mechanical devices. This trap is used by immigrant Dinka in most parts of Nuerland and by some of the Lou Nuer, who, nevertheless, regard it as a Dinka contrivance and accordingly tend to despise it, regarding its use as unworthy of men possessing cattle but allowable to poor persons who can thereby obtain meat and even cattle, for giraffe-hair is highly valued for necklaces, such as those which can be seen on Nuer in many plates (especially Plates I and XXVIII(b)). Hence one finds a few members of a camp setting traps while the rest abstain. They are set around drinking-pools at the end of the dry season or in the early rains when surface water is still restricted and the ground is not yet moist enough to rot the leather nooses. In 1930 on the Sobat large numbers of giraffe were captured by means of spiked-wheel traps, but it appears to have been an exceptional year. If game-pits are dug at all by Nuer they are very rare and found only on the borders of Dinka tribes, and the burning of stretches of grass that have survived the annual firing in order to spear or club the animals that flee the flames is a very casual practice. In the dry season in Western Nuerland, and probably in other parts, though not on the Sobat, men harpoon hippopotami along the tracks to their nightly grazing grounds. Hippopotamus hunting is not, however, considered a Nuer practice, but a habit of Shilluk and some of the Dinka tribes; and even in those parts where Nuer hunt them it is said to be only men with a few cattle who do so. We may conclude that hunting does not give Nuer much meat and that they do not greatly esteem it as a sport.

VII

In most years wild fruits, seeds, and roots are not an important
item in Nuer diet. Their country is mainly treeless and fruits
therefore few; only 'wild dates' (*Balanites aegyptiaca*), found in
occasional patches to the west of the Nile and in more extensive
stretches to the east, provide much sustenance. The fruits ripen
from about January to March and both the kernels and their
sweet fleshy covering are eaten. A number of other fruits are
eaten, mainly by children. Initiated youths refuse most of them.
The seeds and roots of water-lilies (*Nymphaea lotus*), which are
found in pools and lagoons in the early dry season are much
relished. The seeds of 'wild rice' (*Oryza Barthii*) are collected
and a number of wild plants that grow on village sites are used
as seasoning for porridge. In famine years much greater attention is paid to the wild harvest. 'Wild dates' are then a great
stand-by and people eat a wide range of fruits, ripening mainly
in the early part of the drought, which they neglect when hunger
is not severe, and make use of bush-yams and the seeds of wild
sorghum and other grasses.

VIII

It will have been noted that fishing, hunting, and collecting
are dry-season occupations and produce during that season the
necessary supplement to an insufficient milk diet. In the wet
season, when these activities are no longer profitable and the
milk yield tends to fall off, the heavy rains, which cause the
changes responsible for these losses in supply, produce conditions
suitable for horticulture, impossible in the drought, that will
replace them. The variation in food-supply throughout the year
and its sufficiency for life at all seasons is thus determined by
the annual cycle of oecological changes. Without grain in the
wet season Nuer would be in a parlous state; and since it can be
stored they can, also, to a small extent, make provision against
famine in the drought.

Climatic conditions together with flooding and the flatness
of the country make it impossible to cultivate most Central
African food plants in Nuerland, and the Nuer are especially
unfortunate in having no root crop as a reserve in famine years.

It may be doubted whether they could cultivate any crops other than those they now sow, without extensive irrigation in the dry season, and this is incompatible with their nomadism. These crops do not make an imposing list. The staple crop is millet (*Sorghum vulgare*), from which they reap two harvests, and they sow some maize near their huts and a few beans (*Vigna*), their only garden vegetable, among the millet. Besides these three food plants they cultivate a little tobacco under the eaves of their huts and plant some gourds to grow up kraal fences. The millet is consumed as porridge and beer; the maize is mainly roasted, though some is eaten as porridge; the beans are eaten stewed or cooked with porridge; the tobacco is used for smoking in pipes, as snuff, and for chewing; and the gourds are, according to their species, either eaten or fashioned into dairy vessels.

Millet, the main crop, is the only one of these plants to the cultivation of which we need make more than a passing reference. Once it is established it stands up well to conditions which would be fatal to most plants, and it is worthy of notice that wild species of sorghum flourish in this latitude. Maize is also hardy but, although it is important to Nuer because it is the first grain to be harvested when their supplies are running short or are exhausted, its quantity is negligible except on the banks of the Baro. Nuer distinguish between many types of millet, mainly by the colour of their seeds, and know which are early, and which late, varieties, in what order they ripen, which give good flour for porridge, and which have sweet stalks for chewing. The plant thrives in black clays which hold up water, but shows much adaptability and ripens also on the more sandy stretches on which the Nuer build their villages, though in such spots it has less resistance to drought and a second sowing is very uncertain. Eastern Jikany is probably the best millet country in Nuerland, and, although in many parts it is too flooded for a second crop, it is the only section I have seen which can generally be relied on to yield sufficient grain to support the population. Lak and Thiang tribal areas in the Zeraf Island, which I have not visited, are said to be good grain country.

Even millet will not flourish in standing water, so that the gardens have to be made on higher land. Where circumstances permit homesteads to be built over a wide stretch of country gardens can be made almost anywhere between them, but where they are strung out along a ridge there is less choice, for the back of the ridge is too hard, does not retain enough water, and is required for grazing. Cultivations are therefore made behind the huts and byres between the summit of the ridge and the sunken plain. Among the Western Nuer, in the higher parts where there is a slight slope, small dams are often constructed to prevent the water running from the gardens. If, on the contrary, the millet is likely to be flooded where the ridge slopes into the plain, drainage canals, sometimes several feet deep and over fifty yards in length, are dug to take excess of water into the bush. These gardens form a continuous line behind the homesteads and if there is sufficient land there for cultivation people do not cultivate elsewhere. If there is not enough land they cultivate along the ridge beyond the confines of the village where it is too damp for building but not too flooded for millet gardens, or in near-by forest.

There is enough land for everybody on the Nuer scale of cultivation and consequently questions of tenure do not arise. It is taken for granted that a man has a right to cultivate the ground behind his homestead unless some one is already using it, and a man can choose any spot outside the village which is not occupied by the gardens of others. New-comers are always in some way related to some of the villagers, and kinsmen do not dispute about gardens. Moreover, owing to the conformation of Nuer villages, there is a rough correlation between the size of population and the area of cultivable land, for where suitable land is limited so is space for building.

It has been remarked that when once established millet shows great resistance to climatic variations. The difficulty is for it to become established. It frequently happens shortly after sowing that there is a short period of drought in which the young shoots wither and die. Sometimes this is due to the hungry people sowing too soon, but it is generally unavoidable, because if they wait too long before planting, the millet becomes subject to smut and neither bears nor ripens properly. It also frequently happens that heavy and violent rain destroys the seedlings by beating them into the sticky clay or by washing the soil from their roots. I have not known a season in Nuerland in which drought or excessive rain did not in some measure destroy the crops after sowing. Elephants do much damage when the millet has passed the vulnerable seedling period and I have known the gardens of a village to be partially destroyed three years in succession by these beasts. Weaver-birds take an annual toll when the millet is ripening, but Nuer do nothing to scare them unless they are in such numbers that they threaten to consume the whole harvest, when they erect bird-watching platforms in the gardens. In some years—I do not know how often—the country is visited by locusts which cause immediate and wholesale destruction. At various stages of growth guinea-fowl, crows, ostriches, and some of the smaller antelopes do much damage, and waterbuck show a great liking for the second crop. Sometimes, though I think rarely, Nuer build huts in their gardens, if they are some way from the village, to guard the millet from these depredations, but generally they show little concern, hoping that the proximity of dwellings will keep animals away and, if it does not, accepting the consequences with a detachment that appears sometimes to be almost indifference.

HORTICULTURAL CALENDAR

Apr.	*May*	*June*	*July*	*Aug.*	*Sept.*	*Oct.*	*Nov.*	*Dec.*	*Jan.*
Sow maize			Harvest maize						
	Sow first millet				Harvest first millet				
		Sow beans				Harvest beans			
			Sow *jaak* millet				Harvest *jaak* millet		
			Sow tobacco			Harvest tobacco			
					Sow second millet			Harvest second millet	

The calendar shown above is an approximation, since the time of sowing and harvesting depends on the commencement of the first heavy rains, which is subject to annual variations. The horticultural season generally begins at the end of March for those who are able to spend the drought in or near their homes on river banks, but most people have to wait till they can return to their villages in April or May before they can start clearing their gardens. Married people usually return to their villages in the first half of

PLATE X

Harpoon-fishing in shallows (Sobat river)

PLATE XI

a. Open savannah in the dry season (Lou)

b. Clearing millet garden for late sowing (Lou)

May and start to prepare the ground around their homesteads for maize. At the end of the month, or in June, the younger people return with the cattle and assist in clearing last year's millet gardens and in the hard work of hoeing new ground. Prolific grasses spring up with the millet which has to be weeded at least three, and maybe four or five, times. The more weeding done for the first crop the less is needed for the second crop.

While the first crop is ripening adjacent strips are cleared for the second crop (Plate XI (b)), which is sown shortly before the first is harvested, at the end of August or in September, and it grows together with the new shoots that spring from the roots of the first crop after its stems have been chopped down. In Eastern Nuerland the second sowing is made among the standing crop or on an extension of the garden, but in Western Nuerland and in parts of the Zeraf Island the ground is so flooded that it is made on prepared mounds of earth. I would again draw attention to Plate XII, where these mounds are illustrated, for it admirably shows what Nuerland is like in the rains and conveys a clear impression of the obstacles confronting Nuer horticulture. The second crop has also to be weeded several times and, as the same garden will be used for the first sowing in the following rains, the more thoroughly it is weeded now the less work there will be to do then. In many parts of Nuerland the second harvest may be almost as big as the first, and it is probably that where local conditions are adverse to one crop they favour the other. It appears that while the sown millet of the second crop requires much moisture and will not flourish if the rains fall off early the millet which sprouts from the old stems does best in drier conditions and may be spoilt by late heavy showers, so that one or the other is likely to ripen, and in moderate conditions both may thrive.

In some districts of the Lou and Eastern Jikany tribes the culture of a slow-maturing millet called *jaak* (*Sorghum durra*) has been copied from the Dinka. The spot chosen for cultivation is not burnt at the annual firing of the bush, but early in the following rains when the new grasses have sprung up among the old. Although this kind of millet has certain disadvantages it has caught on in a few places because it requires less clearing and weeding and is very hardy.

Nuer know nothing of crop rotation, having indeed no crops to rotate, nor of manures, though the droppings of cattle and the ashes of burnt weeds and brushwood no doubt act as fertilizers. They never allow their homestead gardens to lie fallow for a year to enable the soil to recuperate, but plant year after year till it is utterly exhausted, when they change their homestead site, often moving for some years to a new village. Nevertheless, they know that each year of tillage means further deterioration and judge the impoverishment of the soil by the size of the millet plants and of their yield and by the presence of certain weeds which only flourish on exhausted ground. A garden is cultivated annually for from five to ten years and after it has been left fallow for a few seasons it is tested to see whether the soil is still hard and caked, or loose, soft, and ready to bear a new crop. In gardens cultivated in bush sites away from the villages, on the other hand, people are not confined by the gardens of their neighbours, and it is possible to hoe a virgin piece of ground each year at one end and to abandon an exhausted piece at the other end.

Nuer gardens are very small. Measurements do not give so clear an idea of their size as noting that in an average year the people in most parts of Nuerland have just enough grain to last them till the following harvest, if they are very economical during the dry season and subsist mainly on milk and fish, while in a bad year they may have to go without porridge for several weeks. Also it may be noted that Nuer do not build granaries, but find small grass and earthenware bins, kept in their huts, sufficient for storage. However, we may judge how important millet is to them less by its quantity than by its place in their total food-supply, for it is not merely a subsidiary item of diet of high nutritive value but is an essential food, since they would be hard pressed to maintain life without it. Nuer fully acknowledge that this is so and in no way despise horticulture, but are, on the whole, industrious gardeners.

Nevertheless, they consider that horticulture is an unfortunate necessity involving hard and unpleasant labour and not an ideal occupation, and they tend to act on the conviction that the larger the herd the smaller need be the garden. They are herdsmen and not peasants. When I have drawn attention to badly kept gardens or remarked that the crops received no protection from beasts and birds they have been unperturbed, for, while it would be disgraceful to neglect cattle, there are no strong feelings about inattention to gardens. When I have asked them why they do not sow more millet I have often received some such reply as: 'Oh well, such is our custom. We have cattle.'

I wish to emphasize, in conclusion, the following points: (1) that Nuer cultivate only enough grain for it to be one element in their food-supply and not enough to live on it alone; (2) that with their present climate and technology considerable increase in horticulture would be unprofitable; and (3) that the dominance of the pastoral value over horticultural interests is in accord with oecological relations which favour cattle husbandry at the expense of horticulture. Nuer values and oecological relations, therefore, combine to maintain the bias towards cattle husbandry, in spite of rinderpest having rendered it a more precarious occupation than hitherto.

IX

It has been mentioned that Nuer must have a mixed economy in the given oecological relations because no one source of food is sufficient to keep them alive, and that the dominant food-producing activity at each season is determined by the oecological cycle. The different elements of diet, therefore, have an oecologically determined relation to one another and these relations can be roughly plotted.

Milk foods, millet in the form of porridge and beer, a little maize, fish, and meat, are the main items of Nuer diet. Milk is a staple food all the year round, though cows probably tend to give a smaller yield towards the end of the rains owing to insufficiency of pasturage, and it is said that there is a tendency for them to calve in numbers after the first harvest and therefore to cease lactating a few weeks earlier—if this is correct it is possibly due to the hot weather in February and March bringing the cows on heat. This seasonal tendency and the respective contributions of cattle and millet to Nuer food-supply are brought out in a story in which Cow and Millet have a dispute. Cow says that Millet is a person of no importance and that it is her milk that keeps people alive throughout the year, while in time of famine they can eat her flesh and live. Millet replies that Cow's claims are doubtless just, but that when she is ripe the children are glad, for they chew the sweet stems and rub out the grain between their hands and eat it, and there is plenty of porridge and beer. Cow argues that anyhow porridge without milk is unpalatable and that her milk will be finished by the time Millet is ripe. It is difficult to confirm these variations in the yield of milk or to estimate their importance, but the tendency for it to rise slightly in the dry season is indicated in the chart opposite.

Millet is consumed as porridge and beer in large quantities in the months between the first harvest and departure for dry-season camps. If the harvest has been good people like to eat their daily porridge in camps, and when the camp grain-supply runs short women journey to the villages to replenish it. When camps break up and people return to their villages millet consumption increases, beer being again brewed, and in a good year there is sufficient to satisfy requirements till the new harvest is ripe. In a normal year Nuer can just tide over these months if they are economical and have been careful not to use much grain in camp. Only in the most favoured parts of the country are they assured of an adequate supply throughout the year. In most parts there is always a very narrow margin between sufficiency and want, and in a bad year starvation is not infrequent. If the crops fail people survive on milk, fish, and wild fruits, and in extremity may kill some of their beasts. Rinderpest is considered a worse calamity. When rinderpest and failure of crops occur in the same year people expect the older age-sets to be wiped out. Much suffering may be caused by excessive drought or flood, which injure both crops and grazing.

There are good and bad fishing years. Generally, over the greater part of the country, consumption of fish is very low, or entirely absent, at the height of the rains. It rises rapidly to a peak at the commencement of the dry weather, and after descending from this point of great abundance remains fairly constant through the drought, rising again in the early rains. Meat of domesticated stock is mainly eaten after harvest when sacrifices and feasts take place. Cattle are seldom slaughtered in the dry season and, in my experience, Nuer do not kill many wild animals, so that consumption of meat is very low at this time of year, though the deficiency is to some extent made up by bleeding the cows and, in rinderpest years, by eating the carcasses of its victims. On the whole the curve of meat consumption follows that of grain consumption. We need not consider consumption of bush products in a normal year, though it may be kept in mind that they are very useful in famine years, chiefly from January to April.

It will be seen from this chart of relative consumption, which

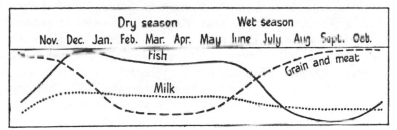

is only presented as a virtual approximation, that fish largely takes the place of grain and meat as the principal food from January to June and that the time when there is most likely to be a shortage of milk and when few, or no, fish are caught is that when there is plenty of porridge and beer. 'The hungry months', as the Nuer call them, are from May to August when the supply of fish quickly diminishes and maize and millet are still ripening. The months of plenty are from September to the middle of December, when there is abundant millet, and generally much meat, while the end of this period is the best time for fishing. Nuer say that they put on flesh in the rains and lose it in the drought. We may conclude, I think, that even in normal years Nuer do not receive as much nourishment as they require. Their diet is well-balanced, but there is not enough of it at some seasons and there is no surplus to fall back on in the all-too-frequent years of scarcity. Much of Nuer custom and thought is to be attributed to this insufficiency of food. It is wistfully related in one of their stories how once upon a time Man's stomach led an independent life in the bush and lived on small insects roasted by the firing of the grasses, for 'Man was not created with a stomach. It was created apart from him.' One day Man was walking in the bush and came across Stomach there and put it in its present place that it might feed there. Although when it lived by itself it was satisfied with tiny morsels of food, it is now always hungry. No matter how much it eats it is soon craving for more.

Seasonal variation in quantity and kind of food is sociologically significant for several reasons, though not all are relevant to the present study. It is, however, important to note that abundance of millet is the main reason for holding ceremonies in the rains, for ritual is seldom complete without porridge and beer and, since it consists of sacrifice, of meat also. Weddings, initiation rites, and religious ceremonies of various kinds take place in the rains and early drought, generally after the first millet harvest. This is also the main season for raiding the Dinka. Nuer say that hunger and war are bad companions and that they are too hungry to fight in the full dry season; and it is evident that they are then not so eager to come to blows over personal and community quarrels as they are in the rainy months, when they are replete with grain and meat and, especially at wedding dances, sometimes slightly intoxicated. Nor do the young men find dancing so attractive in the drought, whereas in the rains they dance as much as possible and think nothing of travelling many miles to attend weddings, at which they dance from eventide till well into the morning. The tempo of village life is different from that of camp life. Owing to flooding at the height of the rains these joint activities take place mainly at the beginning and end—chiefly at the end —of the wet season.

Scarcity of food at times and the narrow margin that for most of the year divides sufficiency from famine cause a high degree of interdependence among members of the smaller local groups, which may be said to have a common stock of food. Although each household owns its own food, does its own cooking, and provides independently for the needs of its members, men, and much less, women and children, eat in one another's homes to such an extent that, looked at from outside, the whole community is seen to be partaking of a joint supply. Rules of hospitality and conventions about the division of meat and fish lead to a far wider sharing of food than a bare statement of the principles of ownership would suggest. Young men eat at all byres in the vicinity; every household gives beer parties which their neighbours and kinsmen attend; the same people are given food and beer at the co-operative work parties that assist in any difficult and laborious task; in camps it is considered correct for men to visit the windscreens of their friends to drink milk, and a special gourd of sour milk is kept for guests; when an ox is sacrificed or a wild animal is killed the meat is always, in one way or another, widely distributed; people are expected to give part of their catch of fish to those who ask them for it; people assist one another when there is a shortage of milk or grain; and so forth. This mutual assistance and common consumption of food, which is especially evident in compact dry-season camps, belongs rather to the subject of domestic and kinship relations than to the present account. I wish here only to stress the following points: (1) This habit of share and share alike is easily understandable in a community where every one is likely to find himself in difficulties from time to time, for it is scarcity and not sufficiency that makes people generous, since everybody is thereby insured against hunger. He who is in need to-day receives help from him who may be in like need to-morrow. (2) While the greatest sharing is in the smaller domestic and kinship groups, there is also so much mutual assistance and hospitality among members of villages and camps that one may speak of a common economy of these communities, which are treated in this book as the smallest political groups in Nuerland and within which are taken for granted ties of kinship, affinity, age-sets, and so forth.

X

I have examined Nuer food-supply in relation to their oecology and I now give a brief account of their material culture in the same terms. When a Nuer is born he enters not only into a natural environment but also into a domesticated environment which is the product of human labour; and this inner world is constructed from the outer world, its form and content being strictly limited by natural resources. I am neither desirous nor capable of describing technological procedures, and to excuse myself in some degree for this omission I am including in this and in a second volume an unusually large number of plates and figures illustrating many examples of Nuer handiwork. However, some general remarks on the limiting conditions of production seem pertinent.

Nuerland lacks the two raw materials that have played so important a part in the manufacture of primitive tools: iron and stone. Nuer have always been poor in iron objects. Till recently they possessed very few iron spears, cherished as heirlooms, but used instead the straightened horns of antelope and buck, ebony wood, and the rib-bones of giraffe, all of which are still used to-day, though almost entirely in dances (Fig. 11). Wooden hoes were used for gardening, and are still sometimes so used to-day. Iron bells (Fig. 4) are rare and highly prized even at the present time, and in the old days iron rings and bracelets were important pieces of property. Wooden bells and ivory and leather rings and bracelets took their place in common use. Nuer have no knowledge of smelting and little of the blacksmith's art. I have never seen a forge and, though there are certainly some blacksmiths, their art is crude and may be regarded as a recent innovation, at any rate in most parts of Nuerland. Spears bought from Arab merchants are beaten out in the cold.

Nuerland also lacks any kind of hard stone. Indeed, outside villages I have never seen a stone. They are sometimes brought from neighbouring areas and employed as hammers, for smoothing metal ornaments, for rubbing skins, and so on. Grinding grain seems to have been a recent introduction. The grinder is made from thornwood and the grindstone from baked marsh mud mixed with finely pounded potsherds (Fig. 12). With clay, mud, and sand, Nuer also make pots, grain-bins, pipes, toys, hearthstones, and firescreens; construct the walls of byres and huts; and coat floors and those parts of homesteads they wish to keep smooth and clean.

Nature, which denies them iron and stone, is niggardly in her gift of wood. Large trees are rare. Thornwood and low brushwood provide timber for building, spear-shafts, harpoon-shafts, clubs (Frontispiece and Plate VIII), pestles, neck-rests, baskets, and winnowing trays. Probably no trees in Nuerland are suitable for carving and Nuer possess no wooden utensils. Even the ebony they use for making spears is not found in their country. Ambatch-trees grow in some parts of the swamp areas and from it is made an object which serves as a parrying stick, tobacco pouch, pillow, and seat (Plate XXIX). Byre and kraal fires are fed with dried dung, and wood fuel is only employed in the kitchen—grasses and millet stalks sometimes being used as a substitute. Grasses, millet stalks, and some plants are also used for various purposes: rafters, windscreens, thatching, cord, basketwork, &c. Gourds are cultivated for dairy utensils.

Lacking iron and stone Nuer thus make use of vegetable and earthy materials instead. Animal products are also a valuable source of material, as may be seen in the list of the uses of the bodies and bodily products of cattle on pp. 28 and 30. The bodies of wild animals replace those of cattle in some, but not many, of these uses, e.g. the skins of tiang and cob are used as sleeping-rugs, waterbuck-skin for the tympana of drums, giraffe-skin for cord, the scrota of giraffe for bags (Fig. 3), the horns of buffalo for spoons (Fig. 14), and the bones and hides of various animals and the tusks of elephants for armlets, leglets, wristlets, finger-rings, &c., and so forth. They can further be employed, though here also to a limited extent, for purposes for which bovine products are unsuitable, e.g. hippopotamus- and buffalo-hide for shields and sandals, elephant-hide also being used for the second purpose; horns and ribs, as mentioned above, for spear-points; leopard- and genet-skins for ritual and ceremonial apparel; and so forth. Ostrich eggs and shells of the giant land snail are manufactured into waist-bands and the second are used for cutting heads of millet in harvesting.

I have indicated a few of the uses to which animal products are put to give the reader a general idea of the limitations imposed on Nuer economy by their environment and of the way they manage to overcome the natural poverty of their country. Taken with the earlier list of uses of cattle we can say that the Nuer do not live in an iron age or even in a stone age, but in an age, whatever it may be called, in which plants and beasts furnish technological necessities.

Deficiency of food and other raw materials can be corrected by trade. However, Nuer seem to have engaged very little in it. Many of their iron weapons and ornaments probably came through Dinka hands from the so-called Jur peoples (Bongo-Mittu group) and the iron-working sections of Dinka tribes to the west of the Nile. Much of it was doubtless booty, though some was certainly traded.[1] The Eastern Gaajak traded iron for ivory with the Galla of Ethiopia, but I doubt whether much iron came from this source before the Abyssinian conquest of the Western Galla towards the end of the nineteenth century. At the beginning of the present century there was some trading of ivory from Nuerland to the Ethiopian markets at Gore and Sayo, and this went on till very recently. A considerable distance separated these markets from the main supply in the Zeraf Island, and people from Eastern Gaajak country in the dry season, at any rate in some seasons, took cattle, tobacco, and spearheads to the Zeraf and returned with ivory. A good tusk fetched up to twenty

[1] Poncet, op. cit., p. 44.

head of cattle.[1] This trade was forbidden some years ago and has probably not a long history, because early writers give no information that might lead us to suppose that it went on previous to the reconquest of the Sudan and the Abyssinian conquest of Western Ethiopia. There was some ivory-trading on the Zeraf between Nuer and Arabs from the middle of the nineteenth century. Metal ornaments and venetian glass beads seem to have been offered in exchange. Nuer may have traded some tobacco, and possibly an occasional canoe, from the Anuak of the Baro and Gila rivers, but it is more likely that they usually acquired these objects by raiding. I do not discuss here the very small trade carried on to-day by Arab shopkeepers who live a hard, and generally unprofitable, life here and there on the main waterways. Nuer obtain from them spears, hoes, fish-hooks, ornaments, and occasionally an anvil, grindstone, &c., and they purchase skins of oxen, and sometimes oxen, from the Nuer. Nuer economy has not been much affected thereby. Nuer do not sell their labour.

We may conclude, therefore, that trade is a very unimportant social process among the Nuer. Many reasons can be adduced to explain this fact. I mention only a few. Nuer have nothing to trade except their cattle and have no inclination to dispose of these; all they greatly desire are more cattle, and, apart from the difficulty that they have nothing to offer in exchange for them, herds are more easily and pleasantly increased by raiding the Dinka; they are seldom on such friendly terms with their neighbours that trade can flourish between them, and, although there may have been sporadic exchange with Dinka and Anuak, it is probable that most objects obtained from these peoples were spoil; they have no money, no markets, and no transport other than human porterage; &c. A further reason, and one that requires emphasis, is the dominant interest of the Nuer in their herds. This narrow focus of interest causes them to be inattentive to the products of other people, for which, indeed, they feel no need and often enough show contempt.

There is very little exchange within Nuerland itself, there being no high specialization and no diversity in the distribution of raw material. The only trading I have seen, apart from the exchange of small commodities and minor services mentioned in the next section, is the exchange of some cattle, mainly oxen, by the Lou for Eastern Gaajok grain in a famine year. I think it most unlikely that such exchanges went on before British occupation of the country, though there was, according to Nuer, sometimes an exchange of an animal for grain in bad years between persons of the same district.

---

[1] Bimbashi H. Gordon, *Sudan Intelligence Report*, no. 107, 1903.

Nuer have, it will be acknowledged, a low technology which, taken with their meagre food-supply and scanty trade, may be supposed to have some effect on their social relations and their character. Social ties are narrowed, as it were, and the people of village and camp are drawn closer together, in a moral sense, for they are in consequence highly interdependent and their activities tend to be joint undertakings. This is seen best in the dry season, when the cattle of many families are tethered in a common kraal and driven as a single herd to the grazing grounds and daily activities are co-ordinated into a common rhythm of life.

I risk being accused of speaking idly when I suggest that a very simple material culture narrows social ties in another way. Technology from one point of view is an oecological process: an adaptation of human behaviour to natural circumstances. From another point of view material culture may be regarded as part of social relations, for material objects are chains along which social relationships run, and the more simple is a material culture the more numerous are the relationships expressed through it. I give, without further explanation, a few examples. The simple family is attached to the hut, the household to the byre, the joint family to the hamlet, the village community to its ridge, and village communities are linked together by paths. Herds of cattle are nuclei around which kinship groups are clustered and the relationships between their members operate through cattle and are expressed in terms of cattle. A single small artifact may be a nexus between persons, e.g. a spear which passes from father to son by gift or inheritance is a symbol of their relationship and one of the bonds by which it is maintained. Thus people not only create their material culture and attach themselves to it, but also build up their relationships through it and see them in terms of it. As Nuer have very few kinds of material objects and very few specimens of each kind, their social value is increased by their having to serve as the media of many relationships and they are, in consequence, often invested with ritual functions. Moreover social relationships instead of being diffused along many chains of material links are narrowed by the meagreness of culture to a few simple foci of interest. This may be supposed to lead to a small range of relationship-forms with a high degree of solidarity in the smaller local and kinship groups and we may expect to find a simple social structure. Some outstanding traits in Nuer character may be said to be consistent with their low technology and scanty food-supply. I again emphasize the crudity and discomfort of their lives. All who have lived with Nuer would, I believe, agree that though they are very poor in goods they are very proud in spirit. Schooled in hardship and hunger—for both they express contempt—they accept the direst calamities with resignation and endure them with courage. Content with few goods they despise all that lies outside them; their derisive pride amazes a stranger. Reliant on one another they are loyal and generous to their kinsmen. One might even to some extent attribute their pronounced individualism to resistance to the persistent claims of kinsmen and neighbours against which they have no protection but stubbornness. The qualities which have been mentioned, courage, generosity, patience, pride, loyalty, stubbornness, and independence, are the virtues the Nuer themselves extol, and these values can be shown to be very appropriate to their simple mode of life and to the simple set of social relations it engenders.

XI

It is unnecessary to write more on what are generally called economics. They can be further considered in an account of kinship and family life. I will only ask the reader to bear in mind the following matters. (1) One cannot treat Nuer economic relations by themselves, for they always form part of direct social relationships of a general kind. Thus, division of labour is part of general relationships between persons of different sexes and of different ages, between spouses, between parents and children, between kinsmen of one order or another, and so forth. (2) There is some specialization, but it is occasional, and there are no occupations which can be called professions. Some women make better pots, grindstones, and baskets than others; only smiths can make certain objects; there are only a few men who understand how to make and put on the arm the tight-fitting bracelets which young men wear to show their endurance, and so on; and people who want these things either ask for them in the name of kinship or give the maker of them some millet for his services, or make him a gift on some future occasion. The man who wants the object

PLATE XII

Millet garden in October (Rengyan)

PLATE XIII

Girl in millet garden (Dok)

and the maker of it always belong to the same local community and conduct the affair between themselves, there being no exchange of objects or services through the medium of a third person, and there is always between them a general social relationship of one kind or another, and their economic relations, if such they may be called, must conform to this general pattern of behaviour. (3) There is little inequality of wealth and no class privilege. A man does not acquire more objects than he can use. Were he to do so he could only dispose of them by giving them away. It is true that cattle can be amassed, but, except for a few sacred herds kept by prophets, in fact they are not. As has been explained, periodic rinderpest levels the herds and, apart from this, when a herd has reached a certain size the owner—if one may speak of an owner of a herd in which many people have rights of one kind and another—is morally bound to dispose of a portion of it by either himself marrying or by assisting a relative to do so. Cattle are sometimes loaned to persons and the owner is entitled to receive back better beasts than those he lent, e.g. a heifer for the loan of an ox ; but people only lend cattle to those with whom they have an established social relationship. (4) In a narrow sense the simple family might be called the economic unit, but we have seen that it is not self-sufficient and the active participation of a wider group is often necessary, e.g. in building, fishing, and hunting. It is also clear that a single family cannot herd its cattle in distant pastures and, at the same time, herd the calves elsewhere, attend to the tiny calves in the kraal, milk, churn, clean the kraal, prepare dung for fuel, cook the food, and so on, by itself. Co-operation is found among neighbours who are also kinsmen. There is also much mutual assistance when co-operation is not essential to the performance of a task, e.g. in weeding and harvesting, for it is conventional to ask people for help, the obligation to assist being part of a general kinship relationship. (5) It must be recognized also that fishing, hunting, herding, and the other activities I have described are always, in a sense, collective actions, for even when there is no active co-operation the whole community passively participates in them. A single man may drive a herd to pasture, a single boy may fish in river shallows, and a single woman may cook, but they can only do these things because they belong to a community and because their actions are related in a productive system. Tradition dictates ends and means and the organization and potential strength of the community gives the co-ordination and security necessary for accomplishment. It has been remarked that seen from the outside a whole village community may be said to be consuming a common stock of food.

From the same angle the whole community may be said to create it.

I may sum up by repeating that economic relations among the Nuer are part of general social relationships and that these relationships, being mainly of a domestic or kinship order, lie outside the scope of this book. I must emphasize, however, that the members of various segments of a village have close economic relations and that all the people of a village have common economic interests, forming a corporation which owns its particular gardens, water-supplies, fishing-pools, and grazing grounds; which herds its cattle in a compact camp in the drought; and operates jointly in defence, in herding, and in other activities; and in which, especially in the smaller villages, there is much co-operation in labour and sharing of food. All this must be taken for granted in future references to villages. It must be further emphasized that climatic conditions together with a pastoral mode of life necessitate relations beyond the limits of a village and give to wider political groups an economic purpose. This statement will later be examined more closely.

XII

I wish to emphasize the following general points in summary of those conclusions reached in the first two chapters which have special relevance to a study of the political institutions of the Nuer.

1. Oecological relations appear to be in a state of equilibrium. As long as present relations exist cattle husbandry, horticulture, and fishing can be pursued but cannot be improved. Man holds his own in the struggle but does not advance.

2. The necessity of a mixed economy follows from the oecological equilibrium. Rinderpest prevents complete dependence upon milk foods; climate prevents complete dependence on grain; and hydrological variations prevent complete dependence on fish. These three elements together enable Nuer to live, and their seasonal distribution determines Nuer modes of life at different periods of the year.

3. The oecology gives to this mixed economy a bias in favour of cattle husbandry, and this bias must have been far stronger

before the introduction of rinderpest. It is in accord with the superlative place of cattle in the Nuer scale of values.

4. A full sedentary and a full nomadic life are alike incompatible with Nuer economy, which demands transhumance. Location and size of wet season villages and the direction of movement in the dry season are determined by their oecology. The oecological rhythm divides the Nuer year into two divisions, the wet season when they live in villages and the dry season when they live in camps, and camp life falls into two parts, the earlier period of small, temporary camps and the later period of large concentrations in sites occupied every year.

5. Scarcity of food, a low technology, and absence of trade makes the members of smaller local groups directly interdependent and tends to make them economic corporations and not merely residential units to which a certain political value is attached. The same conditions and the pursuit of a pastoral life in difficult circumstances produces indirect interdependence between persons living in much larger areas and compels their acceptance of conventions of a political order.

6. The past tendency to migrate, the present transhumance, and the desire to repair losses to stock by raiding the Dinka, enhance the political importance of units larger than villages, for villages cannot, for economic and military reasons, easily maintain a self-sufficient isolation, and permit us to discuss the political system mainly as a set of structural relations between territorial segments larger than village communities.

CHAPTER III

TIME AND SPACE

I

In this chapter we look backwards on our description of Nuer interest in cattle and of their oecology and forwards to an account of their political structure. Their oecology limits and in other ways influences their social relations, but the value given to oecological relations is equally significant in understanding the social system, which is a system within the oecological system, partly dependent on it and partly existing in its own right. Ultimately most, perhaps all, concepts of time and space are determined by the physical ambient, but the values they embody are only one of many possible responses to it and depend also on structural principles, which belong to a different order of reality. In this book we are not describing Nuer cosmology but their political and other institutions, and are, therefore, interested mainly in the influence of oecological relations on these institutions rather than the influence of the social structure on the conceptualization of the oecological relations. Thus, to give one example, we do not describe how Nuer classify birds into various lineages on the pattern of their lineage structure. This chapter is therefore a bridge between the two parts of the book, but we cross it in one direction only.

In describing Nuer concepts of time we may distinguish between those that are mainly reflections of their relations to environment, which we call oecological time, and those that are reflections of their relations to one another in the social structure, which we call structural time. Both refer to successions of events which are of sufficient interest to the community for them to be noted and related to each other conceptually. The larger periods of time are almost entirely structural, because the events they relate are changes in the relationship of social groups. Moreover, time-reckoning based on changes in nature and man's response to them is limited to an annual cycle and therefore cannot be used to differentiate longer periods than seasons. Both, also, have limited and fixed notations. Seasonal and lunar changes repeat themselves year after year, so that a Nuer standing at any point of time has conceptual knowledge of what lies before him and can predict and organize his life accordingly. A man's structural future is likewise already fixed and ordered into different periods, so that the total changes in status a boy will undergo in his ordained passage through the social system, if he lives long enough, can be foreseen. Structural time appears to an individual passing through the social system to be entirely progressive, but, as we shall see, in a sense this is an illusion. Oecological time appears to be, and is, cyclical.

The oecological cycle is a year. Its distinctive rhythm is the backwards and forwards movement from villages to camps, which is the Nuer's response to the climatic dichotomy of rains and drought. The year (*ruon*) has two main seasons, *tot* and *mai*. *Tot*, from about the middle of March to the middle of September, roughly corresponds to the rise in the curve of rainfall, though it does not cover the whole period of the rains. Rain may fall heavily at the end of September and in early October, and the country is still flooded in these months which belong, nevertheless, to the *mai* half of the year, for it commences at the decline of the rains—not at their cessation—and roughly covers the trough of the curve, from about the middle of September to the middle of March. The two seasons therefore only approximate to our division into rains and drought, and the Nuer classification aptly summarizes their way of looking at the movement of time, the direction of attention in marginal months being as significant as the actual climatic conditions. In the middle of September Nuer turn, as it were, towards the life of fishing and cattle camps and feel that village residence and horticulture lie behind them. They begin to speak of camps as though they were already in being, and long to be on the move. This restlessness is even more marked towards the end of the drought when, noting cloudy skies, people turn towards the life of villages and make preparations for striking camp. Marginal months may therefore be classed as *tot* or *mai*, since they belong to one set of activities but presage the other set, for the concept of seasons is derived from social activities rather than from the climatic changes which determine them, and a year is to Nuer a period of village residence (*cieng*) and a period of camp residence (*wec*).

I have already noted the significant physical changes associated with rains and drought, and some of these have been presented in charts on pp. 52 and 53. I have also described, in the last chapter, the oecological movement that follows these physical changes where it affects human life to any degree. Seasonal variations in social activities, on which Nuer concepts of time are primarily based, have also been indicated and, on the economic side, recorded at some length. The main features of these three planes of rhythm, physical, oecological, and social, are charted on the opposite page.

The movements of the heavenly bodies other than the sun and the moon, the direction and variation of winds, and the migration of some species of birds are observed by the Nuer, but they do not regulate their activities in relation to them nor use them as points of reference in seasonal time-reckoning. The characters by which seasons are most clearly defined are those which control the movements of the people: water, vegetation, movements of fish, &c.; it being the needs of the cattle and variations in food-supply which chiefly translate oecological rhythm into the social rhythm of the year, and the contrast between modes of life at the height of the rains and at the height of the drought which provides the conceptual poles in time-reckoning.

Besides these two main seasons of *tot* and *mai* Nuer recognize two subsidiary seasons included in them, being transitional periods between them. The four seasons are not sharp divisions but overlap. Just as we reckon summer and winter as the halves of our year and speak also of spring and autumn, so Nuer reckon *tot* and *mai* as halves of their year and speak also of the seaons of *rwil* and *jiom*. *Rwil* is the time of moving from camp to village and of clearing and planting, from about the middle of March to the middle of June, before the rains have reached their peak. It counts as part of the *tot* half of the year, though it is contrasted with *tot* proper, the period of full village life and horticulture, from about the middle of June to the middle of September. *Jiom*, meaning 'wind', is the period in which the persistent north wind begins to blow and people harvest, fish

May June July August September October November December January February March April

R A I N S   D R O U G H T

R I V E R S   R I S E   R I V E R S   F A L L

H O R T I C U L T U R E

Preparation of gardens for first millet sowing and for maize

Preparation of gardens for second millet sowing

Harvest maize

Harvest first millet crop

BURNING OF THE BUSH

Harvest second millet crop

BUILDING & REPAIRING

F I S H I N G

H U N T I N G   A N D   C O L L E C T I N G

SCARCITY OF FOOD   PLENTY OF FOOD

V I L L A G E S   C A M P S

Older people return to villages

Younger people return to villages

Younger people in early camps

Every one in main dry-season camps

Wedding, initiation, mortuary, and other ceremonies

Main season for raiding Dinka

from dams, fire the bush, and form early camps, from about the middle of September to the middle of December. It counts as part of the *mai* half of the year, though it is contrasted with *mai* proper, from about the middle of December to the middle of March, when the main camps are formed. Roughly speaking, therefore, there are two major seasons of six months and four

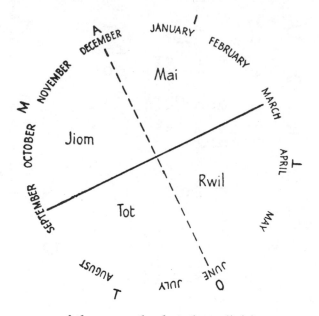

minor seasons of three months, but these divisions must not be regarded too rigidly since they are not so much exact units of time as rather vague conceptualizations of changes in oeco-logical relations and social activities which pass imperceptibly from one state to another.

In the diagram above a line drawn from mid March to mid September is the axis of the year, being an approximation to a cleavage between two opposed sets of oecological relations and social activities, though not entirely corresponding to it, as may be seen in the diagram below, where village life and camp life are shown in relation to the seasons of which they are the focal points. Nuer, especially the younger people, are still in camp for part of *tot* (the greater part of *rwil*) and are still in villages, especially the older people, for part of *mai* (the greater part of *jiom*), but every one is in villages during *tot* proper and in camps during *mai* proper. Since the words *tot* and *mai* are not pure units of time-reckoning but stand for the cluster of social activities characteristic of the height of the drought and of the height of the rains, one may hear a Nuer saying that he is going to '*tot*' or '*mai*' in a certain place.

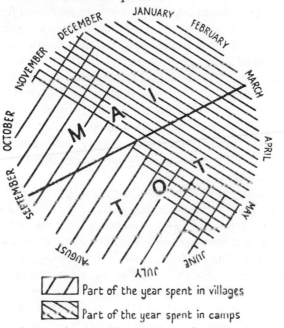

Part of the year spent in villages

Part of the year spent in camps

The year has twelve months, six to each of the major seasons, and most adult Nuer can state them in order. In the list of months given below it has not been possible to equate each Nuer name with an English name, because our Roman months have nothing to do with the moon. It will be found, however, that a Nuer month is usually covered by the two English months equated to it in the list and generally tends to coincide with the first rather than the second.

teer	Sept.–Oct.	*duong*	Mar.–Apr.
lath (*boor*)	Oct.–Nov.	*gwaak*	Apr.–May
kur	Nov.–Dec.	*dwat*	May–June
tiop (*in*) *dit*	Dec.–Jan.	*kornyuot*	June–July
tiop (*in*) *tot*	Jan.–Feb.	*paiyatni* (*paiyene*)	July–Aug.
pet	Feb.–Mar.	*thoor*	Aug.–Sept.

Nuer would soon be in difficulties over their lunar calendar if they consistently counted the succession of moons,¹ but there are certain activities associated with each month, the association sometimes being indicated by the name of the month. The calendar is a relation between a cycle of activities and a conceptual cycle and the two cannot fall apart, since the conceptual cycle is dependent on the cycle of activities from which it derives its meaning and function. Thus a twelve-month system does not incommode Nuer, for the calendar is anchored to the cycle of oecological changes. In the month of *kur* one makes the first fishing dams and forms the first cattle camps, and since one is doing these things it must be *kur* or thereabouts. Likewise in *dwat* one breaks camp and returns to the villages, and since people are on the move it must be *dwat* or thereabouts. Consequently the calendar remains fairly stable and in any section of Nuerland there is general agreement about the name of the current month.

In my experience Nuer do not to any great extent use the names of the months to indicate the time of an event, but generally refer instead to some outstanding activity in process at the time of its occurrence, e.g. at the time of early camps, at the time of weeding, at the time of harvesting, &c., and it is easily understandable that they do so, since time is to them a relation between activities. During the rains the stages in the growth of millet and the steps taken in its culture are often used as points of reference. Pastoral activities, being largely undifferentiated throughout the months and seasons, do not provide suitable points.

There are no units of time between the month and day and night. People indicate the occurrence of an event more than a day or two ago by reference to some other event which took place at the same time or by counting the number of intervening 'sleeps' or, less commonly, 'suns'. There are terms for to-day, to-morrow, yesterday, &c., but there is no precision about them. When Nuer wish to define the occurrence of an event several days in advance, such as a dance or wedding, they do so by

¹ There is some evidence of an intercalary month among the Eastern Jikany, but I cannot be definite on this point, and I have not heard it mentioned in other parts of Nuerland.

reference to the phases of the moon: new moon, its waxing, full moon, its waning, and the brightness of its second quarter. When they wish to be precise they state on which night of the waxing or waning an event will take place, reckoning fifteen nights to each and thirty to the month. They say that only cattle and the Anuak can see the moon in its invisible period. The only terms applied to the nightly succession of lunar phases are those that describe its appearance just before, and in, fullness.

The course of the sun determines many points of reference, and a common way of indicating the time of events is by pointing to that part of the heavens the sun will then have reached in its course. There are also a number of expressions, varying in the degree of their precision, which describe positions of the sun in the heavens, though, in my experience, the only ones commonly employed are those that refer to its more conspicuously differentiated movements: the first stroke of dawn, sunrise, noon, and sunset. It is, perhaps, significant that there are almost as many points of reference between 4 and 6 a.m. as there are for the rest of the day. This may be chiefly due to striking contrasts caused by changes in relations of earth to sun during these two hours, but it may be noted, also, that the points of reference between them are more used in directing activities, such as starting on journeys, rising from sleep, tethering cattle in kraals, gazelle hunting, &c., than points of reference during most of the rest of the day, especially in the slack time between 1 and 3 p.m. There are also a number of terms to describe the time of night. They are to a very limited extent determined by the course of the stars. Here again, there is a richer terminology for the transition period between day and night than during the rest of the night and the same reasons may be suggested to explain this fact. There are also expressions for distinguishing night from day, forenoon from afternoon, and that part of the day which is spent from that part which lies ahead.

Except for the commonest of the terms for divisions of the day they are little used in comparison with expressions which describe routine diurnal activities. The daily timepiece is the cattle clock, the round of pastoral tasks, and the time of day and the passage of time through a day are to a Nuer primarily the succession of these tasks and their relations to one another. The better demarcated points are taking of the cattle from byre to kraal, milking, driving of the adult herd to pasture, milking of the goats and sheep, driving of the flocks and calves to pasture, cleaning of byre and kraal, bringing home of the flocks and calves, the return of the adult herd, the evening milking, and the enclosure of the beasts in byres. Nuer generally use such points of activity, rather than concrete points in the movement of the sun across the heavens, to co-ordinate events. Thus a man says, 'I shall return at milking', 'I shall start off when the calves come home', and so forth.

Oecological time-reckoning is ultimately, of course, entirely determined by the movement of the heavenly bodies, but only some of its units and notations are directly based on these movements, e.g. month, day, night, and some parts of the day and night, and such points of reference are paid attention to and selected as points only because they are significant for social activities. It is the activities themselves, chiefly of an economic kind, which are basic to the system and furnish most of its units and notations, and the passage of time is perceived in the relation of activities to one another. Since activities are dependent on the movement of the heavenly bodies and since the movement of the heavenly bodies is significant only in relation to the activities one may often refer to either in indication of the time of an event. Thus one may say, 'In the *jiom* season' or 'At early camps', 'The month of *Dwat*' or 'The return to villages', 'When the sun is warming up' or 'At milking'. The movements of the heavenly bodies permit Nuer to select natural points that are significant in relation to activities. Hence in linguistic usage nights, or rather 'sleeps', are more clearly defined units of time than days, or 'suns', because they are undifferentiated units of social activity, and months, or rather 'moons', though they are clearly differentiated units of natural time, are little employed as points of reference because they are not clearly differentiated units of activity, whereas the day, the year, and its main seasons are complete occupational units.

Certain conclusions may be drawn from this quality of time among the Nuer. Time has not the same value throughout the year. Thus in dry season camps, although daily pastoral tasks follow one another in the same order as in the rains, they do not take place at the same time, are more a precise routine owing to the severity of seasonal conditions, especially with regard to water and pasturage, and require greater co-ordination and co-operative action. On the other hand, life in the dry season is generally uneventful, outside routine tasks, and oecological and social relations are more monotonous from month to month than in the rains when there are frequent feasts, dances, and ceremonies. When time is considered as relations between activities it will be understood that it has a different connotation in rains and drought. In the drought the daily time-reckoning is more uniform and precise while lunar reckoning receives less attention, as appears from the lesser use of names of months, less confidence in stating their order, and the common East African trait of two dry-season months with the same name (*tiop in dit* and *tiop in tot*), the order of which is often interchanged. The pace of time may vary accordingly, since perception of time is a function of systems of time-reckoning, but we can make no definite statement on this question.

Though I have spoken of time and units of time the Nuer have no expression equivalent to 'time' in our language, and they cannot, therefore, as we can, speak of time as though it were something actual, which passes, can be wasted, can be saved, and so forth. I do not think that they ever experience the same feeling of fighting against time or of having to co-ordinate activities with an abstract passage of time, because their points of reference are mainly the activities themselves, which are generally of a leisurely character. Events follow a logical order, but they are not controlled by an abstract system, there being no autonomous points of reference to which activities have to conform with precision. Nuer are fortunate.

Also they have very limited means of reckoning the relative duration of periods of time intervening between events, since they have few, and not well-defined or systematized, units of time. Having no hours or other small units of time they cannot measure the periods which intervene between positions of the sun or daily activities. It is true that the year is divided into twelve lunar units, but Nuer do not reckon in them as fractions of a unit. They may be able to state in what month an event occurred, but it is with great difficulty that they reckon the relation between events in abstract numerical symbols. They think much more easily in terms of activities and of successions of activities and in terms of social structure and of structural differences than in pure units of time.

We may conclude that the Nuer system of time-reckoning within the annual cycle and parts of the cycle is a series of conceptualizations of natural changes, and that the selection of points of reference is determined by the significance which these natural changes have for human activities.

II

In a sense all time is structural since it is a conceptualization of collateral, co-ordinated, or co-operative activities: the movements of a group. Otherwise time concepts of this kind could not exist, for they must have a like meaning for every one within a group. Milking-time and meal-times are approximately the same for all people who normally come into contact with one another, and the movement from villages to camps has approximately the same connotation everywhere in Nuerland, though it may have a special connotation for a particular group of persons. There is, however, a point at which we can say that time concepts cease to be determined by oecological factors and become more determined by structural interrelations, being no longer a reflection of man's dependence on nature, but a reflection of the interaction of social groups.

The year is the largest unit of oecological time. Nuer have words for the year before last, last year, this year, next year, and the year after next. Events which took place in the last few years are then the points of reference in time-reckoning, and these are different according to the group of persons who make use of them: joint family, village, tribal section, tribe, &c. One of the commonest ways of stating the year of an event is to mention where the people of the village made their dry season camps, or to refer to some evil that befell their cattle. A joint family may reckon time in the birth of calves of their herds. Weddings and other ceremonies, fights, and raids, may likewise give points of time, though in the absence of numerical dating no one can say without lengthy calculations how many years ago an event took place. Moreover, since time is to Nuer an order of events of outstanding significance to a group, each group has its own points of reference and time is consequently relative to structural space, locally considered. This is obvious when we examine the names given to years by different tribes, or sometimes by adjacent tribes, for these are floods, pestilences, famines, wars, &c., experienced by the tribe. In course of time the names of years are forgotten and all events beyond the limits of this crude historical reckoning fade into the dim vista of long long ago. Historical time, in this sense of a sequence of outstanding events of significance to a tribe, goes back much farther than the historical time of smaller groups, but fifty years is probably its limit, and the farther back from the present day the sparser and vaguer become its points of reference.

However, Nuer have another way of stating roughly when events took place; not in numbers of years, but by reference to the age-set system. Distance between events ceases to be reckoned in time concepts as we understand them and is reckoned in terms of structural distance, being the relation between groups of persons. It is therefore entirely relative to the social structure. Thus a Nuer may say that an event took place after the *Thut* age-set was born or in the initiation period of the *Boiloc* age-set, but no one can say how many years ago it happened. Time is here reckoned in sets. If a man of the *Dangunga* set tells one that an event occurred in the initiation period of the *Thut* set he is saying that it happened three sets before his set, or six sets ago. The age-set system is discussed in Chapter VI. Here it need only be said that we cannot accurately translate a reckoning in sets into a reckoning in years, but that we can roughly estimate a ten-year interval between the commencement of successive sets. There are six sets in existence, the names of the sets are not cyclic, and the order of extinct sets, all but the last, are soon forgotten, so that an age-set reckoning has seven units covering a period of rather under a century.

The structural system of time-reckoning is partly the selection of points of reference of significance to local groups which give these groups a common and distinctive history; partly the distance between specific sets in the age-set system; and partly distances of a kinship and lineage order. Four generation-steps (*kath*) in the kinship system are linguistically differentiated relations, grandfather, father, son, and grandson, and within a small kinship group these relationships give a time-depth to members of the group and points of reference in a line of ascent by which their relationships are determined and explained. Any kinship relationship must have a point of reference on a line of ascent, namely a common ancestor, so that such a relationship always has a time connotation couched in structural

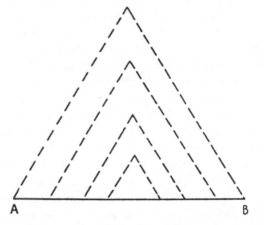

A   B

terms. Beyond the range of the kinship system in this narrow sense the connotation is expressed in terms of the lineage system. As this subject is treated in Chapter V, we limit further discussion of it to an explanatory comment on the diagram above. The base line of the triangle represents a given group of agnates and the dotted lines represent their ghostly agnatic forebears, running from this base to a point in lineage structure, the common ancestor of every member of the group. The farther we extend the range of the group (the longer becomes the base line) the farther back in lineage structure is the common ancestor (the farther from the base line is the apex of the triangle). The four triangles are thus the time depths of four extensions of agnatic relationship on an existential plane and represent minimal, minor, major, and maximal lineages of a clan. Lineage time is thus the structural distance between groups of persons on the line *AB*. Structural time therefore cannot be understood until structural distance is known, since it is a reflection of it, and we must, therefore, ask the reader to forgive a certain obscurity at this point and to reserve criticism till we have had an opportunity of explaining more clearly what is meant by structural distance.

We have restricted our discussion to Nuer systems of time-reckoning and have not considered the way in which an individual perceives time. The subject bristles with difficulties. Thus an individual may reckon the passage of time by reference to the physical appearance and status of other individuals and to changes in his own life-history, but such a method of reckoning time has no wide collective validity. We confess, however, that our observations on the matter have been slight and that a fuller analysis is beyond our powers. We have merely indicated those aspects of the problem which are directly related to the description of modes of livelihood which has gone before and to the description of political institutions which follows.

We have remarked that the movement of structural time is, in a sense, an illusion, for the structure remains fairly constant and the perception of time is no more than the movement of persons, often as groups, through the structure. Thus age-sets succeed one another for ever, but there are never more than six in existence and the relative positions occupied by these six sets at any time are fixed structural points through which actual sets of persons pass in endless succession. Similarly, for reasons which we explain later, the Nuer system of lineages may be considered a fixed system, there being a constant number of steps between living persons and the founder of their clan and the lineages having a constant position relative to one another. However many generations succeed one another the depth and range of lineages does not increase unless there has been structural change. These statements are discussed more fully on pp. 198–200.

Beyond the limits of historical time we enter a plane of tradition in which a certain element of historical fact may be supposed to be incorporated in a complex of myth. Here the points of reference are the structural ones we have indicated. At one end this plane merges into history; at the other end into myth. Time perspective is here not a true impression of actual distances like that created by our dating technique, but a reflection of relations between lineages, so that the traditional events recorded have to be placed at the points where the lineages concerned in them converge in their lines of ascent. The events have therefore a position in structure, but no exact position in historical time as we understand it. Beyond tradition lies the horizon of pure myth which is always seen in the same time perspective. One mythological event did not precede another, for myths explain customs of general social significance rather than the interrelations of particular segments and are, therefore, not structurally stratified. Explanations of any qualities of nature or of culture are drawn from this intellectual ambient which imposes limits on the Nuer world and makes it self-contained and entirely intelligible to Nuer in the relation of its parts. The world, peoples, and cultures all existed together from the same remote past.

It will have been noted that the Nuer time dimension is shallow. Valid history ends a century ago, and tradition, generously measured, takes us back only ten to twelve generations in lineage structure, and if we are right in supposing that lineage structure never grows, it follows that the distance between the beginning of the world and the present day remains unalterable. Time is thus not a continuum, but is a constant structural relationship between two points, the first and last persons in a line of agnatic descent. How shallow is Nuer time may be judged from the fact that the tree under which mankind came into being was still standing in Western Nuerland a few years ago!

Beyond the annual cycle, time-reckoning is a conceptualization of the social structure, and the points of reference are a projection into the past of actual relations between groups of persons. It is less a means of co-ordinating events than of co-ordinating relationships, and is therefore mainly a looking-backwards, since relationships must be explained in terms of the past.

III

We have concluded that structural time is a reflection of structural distance. In the following sections we define further what we mean by structural distance, and make a formal, preliminary, classification of Nuer territorial groups of a political kind. We have classified Nuer socio-temporal categories. We now classify their socio-spatial categories.

Were a man to fly over Nuerland he would see, as on Plate XVI, taken by the Royal Air Force in the dry season, white patches with what look like tiny fungoid growths on them. These are village sites with huts and byres. He would see that between such patches are stretches of brown and black, the brown being open grassland and the black being depressions which are swampy in the rains; and that the white patches are wider and more frequent in some parts than in others. We find Nuer give to these distributions certain values which compose their political structure.

It would be possible to measure the exact distance between hut and hut, village and village, tribal area and tribal area, and so forth, and the space covered by each. This would give us a statement of spatial measurements in bare physical terms. By itself it would have very limited significance. Oecological space is more than mere physical distance, though it is affected by it, for it is reckoned also by the character of the country intervening between local groups and its relation to the biological requirements of their members. A broad river divides two Nuer tribes more sharply than many miles of unoccupied bush. A distance which appears small in the dry season has a different appearance when the area it covers is flooded in the rains. A village community which has permanent water near at hand is in a very different position to one which has to travel in the dry season to obtain water, pasturage, and fishing. A tsetse belt creates an impassable barrier, giving wide oecological distance between the peoples it separates (p. 133), and presence or absence of cattle among neighbours of the Nuer likewise determines the oecological distance between them and the Nuer (pp. 132–3). Oecological distance, in this sense, is a relation between communities defined in terms of density and distribution, and with reference to water, vegetation, animal and insect life, and so on.

Structural distance is of a very different order, though it is always influenced and, in its political dimension, to a large extent determined by oecological conditions. By structural distance is meant, as we have already indicated in the preceding section, the distance between groups of persons in a social system, expressed in terms of values. The nature of the country determines the distribution of villages and, therefore, the distance between them, but values limit and define the distribution in structural terms and give a different set of distances. A Nuer village may be equidistant from two other villages, but if one of these belongs to a different tribe and the other to the same tribe it may be said to be structurally more distant from the first than from the second. A Nuer tribe which is separated by forty miles from another Nuer tribe is structurally nearer to it than to a Dinka tribe from which it is separated by only twenty miles. When we leave territorial values and speak of lineages and age-sets, structural space is less determined by environmental conditions. One lineage is closer to another than to a third. One age-set is closer to another than to a third. The values attached to residence, kinship, lineage, sex, and age, differentiate groups of persons by segmentation, and the relative positions of the segments to one another gives a perspective that enables us to speak of the divisions between them as divisions of structural space. Having defined what is meant by structural space we may now proceed with a description of its political divisions.

IV

We cannot, owing to lack of adequate population statistics (see p. 117) and survey records, present a map showing the density of the different tribes, but a rough estimate is possible for the whole of Nuerland. Jackson says that the area to the east of the Nile amounts to some 26,000 square miles,[1] and recent censuses put its population at about 144,000, making about 5.5 to the square mile. The area to the west of the Nile is no less sparsely inhabited and possibly has a lower density. The total area of Nuerland is probably about 30,000 square miles and the total population round about 200,000. We may estimate that tribal density probably varies from about 4 to 10 to the square mile and that the average distribution for the whole of Nuerland is from about 5 to 6 to the square mile. Given the hydrological conditions of Nuerland and the present economy

[1] Jackson, op. cit., p. 62.

of the people it may be doubted whether it could support a much larger population than it does. This is particularly the case to the west of the Nile and it is likely, as Nuer themselves suggest, that their expansion eastwards was due to over-population. It is possible for there to be great local concentration in spite of low density for tribal areas, for the estimates of square mileage include vast stretches of land devoid of villages and camps, which is grazed over in the drought or merely traversed in seasonal movements. The degree of actual concentration, in this sense, varies from tribe to tribe and from tribal section to tribal section and from season to season.

I cannot figure such distributions more accurately than the sketch-maps on pp. 56, 58, and 60, and I can only indicate them verbally in the most general terms. As we have seen, the size of a village depends on the space available for building, grazing, and horticulture, and its homesteads are crowded or strung out accordingly, forming in most villages small clusters of huts and byres which we call hamlets, each being separated from its neighbours by gardens and unoccupied land on which calves, sheep, and goats graze. The population of a village—we can make no precise statement—may be anything from fifty to several hundred souls and may cover from a few hundred yards to several miles. A village is usually well demarcated by the contiguity of its residences and the stretches of bush, forest, and swamp which separate it from its neighbours. In my small experience one may, in most parts of Nuerland, traverse five to twenty miles from village to village. This is certainly the case in Western Nuerland. On the other hand, where the nature of the ground allows, villages may be much closer together and follow one another at short intervals over wide areas. Thus the greater part of the Lou are concentrated within thirty miles of Muot tot, the greater part of the Dok within ten miles of Ler, while the Lak, Thiang, and part of the Gaawar run fairly continuously along a wide ridge between the Nile and the Zeraf. Villages are always joined to their neighbours by paths created and maintained by their social interrelations. In every part of Nuerland there are also large areas, inundated in the rains, with no, or very few, villages. Those parts of the tribal areas left blank or shaded to show dry-season occupation in the sketch-maps are mainly, and often entirely, without village sites, and in Western Nuerland the whole area between the Nile and the Bahr el Ghazal is very sparsely dotted with small villages; and the same is probably true of the country to the north of the Bahr el Ghazal.

I am compelled to describe the distribution of dry season camps as vaguely as the distribution of villages. Early camps may be found almost anywhere and often comprise only a few households; but the location of larger camps, formed later in the season, can be known in advance because there are only a few places which provide adequate water. Their size depends largely on the amount of water and grazing and their population varies from about a hundred to over a thousand souls. These concentrations are never tribal but comprise larger or smaller tribal sections. Round a lake a camp may be distributed in several sections with a few hundred yards between each; or one may then speak of contiguous camps. In any camp a few wind-screens are generally adjacent to, almost touching, one another, and such a group may often at a glance be seen to be a distinct unit with its own section of the common kraal. Along the left bank of the Sobat and the right bank of the Baro one may observe from a steamer camps almost anywhere, separated from one another by only a few miles; but up streams, like the Nyan-ding and Filus, in which only isolated pools of water remain, several miles separate camps. Some large camps in the interior of Lou country are separated by more than twenty miles of bush.

Great rivers flow through Nuerland and it is often these natural boundaries which indicate the lines of political cleavage. The Sobat separates the Gaajok tribe from the Lou tribe; the Pibor separates the Lou tribe from the Anuak people; the Zeraf separates the Thiang and Lak from the Dinka; the Ghazal separates the Karlual primary section of the Leek tribe from its other two primary sections; and so forth. Marshes and areas inundated in the rains likewise separate political groups. The Macar swamps divide the Eastern Gaajak from the Gaajok and Gaagwang; water-covered stretches divide, in the rains, the Rengyan from the Wot, Bor, &c.; and so on.

This account of distribution is unavoidably vague, but the main conditions and their significance can easily be summed up.

(1) Physical conditions which are responsible for scarcity of food and a simple technology also cause low density and sparse distribution of settled areas. Lack of political cohesion and development may be related to the density and distribution of the Nuer and, furthermore, in general their structural simplicity may be due to the same conditions. (2) The size of elevated stretches of land and the distances between them permit in some parts of Nuerland larger and closer concentration than in others. In the larger tribes a large population is often compelled by the nature of the country to build their homes within a short radius. (3) Where there is relatively great density of population in the rains there tends also to be greater need in the drought for early and far movement to new pastures. This need compels recognition of a common tribal value over large areas and enables us to understand better how it is that in spite of a necessary lack of political cohesion within the tribes they often have so large a population and occupy so large a territory.

V

We have noted that structural distance is the distance between groups of persons in social structure and may be of different kinds. Those which concern us in our present account are political distance, lineage distance, and age-set distance. The political distance between villages of a tertiary tribal section is less than the distance between tertiary segments of a secondary tribal section, and that is less than the distance between secondary segments of a primary tribal section, and so forth. This forms the subject of Chapter IV. The lineage distance between segments of a minor lineage is less than the distance between minor segments of a major lineage, and that is less than the distance between major segments of a maximal lineage, and so forth. This forms the subject of Chapter V. The age-set distance between segments of an age-set is less than the distance between successive age-sets and that is less than the distance between age-sets which are not successive. This forms the subject of Chapter VI. As we wish to develop our argument and therefore to avoid analysis which does not allow the reader to refer back to statements already made, we will give immediate consideration only to political distance and only to some characteristics of it.

Nuer give values to local distributions. It might be thought a simple matter to discover what these values are, but since they are embodied in words, one cannot understand their range of reference without considerable knowledge of the people's language and of the way they use it, for meanings vary according to the social situation and a word may refer to a variety of local groups. It is, nevertheless, possible to differentiate them and to make a crude formal classification of them, as we have done in the diagram below.

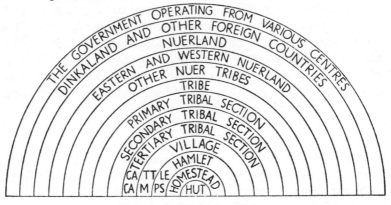

Nuer Socio-Spatial Categories.

A single living hut (*dwil* or *ut*) is occupied by a wife and her children and, at times, by her husband. They constitute a simple residential family group. The homestead, consisting of a byre and huts, may contain a simple family group or a polygamous family and there are often one or two kinsmen living there as well. This group, which we call a household, is often referred to as the *gol*, a word which means 'hearth'. A hamlet with gardens and waste land around it is called *dhor* and each has its special name, often derived from some landmark or from the name of the senior kinsman living there. A hamlet is generally occupied by close agnatic kinsmen, often brothers, and their households, and we call this group of persons a joint family. As these groups are not treated in our account we say no more about them. It must be remembered, however, that a

village is not an unsegmented unit but is a relation between a number of smaller units.

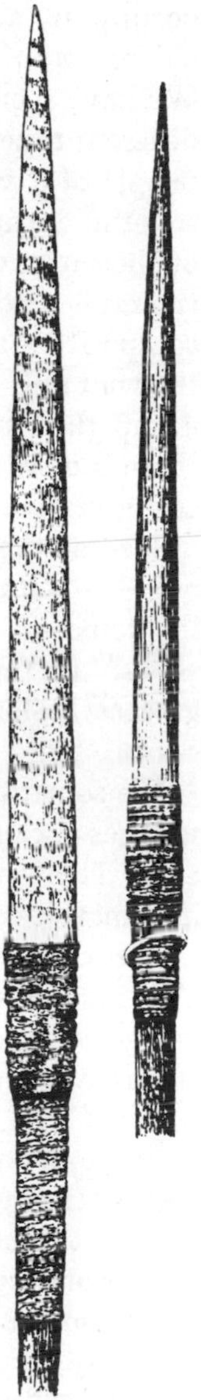

The village is a very distinct unit. It is sometimes referred to as *thur*, a ridge of high ground,
but generally as *cieng*, a word which may be
translated 'home', but which has such a variety
of meanings that we shall devote a special section
to it. A village comprises a community, linked
by common residence and by a network of kinship and affinal ties, the members of which, as
we have seen, form a common camp, co-operate
in many activities, and eat in one another's
byres and windscreens. A village is the smallest
Nuer group which is not specifically of a kinship
order and is the political unit of Nuerland.
The people of a village have a feeling of strong
solidarity against other villages and great affec
tion for their site, and in spite of the wandering
habits of Nuer, persons born and bred in a village
have a nostalgia for it and are likely to return
to it and make their home there, even if they
have resided elsewhere for many years. Members
of a village fight side by side and support each
other in feuds. When the youths of a village go
to dances they enter the dance in a war line (*dep*)
singing their special war chant.

A cattle camp, which people of a village form
in the drought and in which members of neighbouring villages participate, is known as *wec*.
While this word has the meaning of 'camp' in
contrast with *cieng*, 'village', both words are
used in the same general sense of local community. Thus when it is said of a certain clan that
they have no *wec* we are to understand that
they nowhere in a tribal section or village form
a dominant nucleus of the community and that,
therefore, no local community takes its name
from them. A large camp is called after the
dominant lineage in it or after the village community who

FIG. 11. Horn
and ebony
spears.

occupy it, and small camps are sometimes named after an old person of importance who has erected his windscreen there. We have seen that the social composition of a camp varies at different times of the drought from the people of a hamlet to the people of a village, or of neighbouring villages, and that men sometimes camp with kinsmen living in camps other than those of their own villages. Consequently, while local communities of the rains tend to be also local communities in the drought their composition may be somewhat different. We again emphasize that not only are the people of a camp living in a more compact group than the people of a village, but also that in camp life there is more frequent contact between its members and greater co-ordination of their activities. The cattle are herded together, milked at the same time, and so on. In a village each household herds its own cattle, if they are herded at all, and performs its domestic and kraal tasks independently and at different times. In the drought there is increasing concentration and greater uniformity in response to the greater severity of the season.

We sometimes speak of a district to describe an aggregate of villages or camps which have easy and frequent intercommunication. The people of these villages take part in the same dances, intermarry, conduct feuds, go on joint raiding parties, share dry season camps or make camps in the same locality, and so on. This indefinite aggregate of contacts does not constitute a Nuer category or a political group, because the people do not see themselves, nor are seen by others, as a unique community, but 'district' is a term we employ to denote the sphere of a man's social contacts or of the social contacts of the people of a village and is, therefore, relative to the person or community spoken about. A district in this sense tends to correspond to a tertiary or a secondary tribal segment, according to the size of the tribe. In the smallest tribes a whole tribe is a man's district, and a district may even cut across tribal boundaries in that in a large tribe a border village may have more contacts with neighbouring villages of another tribe than with distant villages of its own tribe. The sphere of a man's social contacts may thus not entirely coincide with any structural division.

A number of adjacent villages, varying in number and total

extension according to the size of the tribe, are grouped into small tribal sections and these into larger ones. In the larger tribes it is convenient to distinguish between primary, secondary, and tertiary tribal sections. These sections, of whatever size, are, like a village, spoken of as '*cieng*'. Since the next chapter is devoted to these tribal segments no more is said about them here.

VI

The main Nuer tribes are shown on p. 8. The name 'Jagei' inserted to the west of the Nile includes a number of small tribes—Lang, Bor, Rengyan, and Wot. There are also some small tribes—if they are rightly regarded as tribes, for little research was done in the area—in the vicinity of the Dok Nuer: Beegh, Jaalogh, (Gaan)Kwac, and Rol. A crude census, compiled from various Government sources, gives, in round figures, the more recent estimates for the larger tribes as follows:

Sobat Nuer: Gaajak, 42,000; Gaagwang, 7,000; Gaajok, 42,000; Lou, 33,000. Zeraf Nuer: Lak, 24,000; Thiang, 9,000; Gaawar, 20,000. Western Nuer: Bul, 17,000; Leek, 11,000; the three Western Jikany tribes, 11,000; the various Jagei tribes, 10,000; Dok, 12,000; Nuong, 9,000. These figures are probably more accurate for the Eastern than for the Western Nuer. Estimates show wide discrepancies and there has been much guesswork. On the basis of those recorded, the Sobat Nuer are 91,000, the Zeraf Nuer 53,000, and the Western Nuer 70,000, making a total of 214,000 for the whole of Nuerland. The population of only a few tribal segments is known. Among the Lou the Gun primary section number about 22,000 and the Mor primary section about 12,000; among the Gaawar the Radh primary section number about 10,000 and the Bar primary section about 10,000; and among the Lak tribe the Kwacbur primary section number about 12,000 and the Jenyang primary section number about 12,000.

It will be remarked that the tribes of Western Nuerland are generally smaller than those on the Zeraf, and those on the Zeraf smaller than those on the Sobat. Tribes tend to be larger the farther eastwards one proceeds. Their territories also tend to be more extensive. It may be suggested that the larger population of the Eastern Nuer tribes is due to the integrating effects of conquest and settlement and to the absorption of large numbers of Dinka which resulted therefrom, but we do not think that such explanations account for their maintaining a semblance of tribal unity over such large areas in the absence of any central government. It is evident that the size of tribal populations is directly related to the amount of high land available for wet season occupation, and also to its disposition, for tribes like the Lou and Eastern Gaajok and Gaajak can have a concentration of homesteads and villages on wide stretches of elevated land, which is not possible for the smaller tribes of Western Nuerland, whose only building sites are small and sparsely distributed ridges. But we hold that this fact in itself would not determine the lines of political cleavage, which can only be understood by taking into consideration also the relation between village sites and dry season water-supplies, pasturage, and fishing. We have noted earlier how tribal sections move from their villages to dry season pastures, each having spatial distinction in the rains which is maintained in the drought, but whereas in Western Nuerland there is always plenty of water, grazing, and fishing, generally not far from the villages, and it is possible for wet season village communities, isolated by inundated tracts in the rains, to maintain their isolation and independence in dry season camps, in the larger tribes of Eastern Nuerland, such as the Lou, drier conditions compel greater concentration and wider seasonal movements, with the result that village communities not only have a greater spatial, and we may say also moral, density in the drought than in the rains, but have to mix with one another and share water and pastures and fishing. Distinct villages are found side by side around a pool. Moreover, people of one section have to cross the territories of other sections to reach their camps, which may be situated near the villages of yet another section. Families and joint families often camp with kinsmen and affines who belong to other villages than their own, and it is a common practice to keep cattle in two or more parts of the country to avoid total loss from rinderpest, which is a dry season pestilence. It is understandable, therefore, that local communities which, though they are isolated in the rains, are forced in the drought into relations that necessitate some sense of community and the admission of certain common interests and obligations, should be contained in a common tribal structure. The severer the dry season conditions the greater the need for some measure of contact and therefore of forbearance and recognition of interdependence. The Zeraf tribes move less than the Sobat tribes and more than the Western Nuer tribes, the Gaawar moving more than the Thiang and Lak. We may again point out that on the whole where there is plenty of elevated country which permits concentration in the rains there is likewise the greater need for large concentrations in the dry season, since water, fishing, and pasture are found away from these elevated areas.

These facts seem to explain to some extent the political preponderance of pastoral peoples in East Africa. There may be wide dispersal of communities and low density of population, but there is seasonal contraction and wide interdependence. The variation in their circuits of transhumance also helps us to understand the variation in the size of Nuer tribes. It may be noted that, though the size and cohesion of tribes vary in different parts of Nuerland, nowhere do environmental conditions permit complete autonomy and exclusiveness of small village groups, such as we find among the Anuak, or such high density of population and such developed political institutions such as we find among the Shilluk.

Thus, on the one hand, environmental conditions and pastoral pursuits cause modes of distribution and concentration that provide the lines of political cleavage and are antagonistic to political cohesion and development; but, on the other hand, they necessitate extensive tribal areas within which there is a sense of community and a preparedness to co-operate.

Each tribe has a name which refers alike to its members and to their country (rol), e.g. Leek, Gaawar, Lou, Lak, &c. (see map on p. 8). Each has its particular territory and owns and defends its own building sites, grazing, water-supplies, and fishing-pools. Not only do large rivers or wide stretches of uninhabited country generally divide adjacent sections of contiguous tribes, but these sections tend to move in different directions in the drought. Conditions are doubtless changing in this respect, but we may cite as examples how the Gaawar tribe tend to move eastwards towards the Zeraf and not to come into contact with the Gun primary section of the Lou tribe, who cluster around their inland lakes or move to the Sobat and Pibor; how the Mor tribal section of the Lou move to the Nyanding and Upper Pibor in the direction of the Gaajok, who do not coalesce with them but move to the upper reaches of the Sobat and the lower reaches of the Pibor; and how the Western Jikany move towards the marshes of the Nile, while the Leek move northwest to the junction of the Bahr el Ghazal with its streams and lagoons.

Tribesmen have a common sentiment towards their country and hence towards their fellow tribesmen. This sentiment is evident in the pride with which they speak of their tribe as the object of their allegiance, their joking disparagement of other tribes, and their indication of cultural variations in their own tribe as symbols of its singularity. A man of one tribe sees the people of another tribe as an undifferentiated group to whom he has an undifferentiated pattern of behaviour, while he sees himself as a member of a segment of his own tribe. Thus when a Leek man says that So-and-so is a Nac (Rengyan) he at once defines his relationship to him. Tribal sentiment rests as much on opposition to other tribes as on common name, common territory, corporate action in warfare, and the common lineage structure of a dominant clan.

How strong is tribal sentiment may be gathered from the fact that sometimes men who intend to leave the tribe of their birth to settle permanently in another tribe take with them some earth of their old country and drink it in a solution of water, slowly adding to each dose a greater amount of soil from their new country, thus gently breaking mystical ties with the old and building up mystical ties with the new. I was told that were a man to fail to do this he might die of *nueer*, the sanction that punishes breach of certain ritual obligations.

A tribe is the largest group the members of which consider it their duty to combine for raiding and for defensive action. The younger men of the tribe went, till recently, on joint expeditions against the Dinka and waged war against other Nuer tribes. Wars between tribes were less frequent than attacks on the Dinka, but there are many examples in recent Nuer history of border disputes among tribes and even of one tribe raiding another for cattle, and such fighting is traditional among the Nuer. The Leek tribe raided the Jikany and Jagei tribes, and a Leek tribesman told me, 'The cattle with which my father married were Gee (Jagei) cattle.' Poncet remarks: 'Les Elliab (Dok) se battent avec les Egnan (Nuong) du sud et les Reïan (Rengyan) du nord; les Ror de l'intérieur avec ces derniers et les Bior (Bor) de Gazal (Ghazal river). Toutes leurs querelles viennent des pâturages qu'ils se disputent, ce qui n'empêche pas qu'ils voyagent les uns chez les autres sans aucun danger, à moins cependant qu'on n'ait un parent à venger.'[1] In theory a tribe was regarded as a military unit, and if two sections of different tribes

[1] Op. cit., p. 39.

PLATE XIV

August shower (Lou)

PLATE XV

a. Windscreen (Lou)

b. A well in the bed of the Nyanding (Lou)

were engaged in hostilities each could rely on the support of the
other sections of the same tribe; but, in practice, they would
often only join in if the other side was receiving assistance from
neighbouring sections. When a tribe united for warfare there
was a truce to disputes within its borders.

Tribes, especially the smaller ones, often united to raid
foreigners. The Leek united with the Jagei and Western Jikany,
and the Lou with the Gaawar to attack the Dinka; the Lou with
the Eastern Jikany tribes to attack the Anuak; and so on.
These military alliances between tribes, often under the aegis of
a Sky-god, speaking through his prophet (p. 188), were of short
duration, there was no moral obligation to form them, and,
though action was concerted, each tribe fought separately under
its own leaders and lived in separate camps in enemy country.

Fighting between Nuer of different tribes was of a different
character from fighting between Nuer and Dinka. Inter-tribal
fighting was considered fiercer and more perilous, but it was
subject to certain conventions: women and children were not
molested, huts and byres were not destroyed, and captives were
not taken. Also, other Nuer were not considered natural prey, as
were the Dinka.

Another defining characteristic of a tribe is that within it
there is *cut*, blood-wealth paid in compensation for homicide,
and Nuer explain the tribal value in terms of it. Thus Lou
tribesmen say that among themselves there is blood-wealth, but
not between themselves and the Gaajok or the Gaawar; and
this is the invariable definition of tribal allegiance in every part
of Nuerland. Between tribesmen there is also *ruok*, compensation for torts other than homicide, though the obligation to pay
it is less generally stressed or carried out, while between one
tribe and another no such obligation is acknowledged. We may
therefore say that there is law, in the limited and relative sense
defined in Chapter IV, between tribesmen, but no law between
tribes. If a man commits an offence against a fellow tribesman
he places himself and his kin in a legal position towards this
man and his kin, and the hostile relations that ensue can be
broken down by payment of cattle. If a man commits the same
act against a man of another tribe no breach of law is recognized,
no obligation is felt to settle the dispute, and there is no

machinery to conclude it. Local communities have been classed as tribes or tribal segments by whether they acknowledge the obligation to pay blood-wealth or not. Thus the Gun and the Mor are classed as primary segments of the Lou tribe, while the Eastern Gaajok, Gaajak, and Gaagwang have been classed as three tribes and not as three primary segments of a single Jikany tribe.

It may have happened that border cases between different tribes were sometimes settled by payment of compensation, but I have no record of such settlements other than the doubtful statement given on p. 189, and were they to have taken place it would in no way invalidate our definition of tribal structure. However, it must be understood that we are defining a tribe in the most formal way and that, as we shall show later, the acknowledgement of legal responsibility within a tribe does not mean that, in fact, it is easy to obtain compensation for a tort. There is little solidarity within a tribe and feuds are frequent and of long duration. Indeed, the feud is a characteristic institution of tribal organization.

A tribe has been defined by (1) a common and distinct name; (2) a common sentiment; (3) a common and distinct territory; (4) a moral obligation to unite in war; and (5) a moral obligation to settle feuds and other disputes by arbitration. To these five points can be added three further characteristics, which are discussed later: (6) a tribe is a segmented structure and there is opposition between its segments; (7) within each tribe there is a dominant clan and the relation between the lineage structure of this clan and the territorial system of the tribe is of great structural importance; (8) a tribe is a unit in a system of tribes; and (9) age-sets are organized tribally.

VII

Adjacent tribes are opposed to one another and fight one another. They sometimes combine against Dinka, but such combinations are loose and temporary federations for a specific end and do not correspond to any clear political value. Occasionally a tribe will allow a section of another to camp in its territory and there may be more contacts between persons of border villages or camps of different tribes than between widely separated communities of the same tribe. The first may have more social contacts; the second be structurally nearer. But between Nuer tribes there is no common organization or central administration and hence no political unity that we can refer to as national. Nevertheless, adjacent tribes, and the Dinka who face them, form political systems, since the internal organization of each tribe can only be fully understood in terms of their mutual opposition, and their common opposition to the Dinka who border them.

Beyond these systems of direct political relations the whole Nuer people see themselves as a unique community and their culture as a unique culture. Opposition to their neighbours gives them a consciousness of kind and a strong sentiment of exclusiveness. A Nuer is known as such by his culture, which is very homogeneous, especially by his language, by the absence of his lower incisors, and, if he is a man, by six cuts on his brow. All Nuer live in a continuous stretch of country. There are no isolated sections. However, their feeling of community goes deeper than recognition of cultural identity. Between Nuer, wherever they hail from, and though they be strangers to one another, friendly relations are at once established when they meet outside their country, for a Nuer is never a foreigner to another as he is to a Dinka or a Shilluk. Their feeling of superiority and the contempt they show for all foreigners and their readiness to fight them are a common bond of communion, and their common tongue and values permit ready intercommunication.

Nuer are well aware of the different divisions of their country, even if they have never visited them, and they all look upon the area to the west of the Nile as their common homeland, to the occupants of which they still have distant kinship ties. People also journey to visit kinsmen in other tribes and often settle for long periods far from their homes, sometimes in different tribes, in which, if they stay there long enough, they become permanently incorporated. Constant social intercourse flows across the borders of adjacent tribes and unites their members, especially members of border communities, by many strands of kinship and affinity. If a man changes his tribe he can at once fit himself into the age-set system of the tribe of his adoption, and there is often co-ordination of sets between adjacent tribes. A single clan is sometimes dominant in more than one tribal area, dominant clans are linked in a general clan system, and the principal clans are found in every part of Nuerland. We have noted how in the days of ivory trading Gaajak tribesmen journeyed through the territories of other tribes as far as the Zeraf.

The limits of the tribe are therefore not the limits of social intercourse, and there are many ties between persons of one tribe and persons of another tribe. Through association with the clan system and by proximity the people of one tribe may consider themselves nearer to a second than to a third. Thus the three Eastern Jikany tribes feel a vague unity in relation to the Lou, and so do the Bor and Rengyan in relation to the Leek. But, also, individuals, and through individuals kinship groups and even a village, have a circuit of social relationships that cut across tribal divisions, so that a traveller who crosses the border of his tribe can always establish some links with individuals of the tribe he visits in virtue of which he will receive hospitality and protection. If he is wronged, his host, and not he, is involved in legal action. However, there is a kind of international law, in the recognition of conventions in certain matters, beyond political boundaries and the limits of formal law. Thus, though it is considered more risky to marry outside the tribe than within it, since divorce may prove more detrimental in that the return of bride-wealth is less certain, the rules of marriage are acknowledged on both sides and it would be considered improper to take advantage of political cleavage to break them. Tribes are thus politically exclusive groups, but they are not coterminous with an individual's sphere of social relations, though this sphere tends to follow the lines of political cleavage, in the same way as a man's district tends to be equated to his tribal segment. The relation between political structure and general social relations is discussed in the chapters that follow. Here we may note that it is desirable to distinguish between (1) political distance in the sense of structural distance between segments of a tribe, the largest political unit, and between tribes in a system of political relations; (2) general structural distance in the sense of non-political distance between various social groups in the Nuer-speaking community—non-political structural relations are strongest between adjacent tribes, but a common social structure embraces the whole of Nuerland; and (3) the social sphere of an individual, being his circuit of social contacts of one kind or another with other Nuer.

VIII

The political structure of the Nuer can only be understood in relation to their neighbours, with whom they form a single political system. Contiguous Dinka and Nuer tribes are segments within a common structure as much as are segments of the same Nuer tribe. Their social relationship is one of hostility and its expression is in warfare.

The Dinka people are the immemorial enemies of the Nuer. They are alike in their oecologies, cultures, and social systems, so that individuals belonging to the one people are easily assimilated to the other; and when the balanced opposition between a Nuer political segment and a Dinka political segment changes into a relationship in which the Nuer segment becomes entirely dominant, fusion and not a class structure results.

As far as history and tradition go back, and in the vistas of myth beyond their farthest reach, there has been enmity between the two peoples. Almost always the Nuer have been the aggressors, and raiding of the Dinka is conceived by them to be a normal state of affairs and a duty, for they have a myth, like that of Esau and Jacob, which explains it and justifies it. Nuer and Dinka are represented in this myth as two sons of God who promised his old cow to Dinka and its young calf to Nuer. Dinka came by night to God's byre and, imitating the voice of Nuer, obtained the calf. When God found that he had been tricked he was angry and charged Nuer to avenge the injury by raiding Dinka's cattle to the end of time. This story, familiar to every Nuer, is not only a reflection of the political relations between the two peoples but is also a commentary on their characters. Nuer raid for cattle and seize them openly and by force of arms. Dinka steal them or take them by treachery. All Nuer regard them—and rightly so—as thieves, and even the Dinka seem to admit the reproach, if we attribute correct significance to the statement made to Mr. K. C. P. Struvé in 1907 by the Dinka keeper of the shrine of Deng dit at Luang Deng.

After recounting the myth of the cow and calf, he added, 'And to this day the Dinka has always lived by robbery, and the Nuer by war.'[1]

Fighting, like cattle husbandry, is one of the chief activities and dominant interests of all Nuer men, and raiding Dinka for cattle is one of their principal pastimes. Indeed *jaang*, Dinka, is sometimes used to refer to any tribe whom the Nuer habitually raid and from whom they take captives. Boys look forward to the day when they will be able to accompany their elders on these raids against the Dinka, and as soon as youths have been initiated into manhood they begin to plan an attack to enrich themselves and to establish their reputation as warriors. Every Nuer tribe raided Dinka at least every two or three years, and some part of Dinkaland must have been raided annually. Nuer have a proper contempt for Dinka and are derisive of their fighting qualities, saying that they show as little skill as courage. *Kur jaang*, fighting with Dinka, is considered so trifling a test of valour that it is not thought necessary to bear shields on a raid or to pay any regard to adverse odds, and is contrasted with the dangers of *kur Nath*, fighting between Nuer themselves. These boasts are justified both in the unflinching bravery of the Nuer and by their military success.

The earliest travellers record that Nuer held both banks of the Nile, but it is probable that the entire Zeraf Island was at one time occupied by Dinka and it is certain that the whole of the country from the Zeraf to the Pibor and, to the north of the Sobat, from the confines of Shillukland to the Ethiopian scarp was, with the exception of riverain settlements of Anuak, still in their hands as late as the middle of last century, when it was seized by the Nuer in two lines of expansion, to the north of the Sobat and to the south of it. This is known from the statements of both Nuer and Dinka, the evidence of genealogies and age-sets, and the records of travellers, who frequently refer to the struggle between the two peoples, the dominant position of the Nuer among their neighbours, the awe they inspired in them, and their bravery and chivalry.[2] The conquest, which seems to have resulted in absorp-

[1] *Sudan Intelligence Report*, no. 152, 1907.
[2] Werne, op. cit., p. 163; Abd-el-Hamid, op. cit., pp. 82–3; Philippe Terranuova D'Antonio, 'Relation d'un voyage au Fleuve Blanc', *Nouvelles annales des voyages*, Paris, 1859. Lejean, op. cit., p. 232; Poncet, op. cit., pp. 18, 26, 39, 41–2, and 44; Petherick, op. cit., vol. ii, p. 6; Heuglin, *Reise in das Gebiet*

tion and miscegenation rather than extermination, was so rapid and successful that the whole of this vast area is to-day occupied by Nuer, except for a few pockets of Dinka on the Sobat, Filus, and Atar. Apart from these independent units there are many local communities in Eastern Nuerland of Nuer who acknowledge that they are of Dinka descent, and small lineages of Dinka origin are found in every village and camp. Some Dinka tribes took refuge with compatriots to the south, where the Gaawar and Lou continued to raid them. The Western Nuer likewise persistently raided all the Dinka tribes that border them, particularly those to the south and west, obtained a moral ascendency over them, and compelled them to withdraw farther and farther from their boundaries. To the west of the Nile, as to the east, Dinka captives were assimilated, and there are many small lineages of Dinka descent in every tribe and these are often preponderant in local communities. Of all the Dinka only the Ngok, to the south of the Sobat, were left in peace, probably on account of their poverty of stock and grazing, though their immunity has a mythological sanction. It seems also that the Atwot were not considered such legitimate prey as the Dinka on account of their Nuer origin, and it is probable that they were seldom molested as they are remotely situated.

The favourite season for raiding Dinka was at the end of the rains, though they were also invaded at their commencement. Leek tribesmen told me that when they raided Dinka to the south-west they used to sleep the first night near the villages of the Wot tribe and the second night in the bush. They took no food with them and ate only what fish they might hastily spear on the way, travelling with all speed throughout the day and part of the night. On the third day they attacked the Dinka villages or camps at dawn. The Dinka seldom put up any resistance, but loosened their cattle and tried to drive them away. No one seized cattle till the enemy had been dispersed. Then each took what prizes he could, often not troubling to tether his captures but slashing their rumps in sign of ownership. Afterwards the beasts were tied up

des Weissen Nil und seiner westlichen Zuflüsse in den Jahren 1862-1864, 1869, p. 104. Georg Schweinfurth, *The Heart of Africa* (English translation), 1873, vol. i, pp. 118-19; Gaetano Casati, *Ten Years in Equatoria and the Return with Emin Pasha* (English translation), 1891, vol. i, p. 39; Romolo Gessi Pasha, *Seven Years in the Soudan* (English translation), 1892, p. 57. The maps intended by travellers to show the positions of the peoples of this area are rather vague and are not in entire agreement. The reader may consult those in Marno, op. cit., Poncet, op. cit., Heuglin, op. cit., the map compiled by Lejean from information supplied by the Poncet brothers in *Bulletin de la Société de Géographie* (Paris), 1860; the maps prepared by V. A. Malte-Brun in *Nouvelles annales des voyages*, 1855 and 1863, and others of this period.

in the enemy's kraal, the oxen being mainly slaughtered for food. If the Dinka gathered reinforcements and returned to fight they were met in full battle formation. Nuer fight in three divisions with two or three hundred yards between each, and if one division is engaged the others advance or retreat parallel to it according to the fortunes of war. A party of scouts are in advance of the central division and they charge up to the enemy, hurl their spears at them, and fall back on the main body.

The raiders spent several weeks in Dinkaland and sometimes remained there throughout the dry season, living on the milk and flesh of captured cattle, on pillaged grain, and on fish. Using a captured kraal as a base they extended their raid against distant camps. Nuer migrations seem to have been conducted on these lines, the raiders settling permanently in Dinka country and by systematic raiding compelling the inhabitants to withdraw farther and farther from the points of occupation. In the following season a new series of raids was initiated and the process was repeated till the Dinka were compelled to seek refuge with their kinsfolk of another tribe and leave their country to its invaders. If settlement was not contemplated, however, the raiders returned home when they considered that they had sufficient booty.

Before camp was broken up there took place a custom highly indicative of Nuer sense of equality and justice. It was recognized that the whole force was jointly responsible for the success of the raid and there was therefore a redistribution of the booty. The prophet whose revelations sanctioned the raid first made a round of the camp and selected from each household a cow for the divine spirit of whom he was the mouthpiece. By this time a household possessed some fifty head, so that it was no hardship to be asked to give one to the spirit. There then took place a general scramble and everybody rushed amid the herd to earmark beasts for himself. A man who could first seize an animal, tether it, and cut its ear had absolute claim to it. The man who originally captured a cow had the advantage that it was tethered near his windscreen, but if he and members of his household had an undue share of the booty they could not earmark all the beasts before they were seized by others. As might be supposed, men frequently sustained injury in these scrambles, for if two men seized the same cow they fought with clubs for possession of it. One must not use the spear on these occasions. Men of neighbouring camps took part in one another's redistributions and there must have been great confusion. Captives, women of marriageable age, boys, and girls, were not redistributed but belonged to their original captor. Older women and babies were clubbed and, when the raid was on a village, their bodies were thrown on the flaming byres and huts. Captives were placed in the centre of the camp, the women being sometimes bound at night to render them more secure. Sexual intercourse is taboo on a raid. Nor may Nuer eat with a captive. A boy captive may not even draw water for them to drink. Only when

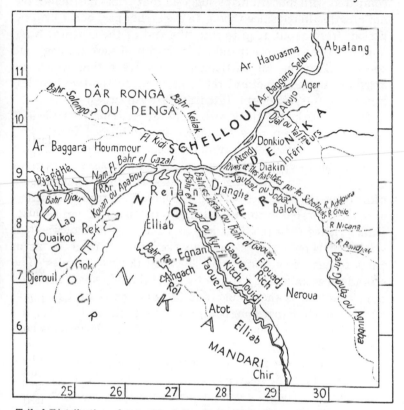

Tribal Distribution about 1860 (after V. A. Malte-Brun, *Nouvelles annales des voyages*, 1863).

an ox has been sacrificed in honour of the ghosts, after the return home, and they have been informed that strangers have entered their homesteads, may Nuer have sexual relations with captives or eat with them.

In the following section we describe other foreign contacts, but till European conquest the only foreign relations which may be said to have been expressed in constant warfare were those with the various Dinka tribes which border Nuerland.

We have not enumerated them, for their names are irrelevant. The fighting between the two peoples has been incessant from time immemorial and seems to have reached a state of equilibrium before European conquest upset it. (Malte-Brun's map compared with modern maps suggests that tribal positions have not greatly altered since 1860.) In the earlier part of the historic period, from about 1840 to near the end of the century, Nuer appear to have been expanding in search of new grazing, but continued raiding for cattle, an aggressive action which we attribute to the structural relations between the two peoples, but which was, no doubt, intensified by rinderpest.

Though Dinka relations with Nuer are extremely hostile and war between them may be called an established institution, they have, nevertheless, united occasionally to make war against the Egyptian Government and there have sometimes been joint social gatherings. In times of famine Dinka have often come to reside in Nuerland and have been readily accepted and incorporated into Nuer tribes. In times of peace, also, Dinka visited their relations who had been captured or who had settled in Nuerland, and, as remarked earlier, there seems in parts to have been some trade between the two peoples. The strands of social relationships of a general kind, which are often numerous across the boundaries of adjacent Nuer tribes and which stretch across Nuerland, are thus prolonged weakly beyond the limits of Nuerland in occasional and hazardous contacts with foreigners.

All Dinka come into the category of *Jaang*, and Nuer feel that category to be nearer to themselves than other categories of foreigners. These foreign peoples, with all of whom the Nuer have reached a state of balanced hostility, an equilibrium of opposition, expressed occasionally in fighting, are, with the exception of the Beir, generally classed as *Bar*, cattleless people or people possessing very few cattle. A further category are the *Jur*, cattleless people whom the Nuer regard as lying on the periphery of their world, such as the Bongo-Mittu group of peoples, the Azande, the Arabs, and ourselves. However, they have separate names for most of these peoples.

We have remarked that Nuer feel Dinka to be nearer to themselves than other foreigners, and in this connexion we draw attention to the fact that Nuer show greater hostility towards, and more persistently attack, the Dinka, who are in every respect most akin to themselves, than any other foreign people. This is undoubtedly due, in some degree, to the ease with which they can pillage the vast Dinka herds. It may also, in part, be attributed to the fact that of all neighbouring areas Dinkaland alone opposes no serious oecological handicaps to a pastoral people. But it may be suggested further that the kind of warfare that exists between Nuer and Dinka, taking into consideration also the assimilation of captives and the intermittent social relations between the two peoples between raids, would seem to require recognition of cultural affinity and of like values. War between Dinka and Nuer is not merely a clash of interests, but is also a structural relationship between the two peoples, and such a relationship requires a certain acknowledgement on both sides that each to some extent partakes of the feelings and habits of the other. We are led by this reflection to note that political relations are profoundly influenced by the degree of cultural differentiation that exists between the Nuer and their neighbours. The nearer people are to the Nuer in mode of livelihood, language, and customs, the more intimately the Nuer regard them, the more easily they enter into relations of hostility with them, and the more easily they fuse with them. Cultural differentiation is strongly influenced by oecological divergences, particularly by the degree to which neighbouring peoples are pastoral, which depends on their soils, water-supplies, insect life, and so forth. But it is also to a considerable extent independent of oecological circumstances, being autonomous and historical. The cultural similarity of Dinka and Nuer may be held largely to determine their structural relations; as, also, the relations between the Nuer and other peoples are largely determined by their increasing cultural dissimilarity. The cultural cleavage is least between Nuer and Dinka; it widens between Nuer and the Shilluk-speaking peoples; and is broadest between the Nuer and such folk as the Koma, Burun, and Bongo-Mittu peoples.

Nuer make war against a people who have a culture like their own rather than among themselves or against peoples with cultures very different from their own. The relations between social structure and culture are obscure, but it may well be that had the Nuer not been able to expand at the expense of the Dinka, and to raid them, they would have been more antagonistic to people of their own breed and the structural changes which would have resulted would have led to greater cultural heterogeneity in Nuerland than at present exists. This may be an idle speculation, but we can at least say that the vicinity of a people like themselves who possess rich herds that can be plundered may be supposed to have had the effect of directing the aggressive impulses of Nuer away from their fellow-countrymen. The predatory tendencies, which Nuer share with other nomads, find an easy outlet against the Dinka, and this may account not only for the few wars between Nuer tribes but also, in consequence, be one of the explanations of the remarkable size of many Nuer tribes, for they could not maintain what unity they have were their sections raiding one another with the persistence with which they attack the Dinka.

IX

Nuer had little contact with the Shilluk, a buffer of Dinka dividing them in most places, and where they have a common border, warfare seems to have been restricted to incidents involving only frontier camps. The powerful Shilluk kingdom, well organized and comprising over a hundred thousand souls, could not have been raided with the same impunity as the Dinka tribes, but the characteristic reason Nuer give for not attacking them is otherwise: 'They have no cattle. The Nuer only raid people who possess cattle. If they had cattle we would raid them and take their cattle, for they do not know how to fight as we fight.' There is no actual or mythological enmity between the two peoples.

The Anuak, who also belong to the Shilluk-Luo group, border the Nuer to the south-east. Though they are almost entirely horticultural to-day, they possessed herds in the past and in Nuer opinion their country has better grazing than Shillukland. It was overrun by the Nuer over half a century ago as far as the foothills of the Ethiopian scarp, but was quickly abandoned, probably because of tsetse, for the Anuak put up little resistance. Nuer continued to raid them up to thirty years ago, when they obtained rifles from Abyssinia and were better able to resist and even to take the offensive. In spite of two reverses they finally succeeded in penetrating Lou country, where they inflicted heavy casualties and captured many children and cattle, a feat which brought the Government down the Pibor, thereby closing hostilities. Many evidences show that at one time the Anuak extended far westward of their present distribution and were displaced from these sites, or assimilated, by the Nuer.

The other peoples with whom Nuer come into contact may be mentioned very briefly as their interrelations have little political importance. Another south-eastern neighbour is the Beir (Murle) people. As far as I am aware the Nuer did not raid them often and those few who know something of them respect them as devoted herdsmen. To the north-east of Nuerland the Gaajak have for several decades had relations with the Galla of Ethiopia. These appear to have been peaceful and there was a certain amount of trade between the two peoples. Absence of friction may be attributed largely to the corridor of death that divides them, for when the Galla descend from their plateau they quickly succomb to malaria while any attempt on the part of the Nuer to move eastwards is defeated by the tsetse belt that runs along the foot-hills. The Gaajak raided the Burun and Koma (both often referred to vaguely as 'Burun') for captives, and they were too small in numbers and too unorganized to resist or retaliate. To the north-west the Jikany, Leek, and Bul tribes occasionally raided the Arabs and the communities of the Nuba Mountains; and, to judge from a statement by Jules Poncet, the trouble over water and grazing in the dry season that occurs to-day between Nuer and Arabs has long occurred.[1]

The Arab slavers and ivory traders, who caused so much misery and destruction among the peoples of the Southern Sudan after the conquest of the Northern Sudan by Muhammad Ali in 1821, very little inconvenienced the Nuer. They sometimes pillaged riverside villages, but I know of no record of their having penetrated far inland, and it was only the more accessible sections of the Zeraf River tribes that appear to have suffered to any extent from their depredations. I do not believe that anywhere were the Nuer deeply affected by Arab contact.[2] The Egyptian Government and, later, the Mahdist Government, which were supposed to be in control of the Sudan from 1821 to the end of the century, in no way administered the Nuer or exercised control over them from the riverside posts they established on the fringes of their country.

[1] Poncet, op. cit., p. 25.

[2] I find myself unable to accept Casati's statement of the position, (op. cit, vol. i, p. 38), but consider that greater reliance should be placed on the opinion of other authorities. See Romolo Gessi's letter to the Editor of *Esploratore* in 1880 (op. cit., p. xx), and Lejean's report from Khartoum in 1860 (op. cit., p. 215).

The Nuer sometimes raided these posts and were sometimes raided from them,[1] but on the whole it may be said that they pursued their lives in disregard of them. This disregard continued after the reconquest of the Sudan by Anglo-Egyptian forces and the establishment of the new administration. The Nuer were the last important people to be brought under control and the administration of their country cannot be said to have been very effective till 1928, before which year government consisted of occasional patrols which only succeeded in alienating them further. The nature of the country rendered communications difficult and prevented the establishment of posts in Nuerland itself, and the Nuer showed no desire to make contact with those on its periphery. Little control was exercised and it was impossible to enforce decisions.[2] A further difficulty was the absence of Nuer who had travelled in foreign parts and spoke Arabic, for their place was usually taken, as interpreters and in other capacities, by Dinka and Anuak, who were distrusted, and rightly so, by the Nuer against whom they lodged every kind of complaint.

The truculence and aloofness displayed by the Nuer is conformable to their culture, their social organization, and their character. The self-sufficiency and simplicity of their culture and the fixation of their interests on their herds explain why they neither wanted nor were willing to accept European innovations and why they rejected peace from which they had everything to lose. Their political structure depended for its form and persistence on balanced antagonisms that could only be expressed in warfare against their neighbours if the structure were to be maintained. Recognition of fighting as a cardinal value, pride in past achievements, and a deep sense of their common equality and their superiority to other peoples, made it impossible for them to accept willingly domination, which they had hitherto never experienced. Had more been known about them a different policy might have been instituted earlier and with less prejudice.[3]

[1] See, for example, Casati, op. cit., p. 221.

[2] For an account of conditions at this time see the *Sudan Intelligence Reports*, especially those by Kaimakam F. J. Maxse (no. 61, 1899), Capt. H. H. Wilson (no. 128, 1905), and O'Sullivan Bey (no. 187, 1910).

[3] For abusive references to the Nuer see Sir Samuel Baker, *The Albert N'Yanza*, 1913 (first published in 1866), pp. 39–42; Capt. H. H. Austin, *Among Swamps and Giants in Equatorial Africa*, 1902, p. 15; Count Gleichen, op. cit., 1905, vol. i, p. 133; C. W. L. Bulpett, *A Picnic Party in Wildest Africa*, 1907, pp. 22–3 and 35; Bimbashi Coningham, *Sudan Intelligence Report*, no. 192, 1910; H. Lincoln Tangye, *In the Torrid Sudan*, 1910, p. 222; E. S. Stevens, *My Sudan Year*, 1912, pp. 215 and 256–7; H. C. Jackson, op. cit., p. 60; *The Story of Fergie Bey. Told by himself and some of his Friends*, 1930, p. 113; and J. G. Millais, *Far away up the Nile*, 1924, pp. 174–5.

In 1920 large-scale military operations, including bombing and machine-gunning of camps, were conducted against the Eastern Jikany and caused much loss of life and destruction of property. There were further patrols from time to time, but the Nuer remained unsubdued. In 1927 the Nuong tribe killed their District Commissioner, while at the same time the Lou openly defied the Government and the Gaawar attacked Duk Faiyuil Police Post. From 1928 to 1930 prolonged operations were conducted against the whole of the disturbed area and marked the end of serious fighting between the Nuer and the Government. Conquest was a severe blow to the Nuer, who had for so long raided their neighbours with impunity and whose country had generally remained intact.

X

In our account of Nuer time-reckoning we noted that in one department of time their system of reckoning is, in a broad sense, a conceptualization, in terms of activities, or of physical changes that provide convenient points of reference for activities, of those phases of the oecological rhythm which have peculiar significance for them. We further noted that in another department of time it is a conceptualization of structural relations, time units being co-ordinate with units of structural space. We have given a brief description of these units of structural space in its political, or territorial, dimension and have drawn attention to the influence of oecology on distribution and hence on the values given to the distribution, the interrelation between which is the political system. This system is not, however, as simple as we have presented it, for values are not simple, and we now attempt to face some of the difficulties we have so far neglected. We start this attempt by asking what it is the Nuer mean when they speak of their *cieng*.

Values are embodied in words through which they influence behaviour. When a Nuer speaks of his *cieng*, his *dhor*, his *gol*, &c., he is conceptualizing his feelings of structural distance, identifying himself with a local community, and, by so doing, cutting himself off from other communities of the same kind. An examination of the word *cieng* will teach us one of the most fundamental characteristics of Nuer local groups and, indeed, of all social groups: their structural relativity.

What does a Nuer mean when he says, 'I am a man of such-and-such a *cieng*'? *Cieng* means 'home', but its precise significance varies with the situation in which it is spoken. If one meets an Englishman in Germany and asks him where his home is, he may reply that it is England. If one meets the same man in London and asks him the same question he will tell one that his home is in Oxfordshire, whereas if one meets him in that county he will tell one the name of the town or village in which he lives. If questioned in his town or village he will mention his particular street, and if questioned in his street he will indicate his house. So it is with the Nuer. A Nuer met outside Nuerland says that his home is *cieng Nath*, Nuerland. He may also refer to his tribal country as his *cieng*, though the more usual expression for this is *rol*. If one asks him in his tribe what is his *cieng*, he will name his village or tribal section according to the context. Generally he will name either his tertiary tribal section or his village, but he may give his primary or secondary section. If asked in his village he will mention the name of his hamlet or indicate his homestead or the end of the village in which his homestead is situated. Hence if a man says '*Wa ciengda*', 'I am going home', outside his village he means that he is returning to it; if in his village he means that he is going to his hamlet; if in his hamlet he means that he is going to his homestead. *Cieng* thus means homestead, hamlet, village, and tribal sections of various dimensions.

The variations in the meaning of the word *cieng* are not due to the inconsistencies of language, but to the relativity of the group-values to which it refers. I emphasize this character of structural distance at an early stage because an understanding of it is necessary to follow the account of various social groups which we are about to describe. Once it is understood, the apparent contradictions in our account will be seen to be contradictions in the structure itself, being, in fact, a quality of it. The argument is here introduced in its application to local communities, which are treated more fully in the next chapter, and its application to lineages and age-sets is postponed to Chapters V and VI.

A man is a member of a political group of any kind in virtue of his non-membership of other groups of the same kind. He sees them as groups and their members see him as a member of a group, and his relations with them are controlled by the structural distance between the groups concerned. But a man does not see himself as a member of that same group in so far as he is a member of a segment of it which stands outside of and is opposed to other segments of it. Hence a man can be a member of a group and yet not a member of it. This is a fundamental principle of Nuer political structure. Thus a man is a member of his tribe in its relation to other tribes, but he is not a member of his tribe in the relation of his segment of it to other segments of the same kind. Likewise a man is a member of his tribal segment in its relation to other segments, but he is not a member of it in the relation of his village to other villages of the same segment. A characteristic of any political group is hence its invariable tendency towards fission and the opposition of its segments, and another characteristic is its tendency towards fusion with other groups of its own order in opposition to political segments larger than itself. Political values are thus always, structurally speaking, in conflict. One value attaches a man to his group and another to a segment of it in opposition to other segments of it, and the value which controls his action is a function of the social situation in which he finds himself. For a man sees himself as a member of a group only in opposition to other groups and he sees a member of another group as a member of a social unity however much it may be split into opposed segments.

Therefore the diagram presented on p. 114 illustrates political structure in a very crude and formal way. It cannot very easily be pictured diagrammatically, for political relations are relative and dynamic. They are best stated as tendencies to conform to certain values in certain situations, and the value is determined by the structural relationships of the persons who compose the situation. Thus whether and on which side a man fights in a dispute depends on the structural relationship of the persons engaged in it and of his own relationship to each party.

We need to refer to another important principle of Nuer political structure: the smaller the local group the stronger the sentiment uniting its members. Tribal sentiment is weaker than the sentiment of one of its segments and the sentiment of a segment is weaker than the sentiment of a village which is part of it. Logically this might be supposed to be the case, for if unity within a group is a function of its opposition to groups of the same kind it might be surmised that the sentiment of unity within a group must be stronger than the sentiment of unity within a larger group that contains it. But it is also evident that the smaller the group the more the contacts between its members, the more varied are these contacts, and the more they are co-operative. In a big group like the tribe contacts between its members are infrequent and corporate action is limited to occasional military excursions. In a small group like the village not only are there daily residential contacts, often of a co-operative nature, but the members are united by close agnatic, cognatic, and affinal ties which can be expressed in reciprocal action. These become fewer and more distant the wider the group, and the cohesion of a political group is undoubtedly dependent on the number and strength of ties of a non-political kind.

It must also be stated that political actualities are confused and conflicting. They are confused because they are not always, even in a political context, in accord with political values, though they tend to conform to them, and because social ties of a different kind operate in the same field, sometimes strengthening them and sometimes running counter to them. They are conflicting because the values that determine them are, owing to the relativity of political structure, themselves in conflict. Consistency of political actualities can only be seen when the dynamism and relativity of political structure are understood and the relation of political structure to other social systems is taken into consideration.

CHAPTER IV

THE POLITICAL SYSTEM

I

NUER tribes are split into segments. The largest segments we call primary tribal sections and these are further segmented into secondary tribal sections which are further segmented into tertiary tribal sections. Experience shows that primary, secondary, and tertiary are sufficient terms of definition, and in the smallest tribes probably fewer terms are required. A tertiary tribal section comprises a number of village communities which are composed of kinship and domestic groups.

Thus, the Lou tribe, as shown in the diagram below, is segmented into the Gun and Mor primary sections. The Gun primary section is segmented into the Rumjok and Gaatbal secondary sections. The Gaatbal secondary section is further segmented into the Leng and Nyarkwac tertiary sections. Only a few segments are shown diagrammatically: Gaaliek is split into Nyaak and Buth, Rumjok into Falker, Nyajikany, Kwacgien, &c., and so on.

LOU TRIBE

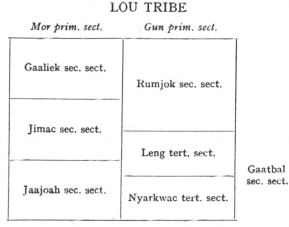

The diagram on p. 140 shows the primary sections of the Eastern Gaagwang tribe and the primary and secondary sections of the Eastern Gaajak and Gaajok tribes. They are presented as accurately as my knowledge permits, but anyone acquainted with the difficulties of unravelling the complex system of Nuer tribal divisions will not be surprised if he discovers sections which he knows under different names or others which he may think should not have been omitted. I am not certain of the secondary sections of the Gaagwang tribe, which I have not visited.

EASTERN JIKANY TRIBES

	Gaajok tribe	Gaagwang tribe	Gaajak tribe	
Laang prim. sect.	Thiur sec. sect.	Gaatcika prim. sect.	Nyayan sec. sect.[1]	Gaagwong prim. sect.
	Dwong sec. sect.		Cany sec. sect.	
	Kwith sec. sect.		Wau sec. sect.	
Wangkac prim. sect.	Minyaal sec. sect.	Nyingee prim. sect.	Kong sec. sect.[2]	Reng prim. sect.
	Wang sec. sect.		Col sec. sect.[3]	
	Nyathol sec. sect.		Dhilleak sec. sect.[4]	
Yol prim. sect.	Pwot sec. sect.	Nyaang prim. sect.	Tar sec. sect.	Thiang prim. sect.
	Kwal sec. sect.			
	Yiic sec. sect.		Kang sec. sect.	
	Cam sec. sect.			
	Kwul sec. sect.		Lony sec. sect.	

Among the Western Jikany the Gaagwang appear to be classed as part of the Gaajok tribe whose country stretches on both sides of the Bahr-el-Ghazal, the Gaajak tribe living to the south of that river. The primary sections of these two tribes, Gaagwong, Reng, Thiang, Laang, Wangkac, and Yol, are the same as in the east, but some secondary sections which are important to the north of the Sobat are not to be found, except as very small clusters, on the Bahr-el-Ghazal, and vice versa. The reason for this is that certain lineages migrated eastwards while others remained in the homeland.

After having satisfied myself that the segmentation of other

---

[1] With which goes Nyajaani.
[2] Also called Tiek and Yaar.
[3] Also called Nyaruny.
[4] Also called Gying.

Nuer tribes is on the same pattern as that of the Lou and Jikany tribes I did not make detailed lists of their divisions, being interested in new and different inquiries. I include, however, some diagrammatic representations of tribal segmentation in Gaawar, Lak, and Thiang countries, for which I am indebted to Mr. B. A. Lewis, at one time Commissioner for Zeraf River District.

GAAWAR TRIBE

Radh prim. sect.	*Bar prim. sect.*	
Kerfail sec. sect.	Bang tert. sect.	Lidh sec. sect.
Nyadakwon sec. sect.	Jamogh tert. sect.	
Per sec. sect.	Caam tert. sect.	Gatkwa sec. sect.
Nyaigua sec. sect.	Gatkwa tert. sect.	
Jitheib sec. sect.		

LAK TRIBE

Jenyang prim. sect.	*Kwacbur prim. sect.*	
Kudwop sec. sect.	Nyawar tert. sect.	Tobut sec. sect.
	Dongrial tert. sect.	
Nyapir sec. sect.	Thiang tert. sect.	Lak sec. sect.
	Kar. tert. sect.	
	Cuak tert. sect.	

THIANG TRIBE

Riah prim. sect.	*Bang prim. sect.*	
Juak sec. sect.	Gul tert. sect.	Nyangur sec. sect.
	Bedid tert. sect.	
Manyal sec. sect.	Dwong tert. sect.	
	Kwoth sec. sect.	
Giin sec. sect.	Cuol sec. sect.	

It will have been observed that I have not attempted to list all the sections of each tribe, but have merely tried to indicate the mode of segmentation so that the relation between tribal divisions and lineages may be more clearly understood in the following chapter.

II

Segments of a tribe have many of the characteristics of the tribe itself. Each has its distinctive name, its common sentiment, and its unique territory. Usually one section is clearly divided from another by a wide stretch of bush or by a river. Segments of the same tribe also tend to turn in different directions for their dry season pastures, as is shown on the sketch-maps on pp. 56, 58, and 60, so that the spatial divisions of the rains are maintained, and may be accentuated during the drought, though, as we have pointed out, in the larger tribes to the east of the Nile severity of natural conditions may also produce closer interrelations than in the smaller tribes to the west.

The smaller the tribal segment the more compact its territory, the more contiguous its members, the more varied and more intimate their general social ties, and the stronger therefore its sentiment of unity. As we shall see, a tribal segment is crystallized around a lineage of the dominant clan of the tribe and the smaller the segment the closer the genealogical relationship between members of this clan fragment. Also the smaller the segment the more the age-set system determines behaviour and produces corporate action within it. Political cohesion thus not only varies with variations of political distance but is also a function of structural distance of other kinds.

Each segment is itself segmented and there is opposition between its parts. The members of any segment unite for war against adjacent segments of the same order and unite with these adjacent segments against larger sections. Nuer themselves state this structural principle clearly in the expression of their political values. Thus they say that if the Leng tertiary section of the Lou tribe fights the Nyarkwac tertiary section—and, in fact, there has been a long feud between them—the villages which compose each section will combine to fight; but if there is a quarrel between the Nyarkwac tertiary section and the Rumjok secondary section, as has occurred recently over water rights at Fading, Leng and Nyarkwac will unite against their common enemy Rumjok which, in its turn, forms a coalition of the various segments into which it is divided. If there is a fight between the Mor and the Gun primary sections, Rumjok and Gaatbal will unite against the combined Mor sections: Gaaliek, Jimac, and Jaajoah. If there is fighting against the Gaajok or the Gaawar the primary sections, Gun and Mor, will, at any rate in theory, combine and a united Lou tribe will take the field, since both sections belong to the same political group and since their dominant lineages belong to the same clan. Certainly they used to unite in raids on the Dinka.

Among the Eastern Gaajok, Minyal, Wang, and Nyathol sections combine against Yol. Also Thiur, Dwong, and Kwith sections unite for war. These fights between tribal sections and the feuds that result from them, though based on a territorial principle, are often represented in terms of lineages, since there is a close relation between territorial segments and lineage segments, and Nuer habitually express social obligations in a kinship idiom. Thus in telling me that Wangkac and Yol would unite for war against any other section Nuer stated the proposition by saying that the WANGKAC and YOL lineages, which are the dominant lineages in these sections, would unite because their ancestors were sons of the same mother. We shall see in Chapter V that Nuer generally speak in such terms.

This principle of segmentation and the opposition between segments is the same in every section of a tribe and extends beyond the tribe to relations between tribes, especially among the smaller Western Nuer tribes, which coalesce more easily and frequently in raiding the Dinka and in fighting one another than the larger tribes to the east of the Nile. Thus a man of the Fadang section of the Bor tribe exemplified it when he told me, 'We fight against the Rengyan, but when either of us is fighting a third party we combine with them'. It can be stated in hypothetical terms by the Nuer themselves and can best be represented in this way. In the diagram on p. 144, when Z^1 fights Z^2 no other section is involved. When Z^1 fights Y^1, Z^1 and Z^2 unite as Y^2. When Y^1 fights X^1, Y^1 and Y^2 unite, and so do X^1

and X^2. When X^1 fights A, X^1, X^2, Y^1, and Y^2 all unite as B. When A raids the Dinka A and B may unite.

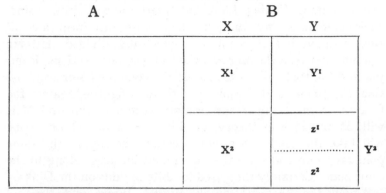

The larger tribal sections were almost autonomous groups and acted as such in their enmities and alliances. At one time they would be fighting among themselves and at another would be combining against a third party. These combinations were not always as regular and simple as they were explained to me and as I have stated them. I give a few examples of fighting between tribal sections. One of the worst wars in Nuer history occurred in the last generation between the Gun and the Mor moieties of the Lou tribe. It was known as *kur luny yak*, the war of letting loose the hyena, because so many people were killed that the dead were left for the hyenas to eat. It is said that in this struggle men displayed unusual ferocity, even cutting off arms to seize quickly ivory armlets. There was a lengthy, and more recent, feud between the Leng and the Nyarkwac tertiary sections of the Lou tribe which has continued up to the present. It sprang out of an earlier fight between Thiang and Yol which once formed sub-sections of the Nyarkwac. The ancestors of the dominant lineages in the Leng and Yol divisions were brothers, whereas the ancestor of the dominant lineage of the Thiang division stood to these brothers in the relationship of sister's son. For a long while Yol and Thiang lived peaceably together, but some thirty years ago a fight broke out between them, and Thiang, defeated, fled to seek protection among the Leng section. The Yol sent messages to the Leng telling them that they were not to receive their enemies or give them asylum. The Leng replied that the ancestor of the LENG lineage was the maternal uncle of the ancestor of the THIANG lineage and that they could not refuse asylum to their sisters' sons. This attitude involved Yol (Nyarkwac) in a second war, this time against a combination of Leng and Thiang. Other recent Lou feuds were between the

Falkir and Nyajikany divisions of the Rumjok secondary section and between various local communities of the Mor primary section, particularly between two divisions of the Jimac secondary section.

In Eastern Gaajok country the Yol primary section joined the Gaagwang tribe, who seem to have identified themselves so much with the Gaajok tribe that we may almost speak of them, as we can to the west of the Nile, as a single tribe separated from the Gaajak by the wide Macar swamps, against several, if not all, sections of the Gaajak tribe. Yol fought Nyayan while Gaagwang fought Reng and Kang. About half a century ago the Laang and Wangkac primary sections of the Gaajok tribe were involved in a long feud and there was also warfare between the Yol and Wangkac sections in which Yol, assisted by their allies the Gaagwang tribe, were victorious; the Wangkac being so heavily defeated that they moved southwards to the banks of the Pibor river. Here, they say, they were attacked by *Turuk* (Arabs of some kind) and moved north again to the site of their old homes. They were too exhausted to resume their feud with the Yol section. In spite of these internal feuds, if any section of the Gaajok tribe is engaged in warfare with the Lou tribe all its sections will come to assist the threatened section if it is not strong enough to resist whatever section of the Lou is opposed to it. There have also been feuds between the Eastern Gaajak sections, e.g. between Thiang and Reng. When two tribes fight, other tribes remain neutral, and if two sections of a tribe are at war with one another the other sections of each may leave them to fight it out if they are well matched and do not appeal for assistance. Some of Miss Soule's informants pointed out that when there was trouble a few years ago between the Yol section of the Gaajok tribe and the Lony section of the Gaajak tribe they were strong enough to fight their own battle, but had Lony not been strong enough to fight single-handed then the Kaang and Tar, and possibly other, sections of the Gaajak would have come to its assistance, in which case the Gaajok sections would have joined Yol. They also pointed out that at present there is trouble between the Luluaa section and the Wang section. There is also trouble between various sections of Wangkac. If Luluaa and Wang begin to fight then the Wangkac sections will compose their differences and join Luluaa.

In accordance with the general tendency to the west of the Nile the Western Gaajok and Gaajak tribes are not only smaller but less united than the Eastern Gaajok and Gaajak. Both, on the Bahr-el-Ghazal, had frequent and bitter internal feuds. There was a fierce battle between the Gai division of the Gaagwong primary section and two other divisions of the same section, the Kwoth and the

Bor, whose dominant lineages spring from one mother. The Kwoth and Bor divisions were defeated and migrated southwards to settle at Kwac in Rengyan country. The same Gai division also had a feud with the Reng primary division, after which it moved into Karlual country. There were numerous other feuds in the Gaajak tribe. The Gaajok tribe once lived entirely on the left bank of the Bahr-el-Ghazal and their present extension on the right bank is a consequence of migration following feuds.

The Leek tribe once all lived on the right bank of the Bahr-el-Ghazal. Here two of its primary sections, Cuaagh and Deng who lived to the west of the Gany river, fought the third primary section, the Keunyang (Karlual), who lived to the east of that river, and being defeated crossed the Bahr-el-Ghazal and settled on its left bank. The story is that some aristocrats of the Nyapir section and some aristocrats of the Nyawah section used offensive expressions in songs about one another. These songs led to fighting between the young men, one of whom on each side was killed. There was further fighting in consequence, and finally Deng and Cuaagh crossed the river. In the following year they recrossed the Bahr-el-Ghazal to camp in the dry season on the right bank and on their return to their villages they drove before them herds belonging to Keunyang. Six of their girls came back to collect their dairy vessels which they had left in a camp hut and were waylaid and killed by some Keunyang men. This act was considered a serious breach of the rules of war, for the Nuer do not kill their own womenfolk. Because of it the Deng uttered a curse, according to which it is forbidden to an aristocrat of Keunyang who crosses the Bahr-el-Ghazal and settles among the Deng or Cuaagh, and also to an aristocrat of Deng or Cuaagh who moves southwards and settles among the Keunyang, to build a cattle-byre in the usual manner. The curse also causes an aristocrat who thus changes his residence to beget only boys for his first few children because of the slain girls. When the Government raided Karlual (Keunyang) country many Keunyang aristocrats crossed the river to live in Deng and Cuaagh country. At the present day many Deng and Cuaagh spend the dry season in Keunyang country because their own country is not rich in good pasture grasses but consists mainly of marsh grasses which are not so nourishing.

Within each of these primary sections there were constant feuds. Thus in Karlual country, Riaagh, Gom, Jiom, Nyaagh, Jikul, and Ngwol sections have been frequently at feud with one another. It would be tedious to recount the occasions and outcome of these petty feuds. I want only to make it clear that the villages occupied

PLATE XVI

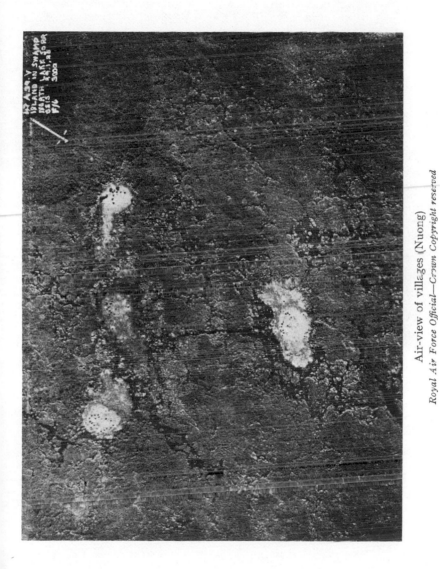

Air-view of villages (Nuong)

PLATE XVII

Boy collecting dung-fuel (Lou)

by these minor sections, Tutgar (Ngwol), Nyang (Riaagh), Nyueny (Juak), Kol (Jikul), &c., are only a few miles from their nearest neighbours, all of them being contained in a radius of five miles. It is between villages and tertiary tribal sections that fights most frequently take place and feuds develop.

I could give many more examples of feuds, but to no purpose, for those I have cited amply illustrate the lack of political control in Nuer tribes. We may conclude that a man's tribe only claims his allegiance in intertribal fighting and in wars against the Dinka. In normal times a man thinks and acts as a member of very much smaller local groups with the members of which he has manifold contacts.

III

We may use the diagram on p. 144 to emphasize the principle of contradiction in political structure. A member of Z^2 tertiary section of tribe B sees himself as a member of Z^2 in relation to Z^1, and all other members of Z^2 see themselves as members of that group in relation to Z^1 and are so regarded by members of Z^1. But he regards himself as a member of Y^2 and not of Z^2 in relation to Y^1 and is so regarded by members of Y^1. Likewise he regards himself as a member of Y and not of Y^2 in relation to X, and as a member of the tribe B, and not of its primary section Y, in relation to tribe A. Any segment sees itself as an independent unit in relation to another segment of the same section, but sees both segments as a unity in relation to another section; and a section which from the point of view of its members comprises opposed segments is seen by members of other sections as an unsegmented unit. Thus there is, as we have pointed out earlier, always contradiction in the definition of a political group, for it is a group only in relation to other groups. A tribal segment is a political group in relation to other segments of the same kind and they jointly form a tribe only in relation to other Nuer tribes and adjacent foreign tribes which form part of the same political system, and without these relations very little meaning can be attached to the concepts of tribal segment and tribe. We make here the same point as we made in discussing the word *cieng*: that political values are relative and that the political system is an equilibrium between opposed tendencies towards fission and fusion, between the tendency of all groups to segment, and the tendency of all groups to combine with segments of the same order. The tendency towards fusion is inherent in the segmentary character of Nuer political structure, for although any group tends to split into opposed parts these parts must tend to fuse in relation to other groups, since they form part of a segmentary system. Hence fission and fusion in political groups are two aspects of the same segmentary principle, and the Nuer tribe and its divisions are to be understood as an equilibrium between these two contradictory, yet complementary, tendencies. Physical environment, mode of livelihood, poor communications, a simple technology, and sparse food-supply—all, in fact, that we call their oecology—to some extent explain the demographic features of Nuer political segmentation, but the tendency towards segmentation must be defined as a fundamental principle of their social structure.

There must always, therefore, be something arbitrary about our formal definition of a tribe by the characters we have earlier listed. The political system is an expanding series of opposed segments from the relations within the smallest tribal section to intertribal and foreign relations, for opposition between segments of the smallest section seems to us to be of the same structural character as the opposition between a tribe and its Dinka neighbours, though the form of its expression differs. Often it is by no means easy to decide whether a group should be regarded as a tribe or as the segment of a tribe, for political structure has a dynamic quality. Using payment of blood-wealth as the principal criterion we class the Eastern Gaajok and Gaajak as distinct tribes because there is no compensation for homicide between them, but they consider themselves to be a single community in relation to the Lou. The tribal value is still recognized throughout Lou country, but, in fact, the Gun and the Mor sections are largely autonomous and it may be doubted whether compensation for homicide would actually be paid between them, though people say that it ought to be paid. It appears that so many people were killed in feuds between the Yol and Wangkac primary sections of the Gaajok tribe that all payments for homicide lapsed. On the other hand, I was told that at the time when the influence of the Lou prophets Ngundeng and Gwek was at its height compensation was for a time paid between the Lou and the Gaajok. In the larger tribes the segments recognize a formal unity, but there may be little actual cohesion. The tribal value is still affirmed, but actual relations may be in conflict with it since they are based on local allegiances within the tribe, and, in our opinion, it is this conflict between rival values within a territorial system which is the essence of the political structure.

Nuer tribes are an evaluation of territorial distribution, and tribal and intertribal and foreign relations are standardized modes of behaviour through which the values are expressed. The tribal value is, therefore, relative and at any time is attached to a certain extension of an expanding series of structural relations without being inevitably fixed to that extension. Moreover, it is not only relative because what we designate a tribe to-day may be two tribes to-morrow, but it can only be said to determine behaviour when a certain set of structural relations are in operation, mainly acts of hostility between tribal segments and between a tribe and other groups of the same structural order as itself, or acts likely to provoke aggression. A tribe very rarely engages in corporate activities, and, furthermore, the tribal value determines behaviour in a definite and restricted field of social relations and is only one of a series of political values, some of which are in conflict with it. The same is true of its segments. We would, therefore, suggest that Nuer political groups be defined, in terms of values, by the relations between their segments and their interrelations as segments of a larger system in an organization of society in certain social situations, and not as parts of a kind of fixed framework within which people live.

We do not doubt that there is an interdependence between the various sectional interrelations and the entire political system of which they form part, but this cannot easily be demonstrated. It has been noted that the smaller the local group the more cohesive it is and the more contacts of various kinds its members have with one another. There is less solidarity the wider we extend the circle from a village to adjacent tribes. It might be assumed, therefore, that there is always greater opposition between two groups than between the segments of either and that the segments are held together, as it were, by this external pressure, but we cannot admit that this view accords with the facts, because greater hostility appears to be felt between villages, groups of villages, and tertiary tribal sections than between larger tribal sections and between tribes. Probably the raids conducted tribally and in tribal federation against the Dinka had an integrating action, but the Dinka were not aggressive against the Nuer and it seems that the maintenance of tribal structure must rather be attributed to opposition between its minor segments than to any outside pressure. If this be so, and a consideration of the institution of the feud suggests that it is so, we arrive at the conclusion that the more multiple and frequent the contacts between members of a segment the more intense the opposition between its parts. However paradoxical this conclusion may at first seem we are led to it both by observation and by reflection on what constitutes a segmentary system.

IV

We have used the term 'feud' in the last section in the sense of lengthy mutual hostility between local communities within a tribe. This broad and slightly vague usage seems justified by convention and also, as we shall show, because, although responsibility for homicide and the duty of exacting vengeance directly fall only on the close agnatic kin of slayer and slain, the communities to which the two parties belong are, in one way or another, involved in the hostility that ensues and, often enough, in any fighting that may result from the dispute. Strictly, however, the word might be considered more appropriately used to describe the relations between the kin on both sides in a situation of homicide, for it then refers to a specific institution. We sometimes, therefore, speak of the 'blood-feud' to emphasize this restricted and more clearly defined meaning.

Blood-feuds are a tribal institution, for they can only occur where a breach of law is recognized since they are the way in which reparation is obtained. Fear of incurring a blood-feud is, in fact, the most important legal sanction within a tribe and the main guarantee of an individual's life and property. If a com-

munity of one tribe attempts to avenge a homicide on a community of another tribe a state of intertribal war, rather than
a state of feud, ensues, and there is no way of settling the dispute
by arbitration.

As Nuer are very prone to fighting, people are frequently
killed. Indeed it is rare that one sees a senior man who does not
show marks of club or spear. A Nuer gave me the following
causes of fighting: a dispute about a cow; a cow or goat eats
a man's millet and he strikes it; a man strikes another's little
son; adultery; watering rights in the dry season; pasturage
rights; a man borrows an object, particularly a dance ornament,
without asking its owner's permission. A Nuer will at once fight
if he considers that he has been insulted, and they are very
sensitive and easily take offence. When a man feels that he has
suffered an injury there is no authority to whom he can make
a complaint and from whom he can obtain redress, so he at once
challenges the man who has wronged him to a duel and the
challenge must be accepted. There is no other way of settling a
dispute and a man's courage is his only immediate protection
against aggression. Only when kinship or age-set status in-
hibits an appeal to arms does a Nuer hesitate to utter a challenge, for it does not occur to him to ask advice first, and no one
would listen to unsolicited advice. From their earliest years
children are encouraged by their elders to settle all disputes by
fighting, and they grow up to regard skill in fighting the most
necessary accomplishment and courage the highest virtue.

Boys fight with spiked bracelets. Men of the same village or
camp fight with clubs, for it is a convention that spears must not
be used between close neighbours lest one of them be killed and
the community be split by a blood-feud. It is also a convention
that no third person may take part in the fight, even though he
be a close kinsman of one of the combatants. Once a fight has
begun neither party can give way and they have to continue
till one or the other is badly injured unless, as generally happens, people pull them away from each other, loudly protesting,
and then stand between them.

When a fight starts between persons of different villages it is
with the spear; every adult male of both communities takes
part in it; and it cannot be stopped before considerable loss of

life has ensued. Nuer know this and, unless they are very angry, are reluctant to start a fight with a neighbouring village and are often willing to allow a leopard-skin chief or the elders to intervene. I have seen a fight of this kind prevented by the mediation of elders on both sides, but it was clear that their mediation would have availed little if the young men had been eager to come to blows. To-day such fights are less common because fear of Government intervention acts as a deterrent, but I have seen camps and even tribal sections massed for war and on the verge of fighting, and at one time fights must have been very frequent.

Tribes sometimes raided each other for cattle, but fighting between them was rare. Inter-community fighting and the feuds that result from it are part of the political relations that exist between segments of a common tribal organization. Thus a Leek man said to me: 'We have our fighting among ourselves and the Gaajok have their fighting among themselves. We do not fight the Gaajok. We fight only among ourselves. They have their own fights.' People are killed in these fights and blood-feuds thereby commence. Within a tribe there is a method by which they can be concluded by arbitration.

V

We give a concise account of the procedure for settling a blood-feud, without describing the detail of ritual. As soon as a man slays another he hastens to the home of a leopard-skin chief to cleanse himself from the blood he has spilt and to seek sanctuary from the retaliation he has incurred. He may neither eat nor drink till the blood of the dead man has been let out of his body, for it is thought to pass into it in some way, and to this end the chief makes one or two vertical incisions on his arm by a downward stroke from the shoulder with a fishing spear. The slayer presents the chief with a steer, ram, or he-goat, which the chief sacrifices. This rite and the mark of Cain on the arm are known as *bir*. As soon as the kinsmen of the dead man know that he has been killed they seek to avenge his death on the slayer, for vengeance is the most binding obligation of paternal kinship and an epitome of all its obligations. It would be great shame to the kinsmen were they to make no effort to avenge the homicide. By living with the chief as his guest from the moment his arm has been cut till the final settlement, the slayer has asylum, for the chief is sacred and blood must not be shed in his homestead. It is possible that men only take refuge with a chief when the danger of vengeance is very great, but it seems to be the general practice.

While the slayer is at the chief's home the avengers keep watch on him (*bim*) from time to time to see if he leaves his sanctuary and gives them a chance to spear him. They take any opportunity that offers to kill him, but they are not very persistent in seeking an opportunity. This state of affairs may go on for some weeks before the chief opens negotiations for settlement with the dead man's people, for his overtures are not likely to meet with a favourable response till the mortuary ceremony has been held and tempers have cooled a little. The negotiations are leisurely conducted. The chief first finds out what cattle the slayer's people (*jithunga*) possess and that they are prepared to pay compensation. I do not think that it would often happen that they would refuse to pay blood-cattle, unless they lived very far from the avengers or there were a number of unsettled feuds between the sections concerned, though they might not have the intention of handing them all over. He then visits the dead man's people (*jiran*) and asks them to accept cattle for the life. They usually refuse, for it is a point of honour to be obstinate, but their refusal does not mean that they are unwilling to accept compensation. The chief knows this and insists on their acceptance, even threatening to curse them if they do not give way, and his exhortations are supported by the advice of distant paternal kinsmen and cognatic relatives who will not receive any of the cattle and need not, therefore, show such pride and stubbornness, but who have a right to make their opinion known in virtue of their relationship to the dead man. The voice of compromise is also supported by the bias of custom. Nevertheless, the close kinsmen must refuse to listen to it till the chief has reached the limit of his arguments, and when they give way they declare that they are accepting the cattle only in order to honour him and not because they are ready to take cattle for the life of their dead kinsman.

In theory forty to fifty head of cattle are paid, but it is

unlikely that they will all be paid at once and the debt may continue for years. The ceremonies of atonement are performed when some twenty have been handed over, and then the slayer's kin may go about without fear of being waylaid, for the time being at any rate, for they are not safe from vengeance till all the cattle have been paid, and possibly not even then. The chief takes the cattle to the dead man's home. The slayer's people would not venture to accompany him. They are partly distributed among the kinsmen of the dead man and partly used to marry a wife to his name to give him heirs. Even if a man on either side has been killed cattle must be paid by both parties, though perhaps only twenty head by each, for the ghosts must be appeased and the honour of the living must be upheld. Also, sacrifices must be performed to rid the villages of death, which is loose in them and must be sent into the bush, and kinsmen on both sides must be purified from their uncleanness. For his part in the proceedings the chief receives, apart from meat of sacrifices, two beasts, but he has to give one of these to an agnatic kinsman who assists him. Often he gains nothing, as he is expected to give the slayer a cow to help him pay compensation and, moreover, he has had the expense of providing him with lengthy hospitality.

A homicide does not concern only the man who has committed it, but his close agnatic kinsmen also. There is mutual hostility between the kinsmen on both sides and they may not, on penalty of death, that will inevitably fall on those who break the injunction, eat or drink with one another or from the same dishes and vessels the other has eaten or drunk from, even if in the home of a man who is not kin to either party. This prohibition ceases after the cattle have been paid and sacrifices made, but close kinsmen on either side will not eat with one another for years, even for a generation or two, for reasons of sentiment. 'A bone (the dead man) lies between them.' Indeed, all Nuer recognize that in spite of payments and sacrifices a feud goes on for ever, for the dead man's kin never cease 'to have war in their hearts'. For years after cattle have been paid close agnates of the slayer avoid close agnates of the dead man, especially at dances, for in the excitement they engender the mere knocking against a man whose kinsman has been slain may cause a fight to break out, because the offence is never forgiven and the score must finally be paid with a life. When the dead man is married a wife the bride is rubbed with ashes by her dead husband's kinsmen and God is invoked by them that she may bear a male child who will avenge his father. Such a child is a *gat ter,* a child of feud. At the sacrifices the ghost is told that his kinsmen have accepted cattle and will marry him a wife with them, but he is assured that one day they will avenge him properly with the spear. 'A Nuer is proud and wants a man's body in vengeance and not his cattle. When he has killed a man he has paid the debt and then his heart is glad.' Hence, though the chief admonishes the relatives of the dead man at the ceremonies of settlement that the feud is ended and must not be reopened, Nuer know that 'a feud never ends'. There may be peace for a time for the reasons that persuaded the kinsmen to accept compensation and on account of the cattle they have received, but enmity continues and the people on both sides remain *jitor*, people who are at feud, even if there is no overt hostility. There is no frequent fighting or continuous unabated hostility, but the sore rankles and the feud, though formally concluded, may at any time break out again.

VI

We have said that feuds create a state of hostility between lineages and thereby, as we shall explain further, between whole tribal sections; and that there is no very great difference between the occasional efforts to exact vengeance when feuds are still unsettled and the latent hostility that persists when they have been settled. This is only true, however, when the homicides are between primary, secondary, and tertiary tribal sections. In smaller groups it is not so, for, in spite of the strength of the feelings aroused and their persistence after compensation has been paid, feuds have there to be settled more quickly and are not so likely to break out again after settlement.

What happens when a man kills another depends on the relationship between the persons concerned and on their structural positions. There are different payments for a true Nuer, for a Dinka living in Nuerland, and, among the Eastern Jikany, for a member of the aristocratic clan (see p. 217). The ability to prosecute a feud and thereby to obtain redress by a life or by payment of cattle depends to some extent on the strength of a man's lineage and on his kin relationships. But the intensity of a feud and the difficulty of settling it depend chiefly on the size of the group concerned in it. If a man kills another who is closely related to him—his paternal cousin, for example—cattle are still paid, though fewer, probably about twenty head. One of the sources of contribution, the father's brothers, or their sons, would be the recipients of compensation and therefore cannot pay it. None the less some cattle have to be paid as it is necessary to compensate the family of the dead man, to provide the ghost with a wife, and to perform the due sacrifices. I was told that in such cases the matter is quickly settled. Probably a blood-feud can be settled more easily if it is within a clan, for Nuer consider it wrong for clansmen to engage in a feud. After payment has been made they say: 'The feud has been cut behind, we have returned to kinship.' It is also said that if there has been much intermarriage between two groups a feud is unlikely to develop.

When a man kills a fellow villager or a man of a nearby village with which his village has close social relations a feud is soon settled, because the people on both sides have got to mix and because there are sure to be between them many ties of kinship and affinity. It is pointed out to the ghost that cattle have been paid and that it is impossible to avenge him by taking life because no one would be left alive if the feud were continued between kinsmen and neighbours. Corporate life is incompatible with a state of feud. When a man spears another of a nearby village it is customary for the people of the wounder's village to send the spear which caused the injury to the wounded man's people so that they can treat it magically to prevent the wound proving fatal. They also send a sheep for sacrifice. By so doing they intimate their hope that the wound will soon heal and that, in any case, they do not want to incur a feud on account of a personal quarrel. After this courtesy, even if the man dies his kinsmen are likely to accept compensation without great reluctance. If a man dies many years after having received a wound the death is attributed to this wound, but compensation is likely to be accepted without demur, and on a reduced scale.

When a man has killed a neighbour a cow is often immediately paid over in earnest so that the community may remain at peace. It must not be supposed, however, that the ease with which feuds are settled is an indication of lack of strong indignation or that the difficulty with which they are settled is an indication of greater indignation.

Feuds are settled with comparative ease in a restricted social milieu where the structural distance between the participants is narrow, but they are more difficult to settle as the milieu expands, until one reaches intertribal relations where no compensation is offered or expected. The degree of social control over feuds varies with the size of the tribal segment, and Nuer themselves have often explained this to me. Long and intense feuds may take place between tertiary tribal sections, but an effort is generally made to close them, for a segment of this size has a strong sense of community, close lineage ties, and some economic interdependence. However, it is far less easy to stop a feud between persons of different tertiary sections than to stop a feud in a village or between neighbouring villages, where a quick and permanent settlement is assured, and unsettled feuds between sections of this size tend to accumulate. This is especially the case where there has not been a single death resulting from a personal quarrel but several deaths in a fight between the two sections. When a fight has taken place between secondary tribal sections there is little chance of exacting vengeance except by a general fight, and people feel less the need to submit to mediation since they have few social contacts and these of a temporary kind, for the relative ease with which feuds are settled is an indication of the cohesion of the community. The larger the segment involved the greater the anarchy that prevails. People say that there is payment of blood-cattle between primary tribal sections, but they do not greatly feel the need of paying it. The tribe is the last stage in this increasing anarchy. It still has nominal political unity, and it is held that feuds between its most distant members can be settled by compensation, but often they are not settled, and if many men are killed in a big fight between large sections nothing is done to avenge them or to pay compensation for their deaths. Their kinsmen abide their time till there is another fight. The political integument may in consequence be stretched eventually to the breaking-point and the tribe split into two. The rent between sections enlarges until they have little to do with each other beyond occasional uniting for raids; and feuds between their members are settled, if at all, with greater difficulty and casualness.

VII

The likelihood of a homicide developing into a blood-feud, its force, and its chances of settlement are thus dependent on the structural interrelations of the persons concerned. Moreover, the blood-feud may be viewed as a structural movement between political segments by which the form of the Nuer political system, as we know it, is maintained. It is true that only close agnatic kin of both sides are immediately and directly involved, but feuds between persons belonging to different tribal sections sooner or later influence the interrelations of the whole communities to which they belong.

The kinsmen of a slain man try to kill the *gwan thunga*, the slayer, but they have a right to kill any of his close agnates (*gaat gwanlen*). They must not kill sons of the mother's brother, father's sister, or mother's sister, because these people do not belong to the slayer's lineage. Also, only the minimal lineages on both sides are directly involved in the feud. However, the significance of the feud may be held to lie less in the ease of settlement within smaller groups than in the difficulties of settlement within larger groups, which participate indirectly in the conflict. We have noted that people at feud may not eat in the same homesteads, and, as a man eats in all the homesteads of his village, the villagers at once come within the scope of the prohibition and enter into a state of ritual opposition to each other. All the people of a village are generally in some way related to one another and have also a strong sense of community, so that if any fighting occurs between their village and another on account of a feud in which some of their members are involved the whole village is likely to be drawn into it. Thus at dances men of each village who attend them arrive in war formation and maintain an unbroken line throughout the dance, so that if one of them is attacked the others are at his side and are bound to assist him. People not directly affected by the feud may thus be compelled to assist the principals.

We have noted, moreover, that the intensity of a feud and the manner of its prosecution depend on the structural relationship of the persons concerned in the political system. A feud cannot be tolerated within a village and it is impossible to maintain one for a long period between nearby villages. Consequently, although fights most frequently occur within a village or be- tween neighbouring villages and camps, a feud, in the sense of a relation between parties between whom there is an unsettled debt of homicide which can be settled either by vengeance or by payment of compensation—a temporary state of active hostility which does not compel immediate settlement but which requires eventual conclusion—can only persist between tribal sections which are near enough to each other for the maintenance of actively hostile relations and far enough from each other for these relations not to inhibit essential social contacts of a more peaceable kind. A feud has little significance unless there are social relations of some kind which can be broken off and resumed, and, at the same time, these relations necessitate eventual settlement if there is not to be complete cleavage. The function of the feud, viewed in this way, is, therefore, to maintain the structural equilibrium between opposed tribal segments which are, nevertheless, politically fused in relation to larger units.

Through the feud whole sections are left in a state of hostility towards one another, without the hostility leading to frequent warfare, for the scope of direct vengeance is limited to small kin- ship groups and their efforts to exact it are not incessant. There is a fight between two sections and some people are killed on either side. Only those lineages which have lost a member are in a state of direct feud with the lineages which they have deprived of a member, but through common residence, local patriotism, and a network of kinship ties, the whole sections participate in the enmity that results, and the prosecution of the feuds may lead to further fighting between the communities concerned and to a multiplication of feuds between them. Thus when the Nyarkwac section of the Lou tribe fought the Leng section, the LAM lineage and the people who live with them were ranged against the MAR, KWOTH, and MALUAL lineages and the people who live with them; the MANTHIEPNI lineage was ranged against the DUMIEN lineage; and so forth. Only these minimal lineages were involved with one another in the feuds that resulted, and not collateral lineages, even though they took part in the fight in other sectors of it, but the hostility between the sections was common to all their members. A good example of how Nuer feel in such matters is furnished by their reactions at Muot Dit cattle camp when the Government seized hostages to compel them to hand over two prophets. Their main complaint to me was that the hostages did not belong to the same lineages as the prophets and were therefore not directly concerned in the issue. The Government was looking at the affair in territorial terms, they in kinship terms on analogy with the conventions of a feud.

Apart from ritual observances, kinship obligations, community sentiment, and so forth, there is a further reason why blood-feuds between small lineages, especially when there are many of them, develop into states of feud, and tend to maintain hostile feelings between communities. As is explained in Chapter V every community is associated with a lineage in such a way that all persons in the community who are not members of the lineage are assimilated to it in political relations which are, therefore, often expressed in lineage values. Hence a blood-feud between small agnatic groups is translated into a feud, in the more general sense, between the lineages with which these groups are associated through the expression of the disturbed relations in terms of their structure, and the communities associated with the lineages are involved in mutual hostility.

Hostility between smaller segments of a tribe may involve the larger segments of which they form part. A quarrel between two villages may thus, as we have noted, bring about a fight between secondary, and even primary, tribal sections. The interrelations between larger sections are operated, as it were, by the interrelations between smaller sections. When a section in which there are unsettled feuds fights another section all quarrels are neglected for the time and the whole section combines for action.

The feud is a political institution, being an approved and

regulated mode of behaviour between communities within a tribe. The balanced opposition between tribal segments and their complementary tendencies towards fission and fusion, which we have seen to be a structural principle, is evident in the institution of the feud which, on the one hand, gives expression to the hostility by occasional and violent action that serves to keep the sections apart, and, on the other hand, by the means provided for settlement, prevents opposition developing into complete fission. The tribal constitution requires both elements of a feud, the need for vengeance and the means of settlement. The means of settlement is the leopard-skin chief, whose role we shall examine later. We therefore regard the feud as essential to the political system as it exists at present. Between tribes there can only be war, and through war, the memory of war, and the potentiality of war the relations between tribes are defined and expressed. Within a tribe fighting always produces feuds, and a relation of feud is characteristic of tribal segments and gives to the tribal structure a movement of expansion and contraction.

There is, of course, no clear-cut distinction between fighting against another tribe and fighting against a segment of one's own tribe. Nuer, however, stress that the possibility of arbitration and payment of blood-wealth for deaths resulting from a fight within a tribe makes it a *ter*, feud, and that this is different from a fight between tribes, *kur*, in which no claims for compensation would be recognized. Both differ from raiding of Dinka, *pec*, and from individual duelling, *dwac*, though all fighting is *kur* in a general sense. But it is obvious that a fight in a village which at once leads to payment of compensation for deaths and a fight between tribes in which there is no compensation for deaths are two poles, and that the further we go from a village community the fights between tribal sections become more like fights between tribes in that blood-wealth is paid with increasing difficulty and infrequency, so that between primary sections the tribal value, the feeling that blood-wealth can, and even ought to, be paid, alone distinguishes their fights from fights between tribes. Here again we would emphasize the conclusion that the tribal value is relative to the structural situation.

We would emphasize further that blood-feuds only directly involve a few persons and that though they sometimes cause violence between whole local communities—a feud in a wider sense—ordinary social contacts continue in spite of them. The strands of kinship and affinity, of age-set affiliations, and of military and even economic interests remain unbroken; and these strands act like elastic between the sections, being capable of considerable expansion by disturbed political relations, but always pulling the communities together and keeping them as a single group in relation to other groups of the same kind. As we have explained, these strands lessen in number and strength the larger the community, but they stretch even beyond tribal frontiers. Increasing anarchy, increasing difficulty in settling feuds, goes together with lessening frequency of social contacts of all kinds. Social cohesion increases as the size of the community narrows.

VIII

There are, of course, disputes between Nuer other than those about homicides, but they can be treated briefly and in direct relation to homicide and the feud. In a strict sense Nuer have no law. There are conventional compensations for damage, adultery, loss of limb, and so forth, but there is no authority with power to adjudicate on such matters or to enforce a verdict. In Nuerland legislative, judicial, and executive functions are not invested in any persons or councils. Between members of different tribes there is no question of redress; and even within a tribe, in my experience, wrongs are not brought forward in what we would call a legal form, though compensation for damage (*ruok*) is sometimes paid. A man who considers that he has suffered loss at the hands of another cannot sue the man who has caused it, because there is no court in which to cite him, even were he willing to attend it. I lived in intimacy for a year with Nuer and never heard a case brought before an individual or a tribunal of any kind, and, furthermore, I reached the conclusion that it is very rare for a man to obtain redress except by force or threat of force. The recent introduction of Government courts, before which disputes are now sometimes settled, in no way weakens this impression, because one well knows how among other African peoples cases are brought before courts under Government supervision which would not previously have been settled in a court, or even settled at all, and how for a long time after the institution of such Government tribunals they operate side by side with the old methods of justice.

Before discussing the chief characteristics of Nuer legal procedure I record that, according to verbal information, for I have never observed the procedure, one way of settling disputes is to use a leopard-skin chief as mediator. Thus, I was told that a man who has a cow stolen may ask a leopard-skin chief to go with him to request the return of the cow. The chief goes first, with several of the elders of his village, to the plaintiff's homestead, where he is given beer to drink. Later they go, with a deputation from the plaintiff's village, to the defendant's village, and here also the chief may be presented with some beer or a goat. The chief is considered to be neutral and a certain sanctity attaches to his person so that there is little likelihood of the deputation being injured. The visiting elders sit with elders of the defendant's village and the chief in one of the byres and talk about the matter in dispute. The owner of the animal gives his view and the man who has stolen it attempts to justify his action. Then the chief, and anybody else who wishes to do so, expresses an opinion on the question. When every one has had his say the chief and elders withdraw to discuss the matter among themselves and to agree upon the decision. The disputants accept the verdict of the chief and the elders and, later, the owner of the animal gives the chief a young steer or a ram unless he is a very poor man, when he gives him nothing.

If a man has a dispute with another of the same neighbourhood they may both go to the homestead of a local leopard-skin chief and lay their spears on the ground in his byre. A man would not plant his spear upright in a chief's byre, and I was told that were he to do so a bystander might appropriate it, as disrespect had thereby been shown to the chief. When both men have stated their views the chief and the elders discuss the matter outside the byre and re-enter it to acquaint the disputants of their decision. The person in whose favour the decision has been given hands his spear to the chief, who either gives it to a friend or spits on it and returns it to its owner. It was clear from the way in which my informants described the whole procedure that the chief gave his final decision as an opinion couched in persuasive language and not as a judgement delivered with authority. Moreover, whilst the sacredness of the chief and the influence of the elders carry weight, the verdict is only accepted because both parties agree to it. No discussion can be held unless both parties want the dispute settled and are prepared to compromise and submit to arbitration, the chief's role being that of mediator between persons who wish other people to get them out of a difficulty which may lead to violence. The man against whom the decision is pronounced may give way to honour the elders and the chief where he would not give way directly and without their intervention, for he does not lose prestige by accepting their verdict. If there is any doubt about the facts, certain oaths, which are in the nature of ordeals, may be employed, such as swearing statements on the chief's leopard skin.

For a dispute to be settled in this way not only is it necessary that both parties should want the matter amicably settled, but it is also necessary that they should themselves reach agreement during the discussion. No one can compel either party to accept a decision, and, indeed, a decision cannot be reached unless there is unanimity, since the elders are of both parties to the dispute. They go on talking, therefore, till every one has had his say and a consensus has been reached.

The five important elements in a settlement of this kind by direct negotiation through a chief seem to be (1) the desire of the disputants to settle their dispute, (2) the sanctity of the chief's person and his traditional role of mediator, (3) full and free discussion leading to a high measure of agreement between all present, (4) the feeling that a man can give way to the chief and elders without loss of dignity where he would not have given way to his opponent, and (5) recognition by the losing party of the justice of the other side's case.

I repeat that I have not seen this method employed and add that I am of the opinion that it is very rarely used and only when the parties are fairly close neighbours and belong to communities closely linked by many social ties. In theory any member of a tribe can obtain redress from any other, but we know of no evidence that leads us to suppose that it was often obtained. Before summing up what we judge to be the nature and scope of legal relations in Nuerland we record a few brief examples of typical acts likely to lead to violence if some reparation is not made.

When a Nuer speaks of a person having stolen (*kwal*) an animal, he means that he has taken it without permission and by stealth and by no means implies that he ought not to have taken it. Within a tribe an abductor of cattle always considers that he is taking what is owing to him. It is a debt (*ngwal*) which he is settling in this way, because the man who owes him cattle has not repaid them of his own accord. The legal issue, therefore, is whether he is right in assuming a debt and whether he should have taken the particular animals he took. So well is this practice of helping yourself to what is owing to you an established habit, that it may be said to be a customary way of settling debts. Thus the final cattle of a homicide-payment are often seized in the pastures, and it often happens that when a bridegroom and his kin do not hand over all the cattle they have promised, the wife's brothers try to seize the animals still owing to them. In other circumstances a man will steal a cow which he is owed, sometimes employing the services of a magician to charm the owner so that he may not guard his herd on the day the theft is planned; for example a man who lent another an ox for sacrifice in sickness, at his daughter's wedding, in time of famine, and so on, and has not received a heifer in return, although the debtor possesses one. Having seized a cow from the debtor's herd he is quite willing to return it if he receives instead the heifer owing to him. The debtor will then either try to steal his cow back again or he will open a discussion which will result in his paying a heifer and receiving back his cow.

The only quarrels within a village or camp about ownership of cattle that I have witnessed have concerned obligations of kinship or affinity and have eventually been settled by one party giving way on account of his relationship to the other. If a man seizes cattle from a kinsman or neighbour he walks into his kraal and takes them. If the owner has a strong case he may resist: otherwise he lets the cattle go, for he knows that the man will be supported by public opinion in the community. If a man seizes cattle from a man of a different village he adopts different tactics. With one or two friends he watches the cattle in their grazing-ground till a suitable opportunity occurs. I have never heard of a Nuer stealing a cow from a fellow tribesman merely because he wanted one. He has, on the other hand, no hesitation in stealing cows from persons belonging to neighbouring tribes and will even go with friends to another tribe in order to steal from them. This theft (*kwal*) is not considered in any way wrong.

If a man commits adultery he pays an indemnity of five cows and an ox, unless the man is impotent, when the adulterer can claim a cow on the marriage of a female child of his adultery. Even when the husband is not impotent, if the adulterer can show that there is fruit of his adultery he can claim back the cattle he has paid as an indemnity, except for a cow known as *yang kule*, the cow of the sleeping-skin, which has ritual significance. But adultery within a small local community is probably rare because the people are all related to one another, and therefore a man considers that not only would it be wrong to commit adultery with their wives but also that it would be, in a greater or lesser degree, incestuous. If the two men are close kinsmen the adulterer provides an ox for sacrifice but is unlikely to pay an indemnity. If they are not close kinsmen the husband may try to seize the adulterer's cattle, but he only takes this step if he actually catches the offender committing adultery. The adulterer, to avoid a fight, runs away, and if he fears that his cattle may be seized he places them in the kraals of friends and kinsmen. This makes it difficult for the husband to seize them, for even if he knows where they are he does not want to involve himself in quarrels with a number of his neighbours by raiding their kraals. Nuer do not consider it immoral to commit adultery with the wives of persons living in other villages. If the husband discovers the offence he may try to seize the offender's cattle, but in doing so he runs the risk of resistance and some one may get killed and a feud result. A herd is the joint property of brothers, even though it is divided among them, and they do not readily acquiesce in the loss of cattle on account of adultery. In my experience it is very seldom indeed that a man obtains compensation for adultery. Adultery with the wife of a man of another tribe is a matter of no importance. What can he do anyhow?

Likewise fornication with an unmarried girl is compensated by payment of a heifer and a steer. But it is most unlikely that the payment will be made. If the girl's kinsmen know that she is having relations with a man who possesses cattle and is likely to marry her they turn a blind eye to the affair. If he has no cattle, or if the girl is already engaged, and one of her brothers catches him in congress with her he fights him, unless, as usually happens, the man runs away, for it is not considered cowardly to run away in these circumstances. The girl's kinsmen may then come to his kraal and, if he possesses them, take a male calf and a female calf, and if they are strong enough they may not be resisted. This is what Nuer tell one, but I have never known any one pay a male and a female calf, although after every dance I have seen the youths and maidens have paired off and there has been much promiscuous intercourse and very little effort to conceal it. It frequently

PLATE XVIII

Building a cattle byre (Eastern Jikany)

PLATE XIX

a. Cattle camp (Leek)

b. Typical swampy depression in November (Western Jikany)

happens that a man impregnates an unmarried girl and he is then expected to marry her. The girl's kinsmen may raid his kraal and seize some of his cattle, but he will try to circumvent this by hiding his beasts in the kraals of relatives and neighbours. If later he marries the girl the cattle her kinsmen have seized count as part of the bride-wealth, and if he refuses to marry her they count as payment for possession of the child, so that in either case he pays no indemnity but only a fee to establish his rights. Here again, in point of fact, it is very difficult for the girl's brothers to seize the man's cattle, unless he is willing to let them do so, and there is always the risk of a fight which may become general. One does not fornicate with the girls of one's own village, for they are generally related to one, so that when an issue of the kind arises it is generally between persons of different villages of the same district. If the young man can avoid being hit over the head with a club at the time of the incident and keeps clear of the girl's village for a few months he is not likely to pay an indemnity or to suffer any other consequences. If he has put the girl in child he will, in normal circumstances, send a kinsman to say that he intends to marry her. The girl is then regarded as engaged and the young man becomes son-in-law to her parents and one does not injure one's son-in-law. Even if he refuses to marry their sister, the brothers hesitate to attack the father of her child.

It is possible to obtain from Nuer a list of compensations for injuries to the person: e.g. ten cattle for a broken leg or skull, ten cattle for the loss of an eye, two cattle for a girl's broken teeth, &c. For a flesh wound, however serious, there is no compensation unless the man dies. In different parts of Nuerland the number of cattle to be paid in compensation varies. I have not recorded any instance of a man receiving such compensation, except from a Government court, but Nuer say that he would receive it if his kinsmen were strong enough to retaliate.

It is alleged that, in the old days, if a man died of magic his kinsmen would try to slay the magician (*gwan wal*), though I have not recorded a case of a magician having been killed. Nuer point out that a magician does not use his magic against persons in his own community but only against persons of other villages, so that it is not easy to revenge yourself on him since he will be supported by his village who regard powerful magic as of value to their community. It is also said that in the old days a witch (*peth*) was sometimes slain, though I cannot say how often, if at all, this occurred.

Many disputes arise about bride-wealth: the husband's people do not pay what they have promised or there is a divorce and the wife's people do not return all the cattle that have been paid. In such circumstances the debtor does not deny the debt but puts forward a counterbalancing claim on some account or says that he has no cattle to settle it. Often enough he says this even when he has got cattle. The claimant can only be sure of getting his due if he takes it by force from the debtor's kraal or from the herd in the grazing-grounds. If he is strong and has the backing of a powerful lineage he is not resisted, since he has right on his side. Such matters are easily settled within a village and among people who share a common dry season camp because every one realizes that some agreement must be reached by discussion and that it must accord with justice. But when the parties belong to different, and maybe hostile, villages, settlement is not so easy. The leopard-skin chief may be employed, in the manner described, to bring the parties together for discussion and some agreement may then be reached, but many such debts are never settled. They are remembered for years. Perhaps some day, maybe in the next generation, an opportunity will occur to steal the cattle.

If a wife dies in her first pregnancy or childbirth the husband is held responsible. There is no question of a feud arising, but the husband loses the bride-cattle he has paid, since these now become blood-cattle for the loss of his wife. The husband is only responsible if the death occurs during childbirth before expulsion of the afterbirth If there is any dispute about the mode of death or the number of cattle that are still owing it is settled by a mediator called *kuaa yiika* or *kuaa yiini*, 'the chief of the mats', an office which pertains to certain lineages. This man has no other office and is not an important person in virtue of his role of arbitrator in disputes of this kind. It is easy to obtain compensation, as the father-in-law has the bride-wealth in his possession. There is, moreover, a tie of affinity and neither party is likely to resort to violence.

Using these brief notes on some exemplifications of the tendencies in Nuer law we may now state what these tendencies are. We speak of 'law' here in the sense which seems most appropriate when writing of the Nuer, a moral obligation to settle disputes by conventional methods, and not in the sense of legal procedure or of legal institutions. We speak only of civil law, for there do not seem to be any actions considered injurious to the whole community and punished by it. The informants who said that witches and magicians were sometimes killed stated that it was always individuals or groups of kin who waylaid them and killed them in vengeance.

The first point to note about Nuer law is that it has not everywhere the same force within a tribe, but is relative to the position of persons in social structure, to the distance between them in the kinship, lineage, age-set, and, above all, in the political, systems. In theory one can obtain redress from any member of one's tribe, but, in fact, there is little chance of doing so when he is not a member of one's district and a kinsman. The wider the area which contains the parties to a dispute the weaker the feeling of obligation to settle it and the more difficult the task of enforcing settlement, and, consequently, the less the likelihood of it being settled. Within a village differences between persons are discussed by the elders of the village and agreement is generally and easily reached and compensation paid, or promised, for all are related by kinship and common interests. Disputes between members of nearby villages, between which there are many social contacts and ties, can also be settled by agreement, but less easily and with more likelihood of resort to force. The nearer we get to the tribe the less the chances of settlement. Law operates weakly outside a very limited radius and nowhere very effectively. The lack of social control to which we have often referred is thus shown in the weakness of law, and the structural interrelations of tribal segments are seen in the relativity of law, for Nuer law is relative like the structure itself.

A cogent reason why there is little chance of redress between members of different secondary and primary tribal sections is that the basis of law is force. We must not be mislead by an enumeration of traditional payments for damage into supposing that it is easy to exact them unless a man is prepared to use force. The club and the spear are the sanctions of rights. What chiefly makes people pay compensation is fear that the injured man and his kin may take to violence. It follows that a member of a strong lineage is in a different position from that of a member of a weak lineage. Also the chances of a man obtaining redress for an injury are less the further removed he is from the man who has injured him, since the opportunity for violence and the effectiveness of kinship backing lessen the wider the distance between the principals. Since self-help, with some backing of public opinion, is the main sanction it is only operative when people are within easy striking distance of one another. This is one of the main reasons why it is difficult to settle feuds when the parties belong to different primary or secondary tribal sections.

Most disputes occur in villages or camps and between persons of nearby villages, since people who live close to one another have more opportunities for dispute than those who live far from

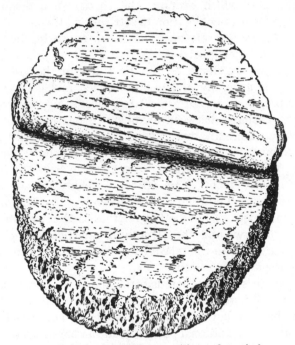

FIG. 12. Baked-mud grindstone with wooden grinder.

one another. Such quarrels are usually complicated by notions of kinship, affinity, age, and so forth and are very often the result of breaches of specific patterns of social behaviour rather than simple breaches of general social regulations. They are, therefore, generally settled in harmony with these traditional patterns. But, if they are not settled by the mediation of kinsmen, they are likely to lead to violence, because, as we have remarked, Nuer are at once prepared to fight if they are wronged or insulted, unless kinship, or great disparity in age, restrains them. If a man refuses to pay compensation for a wrong, therefore, he runs a great risk of his skull being cracked with a club, and even of being speared if excitement runs high. And this is what often happens.

For this reason we have said that Nuer law, in so far as it applies to a study of political relations, must be treated in connexion with the blood-feud. Disputes can often be settled on account of close kinship and other social ties, but between tribesmen as such they are either settled by the aggrieved party using force, and this may result in homicide and blood-feud, or by the debtor giving way in the knowledge that force may be used and a feud result. It is the knowledge that a Nuer is brave and will stand up against aggression and enforce his rights by club and spear that ensures respect for person and property.

The Nuer has a keen sense of personal dignity and rights. The notion of right, *cuong*, is strong. It is recognized that a man ought to obtain redress for certain wrongs. This is not a contradiction of the statement that threat of violence is the main sanction for payment of compensation, but is in accord with it, for a man's kinsmen will only support him if he is right. It is doubtless true that if a man is weak it is unlikely that his being in the right will enable him to obtain satisfaction, but if he is in the right he will have the support of his kin and his opponent will not, and to resort to violence or to meet it the support of one's kin and the approval of one's community are necessary. One may say that if a man has right on his side and, in virtue of that, the support of his kinsmen and they are prepared to use force, he stands a good chance of obtaining what is due to him, so long as the parties to the dispute live near one another.

When we speak of a man being in the right we do not suggest that disputes are mostly a clear issue between right and wrong. Indeed, it would be correct to say that, usually, both parties are to some extent right and that the only question which arises is, Who has the greater right? To state the matter in a different way: a Nuer dispute is usually a balance of wrongs, for a man does not, except in sexual matters, wantonly commit an act of aggression. He does not steal a man's cow, club him, or withhold his bride-cattle in divorce, unless he has some score to settle. Consequently it is very rare for a man to deny the damage he has caused. He seeks to justify it, so that a settlement is an adjustment between rival claims. I have been told by an officer with wide experience of Africans that Nuer defendants are remarkable in that they very seldom lie in cases brought before Government tribunals. They have no need to, since they are only anxious to justify the damage they have caused by showing that it is retaliation for damage the plaintiff has inflicted earlier.

IX

Feuds are settled through the leopard-skin chief and he plays a minor role in the settlement of disputes other than homicide. It might be supposed that this functionary has a position of great authority, but this is not so. Indeed, on the same grounds as we have said that the Nuer have no law we might say that they also have no government. We devote a few lines to stating what are the ritual qualifications of the leopard-skin chief and then assess the part he plays in feuds and quarrels.

The few references in the writings of early travellers about Nuer leaders do not suggest that they were persons of very great authority.[1] The absence of any persons with sufficient authority or, except for a few prophets, with sufficient influence through whom an administrative system might be built up is stated in very direct terms by the earliest British officers to enter Nuerland.[2] The 'sheikhs' described in these early reports as lacking authority are probably the persons who were later known among Europeans as leopard-skin chiefs. A leopard-skin chief, *kuaar muon*, has a sacred association with the earth (*mun*) which gives him certain ritual powers in relation to it, including the power to bless or curse. However, lest it be supposed that the power to utter curses enables a chief to wield great authority I at once record that I have never observed a chief exercise this power. There are stories which recount the dire effects of a curse, but I think that as a rule a chief only ventures to threaten to utter one when he is officiating in a ritual capacity in the settlement of feuds, on which occasions he is expected to do so, the

---

[1] Werne, op. cit., p. 207; Poncet, op. cit., p. 40; Brun-Rollet, op. cit., p. 222. Brun-Rollet's account is unacceptable.

[2] *Kaimakam G. Hawkes, S.I.R.*, no. 98, 1902; *Bimbashi H. Gordon, S.I.R.*, no. 107, 1903.

threat forming part of the proceedings. Certainly to-day chiefs
have no authority in virtue of their power of cursing. He is also
known as *kuaar twac* because he alone wears a leopard-skin
(*twac*) across his shoulders. A chief may be seen wearing one
in Mr. Corfield's photograph on Plate XXIV. The word *kuaar*
has ritual associations in all the Nilotic languages, but, without
discussing further what word might best define its scope of
reference in Nuer, we intend to refer to the person in this
account, as we have done heretofore, as a chief, with the caution
that we do not thereby imply that he has any secular authority,
for we hold that his public acts are mainly ritual.

Nevertheless, his function is political, for relations between
political groups are regulated through him, though he is not
a political authority controlling them. His activities are
chiefly concerned with settlement of blood-feuds, for a feud
cannot be settled without his intervention, and his political
significance lies in this fact. Chiefs sometimes prevent fights
between communities by running between the two lines of combatants and hoeing up the earth here and there. The older men
then try to restrain the youths and obtain a settlement of the
dispute by discussion. However, we think that a fight can only
be prevented in this way when the disputants are close neighbours and anxious not to kill one another.

Besides the part they play in feuds, chiefs perform ritual to
cleanse parties to incestuous congress, and they possess slight
rain-making powers, though Nuer do not attach much importance to the art. On the whole we may say that Nuer chiefs
are sacred persons, but that their sacredness gives them no
general authority outside specific social situations. I have never
seen Nuer treat a chief with more respect than they treat other
people or speak of them as persons of much importance. They
regard them as agents through whom disputes of a certain kind
can be settled and defilement of a certain kind can be effaced,
and I have often heard remarks such as this: 'We took hold of
them and gave them leopard skins and made them our chiefs to
do the talking at sacrifices for homicide.' Their ritual sphere
seldom extends beyond a tribal section.

Only certain lineages are chiefs and only some men of these
lineages practise as such. It is, perhaps, significant that in many

parts of Nuerland, including most of the area with which I am acquainted, chiefs do not belong to the dominant clans in the tribes in which they function, though some of them are said to be aristocrats in parts of Eastern Gaajak, Gaawar, and Leek. Most of those whose clans I know belong to the GAATLEAK and JIMEM clans which nowhere have aristocratic status. Since quarrels between tribal sections are expressed in terms of lineages of the dominant clan associated with the sections, as will be explained in the following chapter, the chief, having no position in the system of dominant lineages, is thereby more fitted to mediate between them. He is not a member of the hereditary owners of the tribal land, but is a stranger living there. A chief may act as such in whatever tribe he resides in. If a chief is killed the ceremonies connected with payment of compensation are performed by an aristocrat of the tribe. This is probably because, even when the chiefs of an area are not all members of one clan, they are believed to have a kind of kinship through their common badge of the leopard skin and cannot marry into one another's families. We regard chiefs as a category of ritual experts and do not consider that they comprise in any way a class or rank. We believe their social function to be a mechanism by which the equilibrium of the political system is maintained through the institution of the feud. The slight authority of chiefs and, in many parts, their position outside the dominant clan, accord with this view.

In taking the view that to regard the leopard-skin chief as a political agent or a judicial authority is to misunderstand the constitution of Nuer society and to be blind to its fundamental principles, we have to account for the part he plays in the settlement of feuds. We have stated that he has no judicial or executive authority. It is not his duty to decide on the merits of a case of homicide. It would never occur to Nuer that a judgement of any kind was required. Likewise he has no means of compelling people to pay or to accept blood-cattle. He has no powerful kinsmen or the backing of a populous community to support him. He is simply a mediator in a specific social situation and his mediation is only successful because community ties are acknowledged by both parties and because they wish to avoid, for the time being at any rate, further hostilities.

Only if both parties want the affair settled can the chief intervene successfully. He is the machinery which enables groups
to bring about a normal state of affairs when they desire to
achieve this end.

It is true that a leopard-skin chief has always in these circumstances to persuade, by exhortations and threats, the kinsmen
of the dead man to accept compensation, but this pressure must
not be regarded as a command. It is quite clear from many
Nuer statements on the matter that the chief's threats are
encouraged to their furthest point in order that by yielding to
his persuasion the kinsmen of the dead man may not dishonour
themselves by neglecting to exact a life for the life of their
kinsman.

A chief's threats might go no further than saying that if the
kinsmen would not listen to him neither would he, when they
were in a similar difficulty, listen to them. But I was told that were
the people to refuse mediation with undue obstinacy the chief
might threaten to leave their homestead and to curse them. He
would take an ox and rub its back with ashes and begin to address
it, saying that if the injured party were to insist on revenge many
of them would be killed in the endeavour and they would throw
spears vainly at their enemies. I was told that he would then
raise his spear to slaughter the animal, but this would be as far
as people would care to let him go. Having asserted their
pride of kin, one of the dead man's family would seize his upraised
arm to prevent him from stabbing the ox, saying: 'No! Do not
kill your ox. It is finished. We will accept compensation.' My
informant, whose statements were supported by others, further
added that if people were to insist on refusing the mediation of a
leopard-skin chief he would take a short-horned ox and, after
invoking God, slay it and rub the hairs off its head so that the
members of the lineage who rejected his mediation might perish
in prosecuting their feud,

We conclude, therefore, that a chief's curse is not in itself the
real sanction of settlement, but is a conventional, ritual, operation in the settlement of feuds, which is known to every one in
advance and is allowed for in their calculations. The threat of
it is compelled by those on whom it would fall were it uttered.
These affairs are like a game in which everybody knows the
rules and the stages of development: when one is expected to
give way, when to be firm, when to yield at the last moment

and so forth. This conclusion is based on many statements (I have only once been present at discussions between a chief and the kinsmen of a slain man, and then the circumstances were unusual). It may, however, be said with certainty that no amount of pressure from a leopard-skin chief, if it is ever exerted, can settle feuds expeditiously, if at all, between the larger tribal sections. In other disputes the chief acts rarely, and only when both sides strongly desire settlement. He has no jurisdiction to hear cases in a locality. Here, again, I was told that if one party refused to accept his decision as arbiter he might pass the man his leopard-skin, an action tantamount to a curse. The man must then make the chief a gift before he will consent to take back the skin. However, this probably happens only when a man refuses to accept a decision to which every one else, including his own elders, have agreed. I was also told that in disputing a chief's words a man will do so respectfully, first spitting into the chief's hands as a sign of goodwill. No doubt a chief is shown respect on such occasions, but the chiefs I have seen were treated in everyday life like other men and there is no means of telling that a man is a chief by observing people's behaviour to him. His role in disputes may be regarded as a means by which neighbours, who wish a difficulty settled without resort to force and who acknowledge that the other side have a good case, can negotiate.

X

We have considered the position of the leopard-skin chief at some length because it is structurally important. He in no way represents or symbolizes the unity and exclusiveness of political groups, but is a mechanism by which, through the institution of the feud, these groups interact and maintain their structural distance. There are other people in Nuerland with ritual powers, of one kind or another, which sometimes make a man well known and, occasionally, very influential, but none of them are politically important, except the prophets whose activities we discuss later. They neither govern nor judge and their sacred functions are not, like those of the leopard-skin chief, specifically related to the interaction of local groups. However, we do not entirely pass them by because sacred powers often give a man prestige from which he may attain local eminence as an important elder, if they are combined with wealth, ability, and wide kinship connexions.

Next to prophets and leopard-skin chiefs the ritual status that carries with it most prestige is that of the *wut ghok*, the Man of the Cattle. Certain lineages have hereditary ritual powers in relation to cattle and are asked to cure sick beasts and to make barren cows fruitful, though only some members of these lineages use their powers. Like leopard-skin chiefs, Men of the Cattle are often members of stranger lineages and not of the aristocratic clan of their tribe. I was told that their curse is feared, as it can be directed to the cattle, and that Nuer do not care to offend them, but, outside tradition, I have not recorded any occasion of its utterance. Apart from the few Men of the Cattle who play a part in the regulation of Age-sets (see Chap. VI), and those who are sometimes consulted about migration to new pastures, they have no public functions. One *wut ghok* of the Eastern Gaajok became very rich and powerful a generation ago, but his prestige was largely due to his possession of magic.

Besides the *kuaa muon*, who has a ritual relationship to the earth and the *wut ghok*, who has a ritual relationship to the cattle, there are a number of totemic specialists whose ritual connexion with lions, crocodiles, weaver birds, &c., enables them to influence the behaviour of these creatures. A totemic specialist is a possessor (*gwan*) of the spirit (*kwoth*) of his totem. Totemic specialists have no political significance and have no social influence in virtue of their powers alone. There is a war specialist whose duty it is to shake a spear in the face of the enemy and to deliver an invocation against them. He is known as *gwan muot*, possessor of the spear, or *ngul*, and is often, perhaps always, a member of a senior lineage of the dominant clan of the tribe, for he invokes the spear by the spear-name of the clan. There are also magicians of various kinds: leeches, diviners, owners of medicines, and owners of fetishes. Of these specialists only owners of fetishes become prominent members of their communities on account of their ritual powers. Nuer are very much afraid of fetish spirits and believe them to be so powerful that they will even purchase them with cattle. A fetish-owner may become the most influential man in the village, and I have been surprised at the respect and fear with which his neighbours sometimes treat him. Nevertheless, he has no defined authority in controlling the relations of the villagers to one another nor does he represent the village in its relations with neighbouring communities.

XI

Ritual status gives a man vague influence in his locality; but authority only in specific ritual situations. Sex and age are two, more general, conditioning attributes of local influence. Women and children have always a position inferior to that of men. Women occasionally gain a reputation as prophets and magicians but, as a rule, they play no leading part in public affairs. Among the Nuer, relations between the sexes, and between man and wife, are more equitable and give females more privilege than in any other tribe I have visited in the Southern Sudan. Nevertheless, they are subject to men: daughters to their fathers and wives to their husbands. Boys are under the command of their parents and elder brothers and only become full tribesmen, with the privileges and responsibilities of such, at initiation. The relations between the sexes and between children and adults belong rather to an account of domestic relations than to a study of political institutions.

When a lad has passed through initiation he becomes 'a man' and when he has married and begotten several children he becomes 'a true man', what we have called an elder. We have from time to time spoken of the part played by elders in homicides and other disputes. When a local community acts corporately and leadership and advice are required, these functions rest with the elders. They decide when seasonal moves are to be made and where camps are to be formed, negotiate marriages, advise on questions of exogamy, perform sacrifices, and so forth. Their opinions on such matters are readily accepted by the younger men, who take little part in the talk unless they are directly concerned in the issue. When the elders disagree there is much shouting and argument, for every one who wishes to speak does so and as often and loud as he pleases. The words of some elders count for more than the words of others and one easily observes that their opinions are usually agreed to.

These elders are members of central age-sets, at the present time the *Maker* and *Dangunga*, for members of the most senior sets, the *Thut* and *Boiloc*, take little part in public life. We discuss in Chapter VI the relations between age-sets. Here we remark only that there is no constituted authority within each set, all members being of equal status, and that, whilst members of junior sets respect those of senior sets, the authority of older men is personal, very indefinite, and based on analogy with domestic relations within the family. Behaviour between individuals is influenced by the distance between them in the age-set system, but age-sets are not a political institution in the sense of the system having an administrative, military, or judicial organization.

Age by itself does not give a man social position. He must have other qualifications as well. Those elders with most influence are the *gaat twot*, the children of bulls. Such a man is called a *tut*, bull, and in strict usage this is equivalent to *dil*, tribal aristocrat. As will be fully explained in Chapter V a *dil* is a member of the dominant clan in each tribe and, in virtue of his membership, has within that tribe a slightly superior social position. This clan is not a ruling class and the enhanced prestige of its members is very indefinite. The clan system has no hereditary leadership; a senior lineage does not rank higher than others; there is no 'father of the clan'; and there is no 'council of clan elders'. *Tut* is also used in a wider sense to refer to men of social position who do not belong to the dominant clan but to other lineages which have long been domiciled in the tribe. A *tut* in this rather wide sense of 'man of good standing', or 'social leader', is usually a scion of an important lineage, the head of his own family, and master of his homestead and herd. He is generally also the eldest surviving son of his father's family and, therefore, head also of the joint family, the master of the hamlet. If he is to gain a social reputation he must also possess sufficient cows to be able to entertain guests and to attract young kinsmen to reside in his byre. Round such a man's homestead are clustered the homesteads of his brothers and married sons and, often enough, the homesteads of his sisters' husbands and daughters' husbands. To be a social leader, whose opinion is readily agreed to, he must also be a man of character and ability.

The authority of a *gat twot*, or *tut wec*, 'bull of the camp', as he is often called, is never formalized. He has no defined status, powers, or sphere of leadership. Lineage, age, seniority in the family, many children, marriage alliances, wealth in cattle, prowess as a warrior, oratorical skill, character, and often ritual powers of some kind, all combine in producing an outstanding social personality who is regarded as head of a joint family and of a cluster of cognatic kinsmen and affines, as a leader in village and camp, and a person of importance in the rather vague social sphere we call a district. It is easy to see in village or camp who are its social leaders, and it is these people who have furnished the administration with most government chiefs, for the influence of the leopard-skin chief is mainly restricted to the circuit of his ritual functions and only if he is also a *gat twot* does he exercise influence beyond these limits.

When we ask, however, in what way a *tut* acts as a leader in his community it is difficult to answer. As the chief man of his family and joint family he takes the most prominent part in settling the affairs of these groups, but he cannot on that account be said to have political authority, for these domestic groups act independently of others in the village, though some co-ordination between them is imposed by their common requirements. A joint family decide on the advice of their *tut* to change camp and the *tut* is supposed to drive in the first tethering peg in the new camp, if he is present, but other joint families of the same camp may decide not to move till another day. Leadership in a local community consists of an influential man deciding to do something and the people of other hamlets following suit at their convenience. When villagers co-operate, there is no appointed leader to organize their activity. If some members of a village are attacked the others rush to their assistance, headed by the swiftest and bravest, but there is no one who calls on them to do so or who organizes their resistance. A village is a political unit in a structural sense, but it has no political organization. There is no headman or other appointed leader invested with authority who symbolizes its unity and no village council. Beyond his domestic groups a *tut* has authority in his village only in the sense that he takes a prominent part in questions of procedure and other discussions. Outside his village he is a well-known person who is generally respected in his district, but he has no political status.

In larger groups than a village and camp there is far less

co-ordination of activities and less scope for leadership. Only in war is there any lengthy direct co-operation. Men noted for their prowess and ability stir up among the youths enthusiasm for a raid against the Dinka or a fight against another tribal section, and direct what simple tactics are employed, but these men have no political status or permanent leadership. The warriors mobilize in local divisions of their own accord, for there are no regiments and companies under officers, and in fighting they follow the most forward and courageous among them. Some of these warriors become renowned and their reputation quickly attracts recruits for raids. Two of the most famous war leaders were Latjor who led the Jikany tribes, and Bidiit who led the Lou, eastwards. Neither had any ritual qualifications, but both were men of outstanding ability who were members of the dominant clans of their tribes. It is not said by Nuer that either established any political control, or even had great authority, in their tribes. The role of prophets in war is examined later. Between tribal segments there are no other joint activities that require organization and direction.

XII

The lack of governmental organs among the Nuer, the absence of legal institutions, of developed leadership, and, generally, of organized political life is remarkable. Their state is an acephalous kinship state and it is only by a study of the kinship system that it can be well understood how order is maintained and social relations over wide areas are established and kept up. The ordered anarchy in which they live accords well with their character, for it is impossible to live among Nuer and conceive of rulers ruling over them.

The Nuer is a product of hard and egalitarian upbringing, is deeply democratic, and is easily roused to violence. His turbulent spirit finds any restraint irksome and no man recognizes a superior. Wealth makes no difference. A man with many cattle is envied, but not treated differently from a man with few cattle. Birth makes no difference. A man may not be a member of the dominant clan of his tribe, he may even be of Dinka descent, but were another to allude to the fact he would run a grave risk of being clubbed.

That every Nuer considers himself as good as his neighbour is evident in their every movement. They strut about like lords of the earth, which, indeed, they consider themselves to be. There is no master and no servant in their society, but only equals who regard themselves as God's noblest creation. Their respect for one another contrasts with their contempt for all other peoples. Among themselves even the suspicion of an order riles a man and he either does not carry it out or he carries it out in a casual and dilatory manner that is more insulting than a refusal. When a Nuer wants his fellows to do something he asks it as a favour to a kinsman, saying, 'Son of my mother, do so-and-so', or he includes himself in the command and says: 'Let us depart', 'Let the people return home', and so forth. In his daily relations with his fellows a man shows respect to his elders, to his 'fathers', and to certain persons of ritual status, within the circuit of its reference, so long as they do not infringe on his independence, but he will not submit to any authority which clashes with his own interests and he does not consider himself bound to obey any one. I was once discussing the Shilluk with a Nuer who had visited their country, and he remarked, 'They have one big chief, but we have not. This chief can send for a man and demand a cow or he can cut a man's throat. Whoever saw a Nuer do such a thing? What Nuer ever came when some one sent for him or paid any one a cow?'

I found Nuer pride an increasing source of amazement. It is as remarkable as their constant aloofness and reticence. I have already described how Nuer would interrupt my inquiries. I mention here three incidents typical of the cavalier way in which they treated me. On one occasion I asked the way to a certain place and was deliberately deceived. I returned in chagrin to camp and asked the people why they had told me the wrong way. One of them replied, 'You are a foreigner, why should we tell you the right way? Even if a Nuer who was a stranger asked us the way we should say to him, "You continue straight along that path", but we would not tell him that the path forked. Why should we tell him? But you are now a member of our camp and you are kind to our children, so we will tell you the right way in future.'

In this same camp, at the end of my stay, when I was sick and being removed by steamer, I asked the people to carry my tent and belongings to the river's edge. They refused, and my servant, a Nuer youth, and I had to do it ourselves. When I asked him why the people were churlish, he replied, 'You told them to carry your belongings to the river. That is why they refused. If you had asked them, saying, "My mother's sons, assist me", they would not have refused.'

On one occasion some men gave me information about their lineages. Next day these same men paid me a visit and one of them asked me, 'What we told you yesterday, did you believe it?' When I replied that I had believed it they roared with laughter and called to others to come and share the joke. Then one of them said, 'Listen, what we told you yesterday was all nonsense. Now we will tell you correctly.' I could relate many such stories.

The Nuer have been rightly described as dour, and they are often gruff and curt to one another and especially to strangers. But if they are approached without a suggestion of superiority they do not decline friendship, and in misfortune and sickness they show themselves kind and gentle. At such moments they permit themselves to show sympathy which their pride stifles at other times, for even when Nuer approve of one they cannot bear that one shall see it and are the more truculent to hide their friendliness. Never are they truckling or sycophantic. When a Nuer wants a gift he asks for it straight out, and if you refuse it he remains in good humour. Their only test of character is whether one can stand up for oneself. One rises in Nuer estimation the more one lives their kind of life and accepts their values.

If you wish to live among the Nuer you must do so on their terms, which means that you must treat them as a kind of kinsmen and they will then treat you as a kind of kinsman. Rights, privileges, and obligations are determined by kinship. Either a man is a kinsman, actually or by fiction, or he is a person to whom you have no reciprocal obligations and whom you treat as a potential enemy. Every one in a man's village and district counts in one way or another as a kinsman, if only by linguistic assimilation, so that, except for an occasional homeless and despised wanderer, a Nuer only associates with people whose behaviour to him is on a kinship pattern.

Kinsmen must assist one another, and if one has a surplus of a good thing he must share it with his neighbours. Consequently no Nuer ever has a surplus. But the European has a surplus and if his possessions are of any use to the Nuer he ought, in their opinion, to share them with the people among whom he is living. Travellers have often remarked that the Nuer have plagued them for gifts. They beg from one another with equal persistence. No Nuer is expected to part with his cattle or household property and, except in special circumstances, these would not be asked for. But were a man to possess several spears or hoes or other such objects he would inevitably lose them. Deng, a Government chief and a man of standing, told me, as I was leaving his village on the Pibor River, that he was grateful for the fishing spears I had distributed among his kinsmen, but added that they would not be able to keep them when his relatives at Fadoi came to spend next dry season on the Pibor.

The only way of keeping tobacco among the Nuer is to deny that one possesses it and to keep it well hidden. When I gave Deng a big lump of Anuak tobacco he managed to place a small piece of it in his pipe, but he had at once to distribute the rest of it. When I used to give tobacco to youths at Yakwac they generally took a small piece for immediate use as snuff and asked me to hide the rest, so that they could come and get a bit when they wanted it without any one knowing that they possessed it. I had hiding-places all over my tent. No Nuer can resist the pleadings of his kinsman for tobacco. Age-fellows do not even ask for snuff or tobacco, but, if they find it in a man's byre, they just take it. My own system was to give away at the first opportunity anything I possessed which Nuer might covet and to rest in poverty and peace. Arab merchants are driven almost crazy by Nuer demands for gifts, but they generally speak Nuer well and have considerable knowledge of Nuer habits and so are able to hold their own. Nevertheless I have often observed that they make gifts where no return is to be expected.

Nuer are most tenacious of their rights and possessions. They take easily but give with difficulty. This selfishness arises from their education and from the nature of kinship obligations. A child soon learns that to maintain his equality with his peers he must stand up for himself against any encroachment on his person and property. This means that he must always be prepared to fight, and his willingness and ability to do so are the only protection of his integrity as a free and independent person against the avarice and bullying of his kinsmen. They protect him against outsiders, but he must resist their demands on himself. The demands made on a man in the name of kinship are incessant and imperious and he resists them to the utmost.

XIII

Some personal recollections and general impressions were recorded in the last section in order that it might be understood what are Nuer feelings about authority. It is the more remarkable that they so easily submit to persons who claim certain supernatural powers. Fetishes are a recent introduction to Nuerland and they inspire much apprehension among the people, so that, in recent years, their owners have often won prestige in their villages and made themselves feared in their

districts, and occasionally even in large tribal sections. These
fetish owners are not, however, in any sense tribal leaders and
cannot compare in social importance with the prophets.

Owing to the fact that Nuer prophets had been the foci of
opposition to the Government they were in disgrace and the
more influential of them under restraint or in hiding during my
visits to Nuerland, so that I was not able to make detailed
observations on their behaviour.[1] Without discussing Nuer
religious categories it may be said that a prophet is a man who
is possessed by one of the sky-spirits, or Gods, whom Nuer
regard as sons of the Sky-god. Nuer have great respect for
these spirits and fear, and readily follow, those whom they
possess. Prophets, consequently, achieved greater sanctity and
wider influence than any other persons in Nuer society. A
prophet is known as *guk* and is sometimes referred to as *cok
kwoth*, an ant of God. He also comes into the general category
of *gwan kwoth*, possessor of a spirit.

The first prophet to have gained great influence appears to have
been Ngundeng who died in 1906. He was a Lou tribesman of the
GAATLEAK clan and an immigrant from the Eastern Jikany. He
had practised as a leopard-skin chief before he had acquired a
reputation as a prophet by prolonged fasts and other erratic
behaviour, by his skill in curing barrenness and sickness, and by
his prophecies. Women came to him to be made fruitful from all
over Lou, from the Eastern Jikany tribes, and even from the west
of the Zeraf and Nile. Many brought oxen which Ngundeng
sacrificed to Deng, the Sky-god which possessed him. He then
anointed them with his spittle. When small-pox threatened the
Lou he went out to meet it and to stay its advance by sacrifice of
oxen. He foretold cattle epidemics and other events and led
expeditions against the Dinka.

When Ngundeng died, the spirit of Deng eventually entered
his son Gwek, who began to prophesy and to cure barrenness and
sickness, as his father had done. However, he never displayed the
pathological qualities of his father, who appears to have been a
genuine psychotic. The spirit of Deng had passed over his elder
brothers, or did not long reside in them. Nuer say that a spirit
eventually returns to the lineage of the man whom it first

[1] The Government has always looked askance at prophets and opposed their
influence. See, for some pejorative references to them, Jackson, op. cit.,
pp. 90-1; Fergusson, Appendix to Jackson, p. 107; C. A. Willis, 'The Cult of
Deng', *S.N. and R.*, vol. xi, 1928, p. 200.

possessed, even if a generation or two later, and the chosen vessel generally becomes aware of its entry by experiencing severe sickness with delirium. Ordinary Nuer, particularly if they are young, do not want to be possessed, and it seems that it is often an abnormal person who is possessed in the first place, while it is the most ambitious of his sons on whom his mantle falls, for he would seem to welcome possession, although not undergoing fasts to procure it. Gwek was killed by Government forces in 1928. Another famous prophet, Diu or Dengleaka, of the Gaawar tribe, was a captured Dinka who set about to acquire a spirit by fasting and solitude. He later achieved fame and power by successful campaigns against the Dinka, whose country his followers occupied, and against Arab slavers. Like Ngundeng he had a reputation for performing miracles. Dengleaka died in 1908 and his son Dwal became possessed with the spirit of the Sky-god, Diu. He is at present a political prisoner. The only prophet I have met, Buom, of Dok country, was possessed by the spirit of a Sky-god, Teeny. He was regarded as selfish and greedy by his neighbours, having been cunning enough to get himself accepted as a Government chief. He showed too great ambition, however, and is now in exile. Well-known prophets, in other parts of Nuerland, were Mut of the Eastern Gaajak, Kulang in Western Nuerland, and others.

Brief reference must be made to the very remarkable pyramid erected by Ngundeng, and added to by Gwek, in the Rumjok section of the Lou tribe. It was fifty to sixty feet high with large elephant tusks planted round the base and at the summit. Dr. Crispin's photograph on Plate XXV, taken in 1901, shows the pallisade of ivory tusks, the type of material of which it was constructed, and weathering, due to rains, round the base. It was blown up by Government forces in 1928. The material used in construction consisted of ashes, earth, and debris excavated from sites of cattle camps. People came from all over Lou and the Eastern Jikany tribes, bringing oxen with them for sacrifice, to assist in the building. Nuer say that it was built in honour of the Sky-god Deng and for the glory of his prophet Ngundeng. There is no doubt that the cult of Deng was of Dinka origin and probably the idea of a mound came from the same source. Besides the famous Lou pyramid there is said to be a smaller one at Thoc in Eastern Jikany country, built by a prophet called Deng, son of Dul.

Nuer are unanimous in stating that these prophets are a recent development. They say that Deng descended from the sky in recent times—within living memory, in fact—and that he was the first, or almost the first, of the Sky-gods to come to

PLATE **XX**

Cattle travelling (Lou)

PLATE XXI

a. Cattle grazing on ridge (Leek)

b. Early dry season cattle camp at forest pool (Lou)

carth. They state that in the old days there were no prophets; only the ritual officials mentioned earlier. The records of European travellers are not explicit enough to confirm or reject this statement. Poncet says that among the Nuer in his day were rich and important persons, honoured after their death, whom he calls *devins ou sorciers* and *jongleurs*,[1] and Brun-Rollet says that the Nuer had a kind of pope for whom they had veneration akin to worship, but his account is too fanciful to carry weight.[2] Whilst it is difficult to believe that there were

FIG. 13. Calf's bell-necklace of palm nuts.

no cases of possession sixty years ago we must, in the absence of conflicting evidence, accept so unanimous a declaration by Nuer that there was no possession by Sky-gods, and it seems fairly certain that if there were any prophets at that time their influence was restricted to small localities and had not the tribal significance of more recent times. There is some evidence that the development of Nuer prophets was related to the spread of Mahdism from the Northern Sudan. However that may be, there is no doubt that powerful prophets arose about the time when Arab intrusion into Nuerland was at its height and that after the reconquest of the Sudan they were more respected and had more influence than any other persons in Nuerland.

Nevertheless, we consider that the power of these prophets, even of the most successful ones, has been exaggerated and that

[1] Poncet, op. cit., p. 40.   [2] Brun-Rollet, op. cit., p. 222.

their tribal position has been misunderstood. The earliest Government officials to enter Lou country have recorded that Ngundeng was greatly feared and respected and were of the opinion that if the Lou were to be administered he would have either to be reconciled or removed. However, his son, Gwek, was not supported against the Government by some sections of the tribe. Mr. Struvé, then Governor of the Upper Nile Province, reported that Dwal, son of Diu, had 'rather shaky authority' among the Gaawar. I received the impression in 1932 that Buom had far more power in Dok country as a government chief than he ever had in pre-government days as a prophet. A prophet's curse is feared, but armed intervention of Government forces is a weightier sanction. Buom was attempting to exercise unprecedented judicial functions and his banishment met with no popular hostility and with little regret. There is no good evidence that the earlier prophets were more than spiritual persons, whose ritual powers were used particularly in warfare, though some of the later ones appear to have begun to settle disputes, at any rate in their own villages and districts. Of them all, perhaps Gwek came nearest to exercising political functions and to imposing his authority outside his own district, but the hostility between tribes and between tribal segments rendered effective personal control impossible.

The only activities of prophets which can truly be called tribal were their initiation of raids against the Dinka and their rallying of opposition to Arab and European aggression, and it is in these actions that we see their structural significance and account for their emergence and the growth of their influence. All the important prophets about whom we have information gained their prestige by directing successful raids on the Dinka, for these raids were carried out in the names of the spirits which promised rich booty by their lips. No extensive raids were undertaken without the permission and guidance of prophets, who received instructions from the Sky-gods in dreams and trances about the time and objective of attack, and often they accompanied them in person and performed sacrifices before battle. They took for themselves part of the spoil and to some extent supervised the division of the rest of it. The warriors sang war hymns to the Sky-gods before starting on raids and the sacrifices to them by their prophets were believed to ensure booty and safety.

For the first time a single person symbolized, if only to a moderate degree and in a mainly spiritual and uninstitutionalized form, the unity of a tribe, for prophets are tribal figures. But they have a further significance, for their influence extended over tribal boundaries. Gwek had great influence in Gaajok, and it is said that because of it the Lou and the Gaajok for a time paid compensation for homicide between them. His influence reached as far as the Eastern Gaagwang and Gaajak. Dengleaka had a similar influence in the valley of the Zeraf, especially among the Thiang. Some of the Western Nuer prophets had a reputation among a number of neighbouring tribes which united for raids at the direction of their spirits. They were not a mechanism of tribal structure like leopard-skin chiefs, but were pivots of federation between adjacent tribes and personified the structural principle of opposition in its widest expression, the unity and homogeneity of Nuer against foreigners. Probably, the coalition of tribes and the organization of joint raids is very largely their achievement—though one cannot be sure of this in the absence of historical records—and has made them important and powerful figures in Nuerland. This interpretation explains how it is that prophets began half a century ago, or at any rate came to the fore then. Certain structural changes were taking place in response to changed conditions: the development of functions that were more purely political than any exercised by individuals before and of a greater degree of unity among neighbouring tribes than there had been hitherto. As Sky-gods passed at the death of prophets into their sons we are further justified in suggesting growth of hereditary political leadership which, with the strong tendency towards federation between adjacent tribes we attribute to the new Arab-European menace. Opposition between Nuer and their neighbours had always been sectional. They were now confronted by a more formidable and a common enemy. When the Government crushed the prophets this tendency was checked. As we understand the situation, the prophets were inevitably opposed to the Government because it was this opposition among the people which led to their emergence and was personified in them.

XIV

We have tried to show how distribution depends on oecology and how the lines of political cleavage tend to follow distribution in relation to modes of livelihood. But consideration of oecology only helps us to understand some demographic features of Nuer tribes and tribal segments and not the nature of their structural relations. These can only be understood in terms of certain structural principles and we have tried to isolate these principles, though not, we admit, at a very deep level of analysis. The chief points we have made are here briefly summarized.

(1) Nuer attach values to their geographical distribution and these evaluations give us socio-spacial units and relate these units into a system. (2) In all such units there is evident a tendency to segment into opposed segments, and also for these segments to fuse in relation to other units. (3) The smaller is the segment the greater is its cohesion, and it is for this reason that a segmentary system exists. (4) The political system of the Nuer can only be understood in relation to a whole structure of which other peoples form part and, likewise, the character of all Nuer communities must be defined by their relations with other communities of the same order within the whole political system. (5) The social system is much wider than spheres of actual political relations and cuts across them. (6) Political values depend on more than residential relations. Political relations can be isolated and studied independently of other social systems, but they are a specific function of the whole set of social relations. These are mainly of a kinship type and the organization of kinship relations into political relations in certain situations is one of our major problems. (7) The structural relations between Nuer tribes and other peoples and between tribe and tribe are maintained by the institution of warfare and the structural relations between segments of the same tribe are maintained by the institution of the feud. (8) There is no central administration, the leopa   kin chief being a ritual agent whose functions are to be interpreted in terms of

the structural mechanism of the feud. (9) Law is relative to the structural distance between persons and has not the same force in different sets of relations. (10) The new conditions of Arab-European intrusion have probably caused the development of prophets, with embryonic juridical functions, and greater intertribal solidarity.

CHAPTER V

THE LINEAGE SYSTEM

I

MANY characteristics of Nuer lineages and clans belong to the study of kinship which we hope to makē in a subsequent volume. Here only those characters which are strictly relevant to the territorial system are discussed. We begin, however, by a formal definition of clan, lineage, and kin. A Nuer clan is the largest group of agnates who trace their descent from a common ancestor and between whom marriage is forbidden and sexual relations considered incestuous. It is not merely an undifferentiated group of persons who recognize their common agnatic kinship, as are some African clans, but is a highly segmented genealogical structure. We refer to these genealogical segments of a clan as its lineages. The relationship of any member of a lineage to any other member of it can be exactly stated in genealogical terms and, therefore, also his relationship to members of other lineages of the same clan can be traced, since the relationship of one lineage to another is genealogically known. A clan is a system of lineages and a lineage is a genealogical segment of a clan. One might speak of the whole clan as a lineage, but we prefer to speak of lineages as segments of it and to define them as such. Alternatively one may speak of a lineage as an agnatic group the members of which are genealogically linked, and of a clan as a system of such groups, the system being, among the Nuer, a genealogical system. In the diagram on p. 193 clan A is segmented into maximal lineages B and C and these bifurcate into major lineages D, E, F, and G. Minor lineages H, I, J, and K are segments of major lineages D and G, and L, M, N, and O are minimal lineages which are segments of H and K. It was found that words to describe four stages of lineage segmentation are sufficient when speaking of even the largest clans. The commonest Nuer word for a lineage is *thok dwiel* and the smallest genealogical unit they describe as a *thok dwiel* has a time depth of from three to five generations from living persons. A whole clan is thus a genealogical structure, and the letters in the diagram represent persons from whom the clan and its segments trace their descent and from whom they often take their names. There must be at least twenty such clans in Nuerland, without taking into account numerous small lineages of Dinka origin.

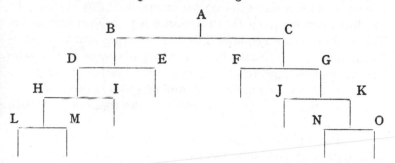

A lineage in the sense in which we generally employ this word is a group of living agnates, descended from the founder of that particular line. Logically it also includes dead persons descended from the founder—and we sometimes use the word to include them also—but these dead persons are only significant in that their genealogical position explains the relationships between the living. It is clear from the context whether the word is used in a more or less inclusive sense.

Clans and lineages have names, possess various ritual symbols, and observe certain reciprocal ceremonial relations. They have spear-names which are shouted out at ceremonies, honorific titles by which people are sometimes addressed, totemic and other mystical affiliations, and ceremonial status towards one another.

Agnatic kinship between lineages is called *buth*. *Buth* is always an agnatic relationship between groups of persons, and only between persons in virtue of their membership of groups. *Buth* agnation is to be distinguished from kinship in the sense of relationship between persons, e.g. between a man and his father's brother and mother's brother. Cognation in this sense the Nuer call *mar*. Any person to whom a man can trace any genealogical link, whether through males or females, is *mar* to him. A man's *mar* are consequently all his father's kin and all his mother's kin, and we call this cognatic category his kindred.

In normal usage the word refers to close relatives only. Therefore, as *mar* includes close agnates, the word *buth* is used only in reference to distant agnates, between whom and the speaker there is lineage cleavage. There is *buth* relationship between lineages of the same clan and also between related clans which have the same ancestor but do not compose an exogamous unit. A Dinka can be given *buth* relationship to a Nuer lineage by being adopted into a collateral lineage. We thus formally distinguish between the lineage system, which is a system of agnatic groups, and the kinship system, which is a system of categories of relationship to any individual; and we speak of these relationships as a man's paternal kin and his maternal kin, and both together as his kindred.

Political and lineage groups are not identical, but they have a certain correspondence and often bear the same name, for a tribal area and its divisions are often called after the clans and lineages which are supposed to have first occupied them. This makes their inter-relation a very difficult problem to investigate and has led to some confusion in writings on the Nuer. Thus Gaawar is the name of a tribal area, of the tribesmen who inhabit it, and of the members of a clan which have in that area a socially dominant status. Likewise Gaajok and Gaajak are names of territories, tribes, and lineages. To clarify description clan and lineage names are therefore printed in small capitals. Hence, when we say that a man is a Gaawar we mean that he is a Gaawar tribesman, a man who resides in Gaawar country, whereas when we say that he is a GAAWAR we mean that he is a member of the GAAWAR clan, a descendant in the male line from War, the founder of the dominant clan in Gaawar country.

II

Three trees of clan descent are presented in the following section in a form conventional to us, and which would also commend itself to Nuer, who sometimes speak of a lineage as *kar*, a branch, as illustrations of the way in which lineages split up, each being a branch of a larger one. The JINACA are the dominant clan in the Lou and Rengyan tribes, the GATGANKIIR are the dominant clan in the Jikany tribes, and the (GAA)THIANG are the dominant clan in the Thiang tribe. Only one line of descent is shown from the roots to the twigs, from the clan ancestor to the minimal lineages, but it is indicated where the other main branches and boughs, the other maximal, major, and minor lineages leave the stem.

III

We have defined lineage and clan and give some examples of them in diagrams. In this section we note some characteristics of both which are germane to our inquiry. It may at once be said that it is not easy to discover a Nuer's clan, for a clan is not to Nuer an abstraction and there is no word in their language that can be translated 'clan' in ours. One may obtain the name of a man's clan by asking him who was his 'ancestor of yore' or his 'first ancestor' (*gwandong*) or what are his 'seeds' (*kwai*), but it is only when one already knows the clans and their lineages and their various ritual symbols, as the Nuer does, that one can easily place a man's clan through his lineage or by his spear-name and honorific salutation, for Nuer speak fluently in terms of lineages. A lineage is *thok mac*, the hearth, or *thok dwiel*, the entrance to the hut, or one may speak of *kar*, a branch. *Thok dwiel* is the commonest expression to denote a line of agnatic descent in those situations when genealogical exactness and precision are relevant, but in normal everyday usage Nuer employ the word *cieng*, as will be explained later. The clan has itself a position analogous to that of a lineage in the clan system, and it is significant to the Nuer not so much as a unique group as a segment in a system of groups, for it acquires its singularity only as part of a system.

A lineage is a relative term, since its range of reference depends on the particular person who is selected as the point of departure in tracing descent. Thus, if we were to begin with a father, the *thok dwiel* would include only sons and daughters, but if we were to take a grandfather as our point of departure, it would include all his sons and daughters and the children of his sons. A larger and larger number of agnates would be included the higher up in the line of ascent we were to take the point of departure for counting descendants. It might be maintained that the smallest possible lineage are the sons and daughters of one man, but Nuer do not refer to them as a *thok dwiel*. They are, with their father and their mother, a family and household. One cannot say definitely how far up a line of ascent Nuer will

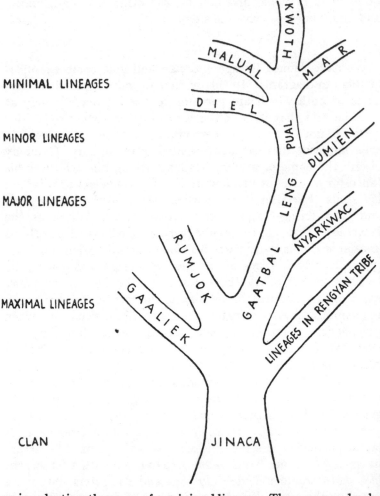

MINIMAL LINEAGES

MINOR LINEAGES

MAJOR LINEAGES

MAXIMAL LINEAGES

CLAN

go in selecting the apex of a minimal lineage. They may go back only two steps, to the grandfather, making in all three generations of agnates, but a minimal lineage of four or five generations is more usual. Apart from Nuer usage, we consider it important to define lineages as groups with a depth of at least three generations, since they are then distinct structural segments in a system of such segments and not easily confused with domestic groups.

The Nuer clan, being thus highly segmented, has many of the characteristics which we have found in tribal structure. Its

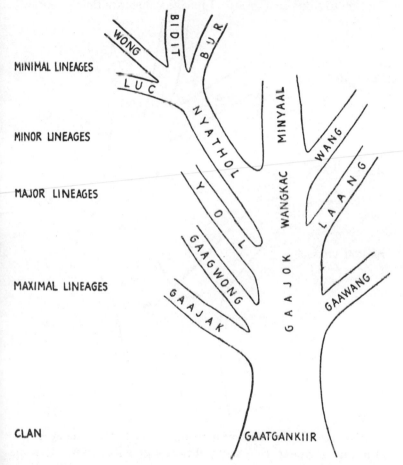

lineages are distinct groups only in relation to each other. Thus, in the diagram on p. 193, M is a group only in opposition to L, H is a group only in opposition to I, D is a group only in opposition to E, and so on. There is always fusion of collateral lineages of the same branch in relation to a collateral branch, e.g. in the diagram, L and M are a single minor lineage, H, in opposition to I, and not separate lineages; and D and E are a single maximal lineage, B, in opposition to C, and not separate lineages. Hence two lineages which are equal and opposite are composite in relation to a third, so that a man is a member of a lineage in relation to a certain group and not a member of it in relation to a different group. Lineage values are thus essentially

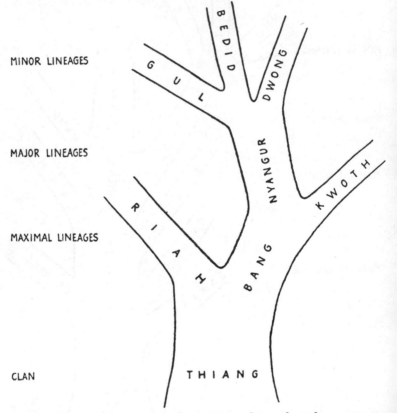

MINOR LINEAGES

MAJOR LINEAGES

MAXIMAL LINEAGES

CLAN

relative like tribal values, and we suggest later that the processes of lineage segmentation and political segmentation are to some extent co-ordinate.

Since humans propagate themselves, the clans might be supposed to be further and further removed from their founder, and the living representatives of a clan to become wider and wider separated in lineage structure. However, we do not believe that this is the case. In theory every man is a potential founder of a lineage, but, in fact, lineages spring from very few names. The others, for one reason or another, drop out, so that only certain lines of descent are remembered. Also, in those lines that persist names drop out of the steps in ascent to the founder of the clan, so that the distance in generations from the founder of a clan to the present day remain fairly constant. We have suggested in our discussion on Nuer time-reckoning that there is always this difference between a true genealogy and a genealogy which Nuer deem to be true. The evidence for the assertion depends partly on a comparative study of East African genealogies and partly on a study of Nuer genealogies. We mention some of the reasons, arising from reflections on Nuer genealogies, that have led us to this conclusion, since the validity of some arguments, developed later in the chapter, depends on their acceptance.

(1) All the main clans have about ten to twelve generations from the present day to the ancestors who gave rise to them. There is no reason to suppose that the Nuer came into existence ten to twelve generations ago. (2) When a Nuer is asked his lineage he gives it by reference to an ancestor, the founder of his minimal lineage, who is from three to six, generally four to five, steps in ascent from the present day. These steps are certain and agreed upon. This is understandable, since five steps represent a man, his father, his grandfather, and his grandfather's father and grandfather, and since a man instructs his children in the names of his immediate forbears. It is evident that after five or six generations the names of ancestors become lost. Young men often do not know them, and there is frequent confusion and disagreement among older persons. The founder of the minor lineage must be placed somewhere between the founder of the minimal lineage and the founder of the major lineage; the founder of the major lineage must be placed somewhere between the founder of the minor lineage and the founder of the maximal lineage; and the founder of the maximal lineage must be placed somewhere between the founder of the major lineage and the founder of the clan. The names of these founders of lineage-branches must go into the line of ascent somewhere, and in a definite order, because they are significant points of reference. It is immaterial whether other names go in or not, and their order is without significance. Consequently some informants put them in and some leave them out, and some put them in one order and others in a different order. It is evident, moreover, that since the minimal lineage consists of four or five actual steps in ascent, there has been telescoping of the agnatic

line from the founder of the minimal lineage further up the line of ascent to the founder of the clan, for the founder of the minimal lineage was himself the extremity of another minimal lineage which has, by increase in generations, become the minor lineage, and so on. Consequently, even were the supposed founder of the clan the real founder of it, there ought to be at least sixteen steps from him to the present day, assuming that minimal lineages have always been of the same character as at the present time. The length of each fork in the tree of descent ought logically to be of equal length, whereas the twig, so to speak, is longer than the branch or stem from which it springs. (3) There is another way in which only significant ancestors, i.e. ancestors who form the apex of a triangle of descent, are denoted in genealogical trees, and irrelevant ancestors, i.e. ancestors who do not give their name to a group of descendants, are obscured and finally forgotten. Not only do links drop out of the direct line of descent, but also collateral lines merge. It is clear from a study of Nuer genealogies that the descendants of one or two brothers become numerous and dominant, that the descendants of others die out, and that the descendants of yet others are relatively few and weak and attach themselves, as is explained in later sections, by participation in local and corporate life, to a stronger and dominant collateral line. They become assimilated to this line in ordinary lineage reference and eventually are grafted on to it by misplacement of their founder, who becomes a son instead of a brother of its founder. The merging of collateral lines higher up a lineage seems to be common, and to be more frequent and necessary the higher up one proceeds. It is necessary because, as will be seen later, the lineage system provides one of the principles of political organization.

The structural form of clans remains constant, while actual lineages at any point in time are highly dynamic, creating new bifurcations and merging old ones. They may therefore be presented as trees. But a presentation more useful for sociological analysis is in terms of structural distance, for lineages are groups of living agnates, and the distance between them varies with their relative positions in clan structure. Thus, in the diagram below, the line A–B represents the JINACA clan. The agnatic distance between the MAR minimal lineage and other lineages of the same clan is represented both on the line A–B and also in its time depth by their point of convergence in ascent on the line B–C. The wider the range of agnation specified the further back their point of convergence, so that the depth of a lineage (the vertical line of ascent) is always in proportion to its width (the base line representing living lineage groups in the clan system).

A Nuer clan, therefore, is a system of lineages, the relationship of each lineage to every other lineage being marked in its structure by a point of reference in ascent. The distance to this

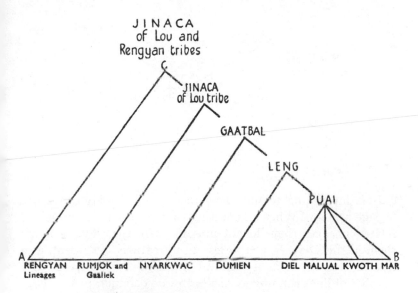

point is what we call the time depth of a lineage. In theory the genealogical relationship between any two clansmen can be traced through this point, and Nuer can actually trace it if they take the trouble. However, they do not consider it necessary to know the exact genealogical relationship between persons who are known to be distantly related by membership of their respective lineages. Thus it is sufficient for a man of the GAATBAL lineage to know that another man is of the GAALIEK lineage without his having to know the man's exact descent, for these two lineages stand to one another in a certain structural relationship, and therefore the two men stand to one another at that distance. Nuer are conversant up to a point—generally up to the founders of their minimal and minor lineages—with the full range of their genealogical relationships. Beyond this point they reckon kinship in terms of lineages. It is necessary for a Nuer to know not only that a man is a fellow clansman, but also to know what lineage he belongs to, in deciding questions of exogamy and ceremonial. The relationship between a lineage and others of the same clan is not an equal relationship, for lineages are structurally differentiated units which stand to one another at different and exact structural distances.

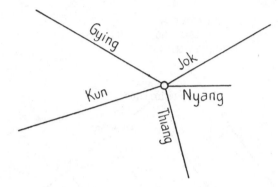

It is interesting to note how the Nuer themselves figure a lineage system. When illustrating on the ground a number of related lineages they do not present them the way we figure them in this chapter as a series of bifurcations of descent, as a tree of descent, or as a series of triangles of ascent, but as a number of lines running at angles from a common point. Thus in Western Nuerland a man illustrated some of the GAATGAN-KIIR lineages, using the names of their founders, by drawing the figure above on the ground. This representation and Nuer comments on it show several significant facts about the way in which Nuer see the system. They see it primarily as actual relations between groups of kinsmen within local communities rather than as a tree of descent, for the persons after whom the lineages are called do not all proceed from a single individual. Jok, Thiang, and Kun are three sons of Kir and founders of the maximal lineages GAAJOK, GAAJAK, and GAAGWONG of the GAATGANKIIR clan. Thiang and Kun are shown next to each other because jointly they form the lineage framework of the Gaajak tribe. The Gying lineage does not belong to the GAAT-GANKIIR clan, but it is shown next to Kun because of the proximity of the Reng section, of which it forms part, to the

Gaagwong section. Nyang is shown as a short line at the side of Jok because, although the lineage which springs from him belongs to the group of lineages founded by Thiang, they live in the Gaagwang tribe together with a lineage descended from Jok, and the Gaagwang tribe is closely associated with the Gaajok tribe. The Nuer, outside certain ritual situations, evaluate clans and lineages in terms of their local relations. Herein lies the importance of these groups for this study.

IV

Nuer lineages are not corporate, localized, communities, though they are frequently associated with territorial units, and those members of a lineage who live in an area associated with it see themselves as a residential group, and the value, or concept, of lineage thus functions through the political system. Every Nuer village is associated with a lineage, and, though the members of it often constitute only a small proportion of the village population, the village community is identified with them in such a way that we may speak of it as an aggregate of persons clustered around an agnatic nucleus. The aggregate is linguistically identified with the nucleus by the common designation of the village community by the name of the lineage. It is only in reference to rules of exogamy, certain ritual activities, and to a very limited extent to responsibility for homicide, that one needs to regard lineages as completely autonomous groups. In social' life generally they function within local communities, of all sizes from the village to the tribe, and as part of them.

A Nuer rarely talks about his lineage as distinct from his community, and in contrast to other lineages which form part of it, outside a ceremonial context. I have watched a Nuer who knew precisely what I wanted, trying on my behalf to discover from a stranger the name of his lineage. He often found great initial difficulty in making the man understand the information required of him, for Nuer think generally in terms of local divisions and of the relations between them, and an attempt to discover lineage affiliations apart from their community relations, and outside a ceremonial context, generally led to misunderstanding in the opening stages of an inquiry.

I must here again refer to the term *cieng*, which has been a source of confusion in Nuer studies. A Nuer does not normally say that he is a man of such-and-such a *thok dwiel* (lineage) when he denotes his social position, but says that he is a man of a certain local community, *cieng*. Thus he says he is a man of *cieng* Mar, *cieng* Pual, *cieng* Leng, *cieng* Gaatbal, and so on (see diagram on p. 196). What he is telling you is that he is a member of a group of people who live together in a village or district or tribal section. In ordinary situations of social life it is irrelevant whether he is, or is not, a member of the lineages from which these local communities derive their names. Moreover, since in ordinary speech a lineage-name has a local rather than a strict kinship connotation, those who share community life with the members of the lineage speak of themselves as though they also were members of it, because politically they are identified with it. Thus the word *cieng* is often used in an ambiguous sense which leaves lineage affiliation uncertain, since it is irrelevant, and it may, in consequence, be difficult, without much probing, to discover to what lineage a man belongs.

A *cieng*, in the sense of 'homestead', is called after the man who owns it, e.g. the homestead of Rainen is called '*cieng* Rainen'. When Rainen is dead and his sons and younger brothers and nephews live in his home they may call the hamlet after him, and it will be said that they are all members of *cieng* Rainen. If Rainen was an important man, and proves to have been the begetter of a strong line of descent, the whole village wherein live his agnatic heirs, and strangers who have intermarried with them or in other ways become attached to them, may thus become known as '*cieng* Rainen'. In course of time his descendants multiply and constitute the nucleus of a tribal section which is called '*cieng* Rainen'. Hence it has come about that many tribal sections are called after persons, e.g. *cieng* Minyaal, *cieng* Dumien, *cieng* Wangkac, &c. A lineage thus becomes identified in speech with the territory it occupies; the district occupied by the major lineage of WANGKAC, for example, being known as *cieng* Wangkac. A Nuer then talks about the local community and the lineage which is its political nucleus as interchangeable terms. He even speaks of *cieng* WANG-KAC when he means the WANGKAC lineage. This habit confuses a European, since the WANGKAC lineage and the people who live in the Wangkac section are by no means the same.

If you ask a Lou man what is his *cieng* you are asking him where he lives, what is his village, or district. Suppose that he replies that his *cieng* is *cieng* Pual. You can then ask him what his *cieng* forms part of, and he will tell you that it is a part of *cieng* Leng, giving the name of a tertiary tribal section. If you continue to interrogate him he will inform you that *cieng* Leng is part of *cieng* Gaatbal, a secondary tribal section, and that *cieng* Gaatbal is a division of the Gun primary section of the Lou tribe. But he has told you nothing about his clan affiliation. He may or may not be a member of the PUAL lineage, which forms part of the LENG lineage, which forms part of the GAATBAL lineage, which is part of the clan of JINACA or GAATGANNACA, the people of Nac or the children of the children of Nac. In the same way, if a Jikany man tells you that he belongs to *cieng* Kwith of the Gaajok it does not follow that he is descended from Kwe (Kwith) who is descended from Jok the founder of the GAAJOK lineage of the GAATGANKIIR clan, the children of the children of Kir. He may merely mean that he lives in a tribal section occupied by the KWITH lineage of this clan. But these men will not tell you that they are not members of the dominant lineages in these sections, and will allow you to assume that they are, for in community relations there is a degree of linguistic assimilation of all residents other than members of the dominant lineage to that lineage, and people do not wish the fact that they are strangers in the tribal area to be publicly stressed, especially if they are of Dinka origin.

The assimilation of community ties to lineage structure, the expression of territorial affiliation in a lineage idiom, and the expression of lineage affiliation in terms of territorial attachments, is what makes the lineage system so significant for a study of political organization.

V

In emphasizing the relations between lineages and local communities we speak mainly of those lineages which are segments of the dominant clans in the different tribes. It is these which have the greater political importance. We speak of them more fully in later sections. Here we give a preliminary account of how they are associated with tribal segments and how they act in those segments as a framework of the political structure.

The two diagrams which follow show the main lineages of the dominant clans among the Lou and Eastern Jikany tribes and the larger tribal sections in which they are dominant. The lines of descent are traced only as far as is necessary to illustrate the argument which follows. They may be compared with the trees of descent of the two clans and with the maps on pp. 56 and 58, which show the distribution of the sections of the two tribes.

LOU TRIBE

Mor primary section *Gun primary section*

Gaaliek secondary section *Gaatbal secondary section* *Rumjok secondary section*

Denac (founder of JINACA clan)

Nyang (founder of GAALIEK maximal lineage) Bal (founder of GAATBAL maximal lineage) Dak (founder of RUMJOK maximal lineage)

Campi Gilgil

Bang (founder of NYARKWAC major lineage) Ling (founder of LENG major lineage)

In the Lou tribe it will be seen that the descendants of Nyang, son of Denac, form the nucleus of the Gaaliek secondary section; that the descendants of Bal, another of his sons, form the nucleus of the Gaatbal secondary section, and that the descendants of Dak, his third son, form the nucleus of the Rumjok secondary section. The sections shown in the map, which are not accounted for in the genealogical tree, are the Jimac and the Jaajoah sections, which have clan nuclei of foreign origin. It must be made clear that when a tribal section is called after a lineage it does not mean that all members of the lineage live in it, though probably most of them do, and it certainly does not mean that they alone live in it, for investigations show that they form only a small minority in the total population of the section. Large stranger lineages are included in the area designated by a title taken from any of the sons of Denac, e.g. the THIANG lineage in the Gaatbal primary section. Also there are innumerable small lineages of Nuer strangers and of Dinka clustered around lineages of GAATNACA descent. Thus, if one visits the villages and cattle camps called after lineages which spring from the GAALIEK maximal lineage, e.g. the lineages of JAANYEN and KUOK, one will find them occupied by a relatively small number of persons of these lineages, while most of the residents will be found to have sprung from other Nuer and Dinka clans. Thus, at the cattle camp at Muot Dit in 1930 there were not only various minimal lineages of the RUE branch of the RUMJOK maximal lineage of the GAATNACA clan, the 'owners' of the site, but also a KAANG lineage from Lang country, a KAN lineage from Bul country, a KONG lineage from Lang country, all segments of clans dominant to the west of the Nile, and many Dinka lineages. Likewise at the village of Par-kur in Leek country in 1930 hamlets were occupied by a NYAPIR lineage of the dominant GAATBOL clan, a CUOR lineage of Dinka which has close association with the JIKUL clan, a GENG lineage from Beegh country, a RUAL lineage from Bul country, a KWACUKUNA lineage of the JIMEM clan, and other lineages.

The descendants of Jok[1]–Kir form the aristocratic nucleus of the Gaajok tribe; the descendants of Thiang[2]–Kir and Kun–Kir form the aristocratic nucleus of the Gaajak tribe; and the descendants of Gwang–Jok and Nyang–Thiang together form the aristocratic nucleus of the Gaagwang tribe. On the map on p. 58 the names of these lineages figure as tribal sections, for they have given their names to the areas in which they are dominant. Thus the names of three major lineages descended from Juk, LAANG, YOL, and WANGKAC appear on the map as Laang, Yol, and Wangkac. None of the foreign lineages is of sufficient size to give its name to a large tribal division, though they give their names to small sections and villages.[3] Here again, it must not be supposed that the descendants of Jok form more than a fragment of the Gaajok tribe. In the same way the Gaagwang tribe comprises many foreign elements which probably far outnumber the descendants of Nyang–Thiang and Gwang–Jok. The same applies to the Gaajak tribe. The GAAGWONG lineage is so closely associated with the GAAJAK lineage in tribal life that they form together a twin nucleus of the Gaajak tribe. The secondary sections of Lony, Kang, and Tar, shown on the map, are all called after lineages which spring from Thiang–Kir. Likewise the secondary sections of Nyayan, Cany, and Wau are all called after lineages which spring from Kun–Kir. Hence the only section in the map not accounted for

---

[1] Also called Majok.   [2] Also called Mathiang.

[3] Village-names are generally place-names and not names of lineages, but one may refer to the communities by the names of their chief lineages. It often happens that these lineages are of stranger or Dinka descent, and though the communities may be referred to by their names, it is recognized that the sites belong to lineages of the dominant clan of the tribe. Hence a village may be associated with two lineages. Thus the JUAK, NGWOL, &c., of the Leek tribe are stranger or Dinka lineages after whom village communities are called, but the sites are the land of the KEUNYANG lineage, and they alone are *diel* in them.

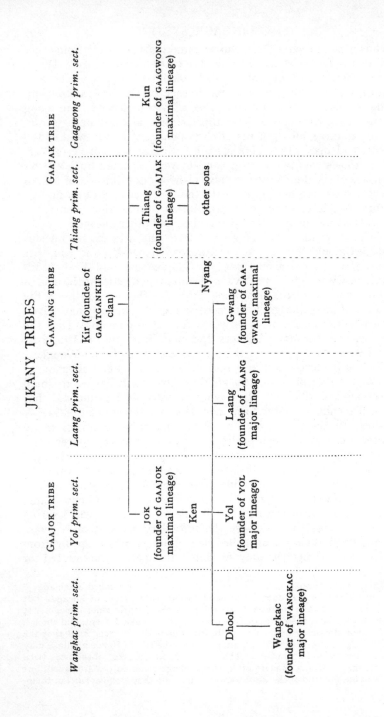

JIKANY TRIBES

in the diagram is the primary section of Reng, the Kong and Dhilleak divisions of which have clan nuclei of different origin to the other sections.

In all these tribes and tribal sections there is much admixture of lineages in communities. The same conditions are found in the Zeraf valley and also, and perhaps to a larger degree, in Western Nuerland. Nuer say that feuds and quarrels between lineages chiefly led to their dispersal, and they can cite many examples. Thus the descendants of Nyang–Thiang left the other sons of Thiang and joined the people with whom they form the Gaagwang tribe, and the NYARUNY lineage left their kinsmen of the Thiang primary section and joined the Reng primary section of the Gaajak tribe. After fights, a whole community, led by its dominant lineage, may in this way move to a different section or tribe and take up permanent residence with them. Migration led to further dispersal, since some lineages remained in the homeland to the west of the Nile and others crossed the Nile and Zeraf and settled to the east of these rivers. Nuer say that in the earliest stages of the migration the warriors used to raid Dinka and return home to their kinsmen after each raid. Then they settled to the east, but kept in close contact with the people of their lineage to the west. But as they shifted farther away the contact lessened and finally, in most cases, ceased altogether. When lineages migrated they must already have been nuclei of heterogeneous accretions and not exclusive groups of agnates: but admixture was no doubt hastened and made more complete by movement.

Two factors other than migration, quarrels, intermarriage, &c., have probably contributed to the dispersal of lineages. The Nuer are mainly a pastoral people with dominant pastoral interests and do not feel themselves bound by economic necessity or by ritual ties to any particular spot. Where his cattle are is the Nuer's home ; his hearth is the droppings of his cattle and his altar a light pole (*riek*) which he plants wherever he may wander, The spirits which give him protection and the ancestral ghosts that watch over his welfare are no more bound to the soil than he is and they are present wherever are the herds. Beasts dedicated to ghosts and spirits are his wandering shrines. Also the Nuer have no organized cult of ancestral ghosts. The dead are buried quickly and crudely in unvisited and unremembered tombs; only in very rare cases are sacrifices offered to them; and there are no sacred places associated with them.

Thus Nuer have always felt themselves free to wander as they pleased, and if a man is unhappy, his family sick, his herds declining, his garden exhausted, his relations with some of his neighbours uncongenial, or merely if he is restless, he moves to a different part of the country and resides with some kinsmen. It is seldom that a man goes alone, for brothers are a corporate group and, especially if they are sons of one mother, stick together. So, frequently as a result of quarrels, a group of brothers will often leave a village and settle elsewhere. Nuer say that they usually make for the home of a married sister, where they are certain to be well received. Here they are respected as *jiciengthu*, in-laws, and their children accepted as *gaat när*, children of the mother's brother, while the people they join are to them *cieng conyimar*, the people of my sister's husband, and *gaat nyal*, children of a female agnate, and *gaat waca*, children of the father's sister. A man who changes his residence thus becomes a member of a different community and enters into intimate relations with the dominant lineage of that community. When a GAATIEK man said to me, 'Now that I have come to settle in *Cieng* Kwoth I am a man of *Cieng* Kwoth', he meant that outside ceremonial situations he identified himself with the KWOTH lineage rather than with his own.

Even one man is a potential lineage and several brothers even more so. A minimal, and then a minor, lineage comes into being which has only ritual status towards the other lineages of its clan, whereas with the people in whose village and district its members have grown up it has a mutuality of interests and a community of experience. The group thus develops into a distinct lineage. It intermarries with the other people of its home and very often it intermarries so frequently with the dominant lineage of the district that further marriage between them becomes impossible without breaking incest regulations. In this way lineages twine around one another and a texture of cognatic relationships unites all members of the community. Only a few such lineages establish themselves and survive as lineages. Many either die out or lose much of their individuality

PLATE XXII

a. Spearing fish from dam (Eastern Gaajok)

b. Harpoon-fishing in Lake Fadio (Lou)

PLATE XXIII

a. Section of camp kraal (Lou)

b. Sobat river in the dry season (Lou)

and become attached to larger and stronger lineages by processes which we will explain later.

Nevertheless, a Nuer lineage never entirely merges into another clan. There are always certain ritual observances which cannot be shared. If intermarriage creates community ties between two lineages, it likewise keeps them distinct, since one may only marry those who are not of one's agnatic group, and even if two lineages intermarry to such an extent that cognatic relationship is a bar to further marriage between them, then each may marry into collateral lineages of the other's clan and children of their daughters. If a mythological link forges a closer union between them it is also a record of their different lines of descent, explaining, indeed, how people of divergent descent are living together amicably. Thus a lineage, however far removed from its homeland and however widely separated from its kinsfolk, never becomes entirely absorbed or loses its ritual heritage. A lineage can only merge with a collateral lineage of the same clan.

But though lineages maintain their autonomy, the lineage value only operates in the restricted field of ceremonial and is, therefore, only occasionally a determinant of behaviour. Community values are those which constantly direct behaviour, and these operate in a different set of social situations to lineage values. While lineage values control ceremonial relations between groups of agnates, community values control political relations between groups of people living in separate villages, tribal sections, and tribes. The two kinds of value control distinct planes of social life.

It is, as we explain in the following sections, only the close association between a tribe and its dominant clan, and lineages in one way or another related to this dominant clan, that makes the agnatic principle in lineage structure politically important, for these lineages function as values in the political system which gives them corporate substance.

VI

In spite of so much dispersion and admixture of clans there is in every tribe a definite relation between its political structure and the clan system, for in each tribe a clan, or a maximal lineage of a clan, is associated with the political group in which it occupies a dominant position among the other agnatic groups that live in it. Moreover, each of its segments tends to be associated with a segment of the tribe in such a way that there is a correspondence, and often linguistic identification, between the parts of a clan and the parts of a tribe. Thus, if we compare the diagram on p. 144 with that on p. 193 and suppose clan A to be the dominant clan in tribe B, then maximal lineages B and C correspond to primary sections X and Y, major lineages D and E correspond to secondary sections X^1 and X^2, major lineages F and G correspond to secondary sections Y^1 and Y^2, and minor lineages J and K correspond to tertiary sections Z^1 and Z^2. Minimal lineages are associated with villages composing the tertiary sections. It is for this reason that we have spoken of the dominant clan as forming a framework on which the political system of the tribe is built up through a complex series of kinship links. The system of lineages of the dominant clan is a conceptual skeleton on which the local communities are built up into an organization of related parts, or, as we would prefer to state it, a system of values linking tribal segments and providing the idiom in which their relations can be expressed and directed.

The JINACA of Lou country lived originally with their kinsmen the JINACA of Rengyan country to the west of the Nile, but they split off from them and, having crossed the Nile, conquered present-day Lou country. Here they were the first occupants, or at any rate the strongest element among the first occupants. Probably JINACA men frequently crossed the Nile to join their kinsmen to the east and amalgamated with them. Such persons would at once be members of the dominant clan and be spoken of as *diel*, members of the aristocratic group of lineages. But members of other clans which settled in Lou country during or after the occupation were classed as strangers (*rul*). In the same manner those lineages of the GAATGANKIIR clan who crossed the Nile and settled to the north of the Sobat held there a privileged position among other Nuer who joined them.

Every Nuer tribe has in this way its *diel*, its superior clan, though in the case of some tribes we are not certain of the correct designation of these clans. Among the Gaawar they are the GAA-WAR, among the Thiang the (GAA)THIANG, among the Leek the GAATBOL, among the Wot, and probably also among the Ror, the

JIDIET, and among the Begh the JIKOI, &c. Where the correct clan name is unknown one may refer to these dominant elements as the aristocrats (*diel*) or the 'bulls' (*tut*) of such-and-such a tribe, as the Nuer themselves frequently do, e.g. a *dil* or *tut* Bura, an aristocrat of the Bor tribe, *dil* or *tut* Wotni, an aristocrat of the Wot tribe, *dil* or *tut* Beeka, an aristocrat of the Beegh tribe, *dil* or *tut* Laka, an aristocrat of the Lak tribe, &c. One may always speak of an aristocratic clan or lineage by its proper name or by reference to the tribe in which it has a privileged position, e.g. GAATNACA, children of Nac, or *diel* Looka, aristocrats of the Lou tribe, GAATBOL, children of Bul, or *diel* Leegni, aristocrats of the Leek tribe.

There are four essential points to be remembered about these aristocratic clans. (1) Not every clan has superior status in a tribe. Some clans, e.g. the JIMEM and the JAKAR, have no *wec*, no local community, as the Nuer say. Others have village-sites where they have resided for a long time and which are called after them, but they are not *diel* in the tribe where these sites are found. Many are like cuttings which have lost all contact with the parent stem, but these may at once be designated Dinka lineages that have sprung from immigrants, whose descendants sometimes know the Dinka country of their origin but do not know their position in its system of lineages. Consequently they cannot trace ascent for as many generations as true Nuer, and their lineages are narrower in range and territorially more restricted. One finds them in little local pockets in a single tribe, whereas the Nuer clans are distributed throughout many tribes.

(2) Not every member of a Nuer clan lives in the tribe where it has superior status, for most clans are found in all parts of Nuerland. Most JINACA live in Lou and Rengyan tribal areas, where they are *diel*, but many are also found among the Eastern Jikany tribes and elsewhere. Likewise, most GAAWAR live in Gaawar country, but they are also found in most, perhaps all, Nuer tribes. Tribes are territorial groups with an unbroken social extension, whereas clans are kinship groups dispersed far and wide. Consequently a tribe is a community and can have corporate functions, but a clan is never a community and can never act corporately. The Lou tribe unite for war. The JINACA never unite. Also a man can change his tribe by changing his place of residence, but he can never change his clan. A

Lou man who goes to live in Gaawar country becomes a Gaawar man. A JINACA man remains a NAC wherever he lives.

(3) A clan is, as we have earlier emphasized, not numerically preponderant in the tribe where it is dominant, e.g. the JINACA are only a small minority in the Lou tribe and the GAAJOK lineage are only a small minority in the Gaajok tribe.

(4) A man is a *dil*, aristocrat, only in the one tribe where his clan has superior status. Thus a *dil Leegni*, an aristocrat of the Leek tribe, is an aristocrat there and nowhere else. If he goes to live in Bul country or in one of the Jikany countries he is no longer a *dil* but a *rul*, stranger. In the same way a member of the JINACA is a *dil* in Lou country, but if he goes, as many of his clan do, to reside in Gaajok country, he is not a *dil* there but a stranger, *rul*. The JINACA are *diel* Looka, but the GAAJOK are *diel* Gaajok. The status of *diel* is dependent on residence on land owned by their clan. The only exception to this statement is to be found in such cases where a clan is dominant in two or more tribes, e.g. the JINACA in Lou and Rengyan and the GAATGAN-KIIR in the Jikany countries to the west and to the east of the Bahr el Jebel. If a man of the JINACA moves from Rengyan to Lou he still remains a *dil*, because both countries belong to his clan. Likewise a man of the GAAJOK lineage of the GAATGAN-KIIR can move from Gaajok to Gaagwang, or Gaajak, country, on either side of the Nile, and still remain a *dil*, for various lineages of his clan are dominant in all these tribes.

Like most words which denote sociological status, *dil* is used by Nuer in various contexts with various meanings. In this book it is used with the precise meaning given to it in the preceding paragraphs. It is, however, permissible to use the word to denote a true member of any lineage, whether dominant in the tribe or not. For example, the JUAK lineage of the Leek tribe are of Dinka origin and are not *diel Leegni*, but a man who dwells among them can obviously be either a *dil Juaka*, a true member of the JUAK lineage, or a person who has attached himself to them for some reason or other. In the same manner one may speak of a *dil* JIMEM, although there is no tribe in which the JIMEM have the status of *diel*, for a man may be a true member of the clan or a Dinka who has attached himself to it. Also a member of the JINACA who leaves Lou and settles in Gaajok still remains a *gat dila Looka*, a child of Lou aristocracy, and will call himself such, meaning that when he is in Lou country he is an aristocrat.

The words 'tut' or 'gat twot', son of a bull, are used in the same manner as 'dil' and 'gat dila'. Here again a man may be a tut of his lineage, in contrast to accretions of strangers and Dinka who live in the district associated with it, without being a tut of the tribe of which that district forms part, e.g. a man may be a tut of the Jaajoah secondary section of the Lou tribe without being a tut Looka, because the aristocratic clan of the whole of Lou country are the JINACA, and the JAAJOAH are not members of this clan. In other words a man may call himself a tut of the Jaajoah to emphasize that he is a JAAJOAH and not merely a Jaajoah, but he does not thereby imply that he is a tut Looka. In a still more general sense tut may, as we have noted, merely mean a paterfamilias or even a male person. One must judge from the context how the expression should be translated. In this book we use the words tut or gat twot in the sense, defined on pp. 179–80, of an elder, and we use the word dil to refer to a tribal aristocrat.

It is difficult to find an English word that adequately describes the social position of diel in a tribe. We have called them aristocrats, but do not wish to imply that Nuer regard them as of superior rank, for, as we have emphatically declared, the idea of a man lording it over others is repugnant to them. On the whole—we will qualify the statement later—the diel have prestige rather than rank and influence rather than power. If you are a dil of the tribe in which you live you are more than a simple tribesman. You are one of the owners of the country, its village sites, its pastures, its fishing pools and wells. Other people live there in virtue of marriage into your clan, adoption into your lineage, or of some other social tie. You are a leader of the tribe and the spear-name of your clan is invoked when the tribe goes to war. Wherever there is a dil in a village, the village clusters around him as a herd of cattle clusters around its bull.

I have described the position of diel as I judged it to be among the Lou tribe. I had the impression that to the west of the Nile their status was less pronounced, whereas among the Eastern Jikany tribes, on the periphery of Nuer expansion, it was more emphasized. In the Karlual area of the Leek tribe, the only part of western Nuerland I know more than superficially, the aristocratic prestige of a dil is recognized, but there are clans of strangers so well and long entrenched in the districts and villages in which they are found to-day that a dil has no legal privilege.

At a cursory glance, I gathered that conditions were elsewhere the same in western Nuerland, except, perhaps, among the Jikany where the status of *diel* may be more enhanced. Among the Eastern Jikany one finds the greatest insistence on social differentiation and legal privilege. The category of *diel* tends to be more stressed in the larger tribes than in the smaller, and when its structural function has been examined it will be understood why this is so.

In a Nuer village or cattle camp there are seldom more than a few families of *diel*. Most people are either *rul*, Nuer of other clans, or *jaang*, persons of Dinka descent who have not been adopted into Nuer lineages. A *rul* is a Nuer who in a certain tribe is not a *dil*, though he may be a *dil* in another tribe. I have already described how lineages split off from their localized kinship groups, wander, join persons of other clans, and become members of a new community. This process was well described to me by a man of the Dok tribe. Members of a lineage beget children and they become numerous and spread over the countryside, wandering here, there, and everywhere. Then their close relationship ends and they go to live in the midst of other clans who are distantly related to them. Here they dwell as friends and slowly forge new cognatic relationships by intermarriage. Hence lineages are much mixed in all local communities.

Also Nuer say that no *dil* dwells in a social milieu composed entirely of fellow aristocrats, for lineages of *diel* split up and segments seek autonomy by becoming the nuclei of new social agglomerations in which they are the aristocratic element. Thus lineages of *diel* split up not only on account of internal dissension, but because a man of personality likes to found his independent settlement where he will be an important person rather than remain a younger brother in a group of influential elder relatives. I was told that this process by which any man, especially a *dil*, could become a local leader is felt to be ingrained in their social system and is a reason why they object to the creation by the Government of a few local 'chiefs' whose position tends to become formalized, permanent, and hereditary. To them this is a rigid interpretation of status, based on territorial rather than personal qualifications, which stabilizes the superiority of a single man or lineage. Every man of standing feels that he should be a 'chief'. It does not follow that a man must be an aristocrat to gain influence among his fellow villagers. He may be a *tut* of some other lineage than the dominant one of his tribe who, by outstanding character, has been able to establish himself and his kin as social leaders in his locality.

There is thus in every tribe some differentiation of status, but the people so differentiated do not constitute classes, and 'strangers' and 'Dinka' are properly to be regarded as categories rather than as groups. Their relation to the aristocrats in the tribal system and the ways in which the different elements are integrated into communities will engage our attention in later sections.

VII

It is only in assessment of blood-cattle that social differentiation between aristocrats and Nuer strangers is of great significance, and then only among the Jikany tribes, principally among the Eastern Jikany. Among the Eastern Jikany the kinsmen of a *dil*, aristocrat, who was killed had to be compensated by payment of more cattle than the kinsmen of a slain *rul*, stranger, or *jaang*, Dinka. It is not easy to know to what extent this privilege could be enforced, or even to discover the relative assessments of blood-cattle. There was undoubtedly considerable elasticity in reckoning who counted as equivalent to a *dil* in situations of homicide and variation in the number of cattle paid for homicide. It was asserted by several informants that in pre-government days a true Nuer, called in the Jikany tribes a *gat Geeka*, counted the same as a *dil* Jikany for purposes of assessing blood-cattle, and I was given the following blood-cattle assessments: a Jikany aristocrat, 40, a Nuer stranger, 40, a Dinka adopted by a Jikany aristocrat, 20, a Dinka who had been adopted by a Nuer stranger, 20, and an unadopted Dinka, 6. In more recent practice the following payments seem to have been regarded as usual: a Jikany aristocrat, 20, a Nuer stranger, 17, a Dinka who has settled permanently in the country, 16, a Dinka who has not been long settled, 10.

I was not long enough among the Eastern Jikany to investigate this matter thoroughly, but I received the impression that the second list was coloured in its variation of assessment, as it was certainly influenced in amounts of assessment, by recent Government decisions; though the informants who gave it insisted that it was in proportion to the ancient assessments. Aristocrats assured me that in the past more cattle were always paid for the homicide of an aristocrat than for that of a Nuer stranger. Members of Nuer clans, other than the GAATGANKIIR, who have settled in Jikany tribes equally assured me that the payments were the same for both. No doubt they were both hoping to influence Government practice by their statements. On the whole, I consider that among the Eastern Jikany there was probably a difference between payments for homicide of an aristocrat and of a stranger, but that there was much flexibility in the assessments, which depended generally on the special circumstances of each case: the length of the dead man's residence in the country, marriage alliances between his family and aristocratic lineages, the strength of his lineage and local community, whether he had been killed by a member of his village or by a man of another village, and so forth. Probably the same is true of the Western Jikany tribes, where I was told that the customary compensation for an aristocrat was from 40 to 50 head of cattle, for a stranger or Dinka who had settled in the country, 30, and for a Dinka who was staying there but had not yet built a homestead, 20. The practice of the Jikany is not typical of Nuerland as a whole.

Nevertheless, all over Nuerland Nuer and Dinka were differentiated by assessment of their value in blood-cattle, though the definition of a Dinka, in this respect, varied in different tribes. Among the Lou the practice was to reckon aristocrats and strangers together at 40 head of cattle. A Dinka who was born in Lou country was said to have become a Nuer (*caa nath*) and a member of the community in which he was living (*caa ran wec*), so that his life also was assessed at 40 head of cattle. On the other hand, a Dinka who had been captured in war and brought to Lou country was reckoned at 16 head of cattle, while a Dinka visiting relatives or affines in Lou country was reckoned at only 6 head of cattle. I was told that a Dinka who had been adopted held an inferior position in this respect to that held by his children, who counted as true Nuer. In the Jagei tribes Nuer strangers and Dinka who were permanent members of a community appear to have been reckoned at 40 head of cattle, like an aristocrat, while a stranger or a Dinka who had not built a byre was reckoned at only 10.

The building of a byre was stressed because a man who built a homestead in a village had clearly the intention of remaining there and the community gained by an addition to its herd. Such a man seems to have been reckoned equal to an aristocrat in all parts of Nuerland, except among the

Jikany where, I was told, a Dinka could never lose his inferior status, which was transmitted to his descendants. The acceptance of a permanent member of a community as equal to an aristocrat conforms to the general tendency among the Nuer for descent to be subordinated to community, a tendency which we shall constantly stress.

We again emphasize the point to which we drew attention in the section on law, that the degree of responsibility acknowledged for a tort, the chances of compensation being offered for it, and the amount of compensation paid, depend on the relations of the persons concerned in social structure. Thus, if a man kills an unadopted Dinka of his own household, who was not born in Nuerland, there is no redress, but his household will protect their Dinka against outsiders and will avenge his death at their hands. Dol, who is himself of Dinka descent, told me: 'If you curse a Dinka of your household, well, you curse him, that is all. If he is angry you tell him that you will kill him and that nothing will happen. You will merely clean your spear on the ground and hang it up. But if another man curses a Dinka of your household you fight him, for the Dinka is your brother. You ask the man whether he is your Dinka or his Dinka.'

The position of a Dinka in his own domestic circle is thus different from his position in relation to members of a wider group. He is only a *jaang* to the joint family which considers him 'their man.' To people standing outside this joint family he is a member of that *gol*, joint family, and it is not their business to differentiate his status within it. I was told that if an outsider called such a Dinka '*jaang*', the sons of the man who had captured him would resent the insult and might start a fight to wipe it out, for to them he is '*demar*', 'my brother', in relation to outsiders. They ask, 'Who is a *jaang*? Did your father seize him or did ours?' The acceptance of Dinka born in Nuerland as full members of Nuer households, hamlets, and villages is even more pronounced.

The status of Dinka is thus a relative one, and a man may be considered to belong to this category in one situation and not in another. This is obviously the case in social life generally, because ordinarily no one differentiates a man of Dinka descent from a man of Nuer descent, but we believe that it was also the case in questions of homicide, since the social situation was composed of the structural relations of the slayer and his kin to the dead man and to other people concerned in the dispute. In our opinion the uncertainty and contradiction which was often evident in the statements of Nuer about assessments of blood-cattle is to be accounted for by relativity of status, it being relative always to the structural distance between persons, and therefore not rigidly definable.

Likewise *rul* is a very plastic concept. If a Leek man goes to Gaajak country to steal cattle and is killed no compensation would be paid for the homicide. A Leek man travelling through Gaajak country without intent to cause loss to its owners would not wantonly be slain. If the man were visiting kinsmen or affines and was killed in a quarrel, his hosts would consider that they were under an obligation to avenge him, though, perhaps, not under a very strong obligation. But a Leek man who has built his homestead in Gaajak country and has married into the village where he resides is a member of that community. If another member of his village kills him, it may be held that he is a *rul* and therefore his death may be paid for with fewer cattle than that of an aristocrat. But if a member of another village kills him, his community are not likely to accept this definition of status, because one does not differentiate between members of one's community on grounds of descent in its relation with other political segments. In political relations community ties are always dominant and determine behaviour.

VIII

We have observed that within a tribe there are three categories of persons: *diel*, *rul*, and *jaang*. The *diel* are an aristocratic clan, numerically swamped in the tribe by strangers and Dinka, but providing a lineage structure on which the tribal organization is built up. The problem is how strangers and Dinka are attached to the dominant clan in such a way that the clan becomes, through the relations of other members of the tribe to it, the framework of the political system. As Nuer reckon all social ties in a kinship idiom it is clear that only the recognition of mutual bonds of kinship could lead to this result. Such recognition is accorded in several ways. We will start by an examination of adoption. A Nuer cannot be adopted into a lineage other than that into which he is born, so that the custom concerns only Dinka.

We have already described how Nuer scorn Dinka and persistently raid them, but they do not treat those Dinka who are permanent members of their community differently from its Nuer members, and we have seen that persons of Dinka descent form probably at least half the population of most tribes. These Dinka are either children of captives and immigrants who have been brought up as Nuer, or are themselves captives and immigrants who are residing permanently among Nuer. They are 'Jaang-Nath', 'Dinka-Nuer', and, it is said, 'caa Nath', 'they have become Nuer'. As we have explained, once their membership of a community is recognized, in most of Nuerland, their legal status is the same as that of a free-born Nuer, and it is only in relation to ritual and rules of exogamy that attention is drawn to their origin. In structural relations of a political kind they are undifferentiated members of a segment. Although in his domestic and kinship relations a Dinka has not so strong a position as a Nuer, because he has not the same range of kinship links, I have never observed that they suffer any serious disabilities, far less degradation. In answer to my question whether a captured Dinka would not work harder in the kraal than a son of the family, I was told that he was a son and would enjoy the same privileges as the other sons, being given an ox by his father at initiation and, later, bride-cattle for a wife. The only foreigners who suffer serious social inequality are certain small pockets of Dinka and Anuak who have been conquered but not absorbed into Nuer society and culture. Such pockets, like the Balak Dinka and the Anuak on the Sobat river, enjoy neither the privileges of Nuer citizenship nor the freedom of foreigners. Such pockets do not truly constitute part of a Nuer tribe.

Captured Dinka boys are almost invariably incorporated into the lineage of their Nuer captors by the rite of adoption, and they then rank as sons in lineage structure as well as in family relations, and when the daughters of that lineage are married they receive bride-cattle. A Dinka boy is brought up as a child of his captor's household. He is already incorporated into the family and joint family by his acceptance as a member of these groups by their other members and by outsiders. People say *'caa dil e cieng'* or *'caa ran wec'*, 'he has become a member of the community', and they say of the man who captured him that 'he has become his father', and of his sons that 'they have become his brothers'. He is already a member of the *gol*, the household and joint family. Adoption gives him a position in lineage structure, and thereby ceremonial status, for by adoption he becomes a member of his captor's *thok dwiel*, lineage.

I was told that the captor will seldom himself give the lad *buth,* agnatic affiliation to his lineage, and that the rite is usually performed by a kinsman at the request of his sons and with the consent of their minimal lineage. A representative of the lineage invites the Dinka, now grown-up and initiated, to attend the sacrifice of an ox or sheep in his kraal. The head of the joint family provides the sacrificial beast and the representative of the lineage drives the tethering-peg into the earth at the entrance to the byre and walks up and down the kraal invoking the spear-name of the clan and calling on the spirits and ancestral ghosts of the lineage to take note that the Dinka is now a member of it and under their protection. He then spears the beast and the Dinka is smeared with the undigested contents of its stomach while the ghosts and spirits are asked to accept him. He is especially smeared on the soles of his feet, for this binds him to his new home. If he leaves it he will die. The beast is then cut up, and a son of the house, or the representative of the lineage, and his new brother divide the skin and the scrotum, which the Dinka cuts. The Dinka also takes the neck as his portion. On all future occasions when animals are sacrificed by members of the lineage the Dinka will receive his share of the meat, for he is now a member of the lineage. The cutting of the scrotum is the symbolic act which makes the man a member of the lineage, because only an agnatic relative may cut the scrotum of a sacrificial beast. 'A man who has cut the scrotum of your beast, if he has sexual relations with your daughter, he will die.'

A girl captive is not adopted into the lineage, but people say *'caa lath cungni'*, 'she is given a right to receive bride-wealth'. 'Her children are become people who partake in the bride-cattle'. This means that when she is married, or her daughters are married, the sons of the family in which she has been brought up will receive the cattle due to brothers and maternal uncles, and that in return, when the daughters of the sons and daughters of this family are married, she, or her sons, can claim the cow due to the paternal aunt and the cow due to the maternal aunt. She has become a daughter to her captor and a sister to his sons, but she is not a member of their lineage.

PLATE XXIV

A leopard-skin chief

PLATE XXV

a. Ngundeng's pyramid (Lou)

b. Ngundeng's pyramid (Lou)

By adoption Dinka men are grafted on to the lineage of their captors. They trace their ascent up the lineage to its ancestor and they become a new point of its growth. The fusion is complete and final. The spirits of the lineage become their spirits, its ghosts become their ghosts, and its spear-name and honorific name become their symbols. Indeed it is almost impossible without a prolonged stay in a Nuer village or camp to discover who are and who are not of pure Nuer origin. I have for weeks considered men to be true Nuer, whereas they were descended from captured Dinka, for a man whose Dinka grandfather had been adopted into a Nuer lineage regards himself as being just as much a member of the lineage as the man whose grandfather adopted his grandsire, and he is so regarded by other members of the lineage and by persons not of it. Thus, when a man gives his descent from E through D and C, and another man gives his descent from E through J and K, one naturally assumed that D and J were sons of E. There is no means of knowing that, in fact, J was a captured Dinka who was adopted into the lineage, unless someone volunteers the information—a most unlikely happening in Nuerland. Moreover, it is impolite to ask strangers whether their grandfathers were captured Dinka, and, even if they were of Dinka origin, they would not readily say so. One can, of course, always ask other people; but only those who are members of the same lineage are likely to be fully acquainted with the man's ancestry, and they, in all probability, will not tell one if he is of Dinka origin, for he is their agnatic kinsman as far as outsiders are concerned.

A very large number of Dinka in all tribes have been incorporated by adoption into Nuer lineages. Since, as mentioned later, adopted Dinka and their descendants can marry into collateral lineages, it would not be accurate to say that they are adopted into clans. Probably most captured Dinka were adopted into Nuer lineages, but there are also many Dinka lineages descended from men who came of their own free will to settle in Nuerland, either to escape famine, largely caused by Nuer raiding, in their own country, to visit captured sisters, or to reoccupy the sites from which Nuer raids had ousted them. Such immigrants were unmolested and were permitted to settle or return to Dinkaland as they might choose. A Dinka who decided to settle became some Nuer's *jaang*, his Dinka, and *rande*, his man, and the Nuer would give him an ox and maybe a cow or two when he had given proof of his fidelity and attachment to his new home. I was told that he might even be given a daughter of the house in marriage without payment of bride-wealth if she were blind or lame and no Nuer would contemplate taking her as a bride. Often a widow lives in concubinage with such a Dinka, who thus obtains a 'wife' in the sense of cook, housekeeper, and mate; and even if the children she may bear him do not count as his descendants he can gain their affection. If a Dinka settles at the home of the husband of his sister, the husband may give him a cow or two in acknowledgement of affinity.

There must also have been pockets of the original Dinka occupants of country overrun by the Nuer who submitted and gave up their language and habits in favour of those of the Nuer. At any rate, there are to-day in all tribes many small Dinka lineages, and villages are often called after them. Such lineages are numerically preponderant in the communities where I spent most of my time, Yakwac camp and Nyueny village. The way in which these lineages are woven into the lineage texture of the dominant clan of the tribe is discussed in the next two sections.

Here we summarize points which have already emerged from our description of the position of Dinka in relation to Nuer. (1) *Jaang*, Dinka, has many meanings: any foreigners whom the Nuer habitually raid; Dinka living in Dinkaland and raided by Nuer; Dinka of unabsorbed pockets in Nuerland or on its confines; recent Dinka immigrants; certain clans which are said to be Dinka in origin, e.g. the GAATGANKIIR; members of small Dinka lineages which are Nuer in every character except in origin; descendants of adopted Dinka; adopted Dinka. One can only judge the meaning Nuer attach to the word by its context and the tone in which it is spoken. (2) It is only those Dinka who are regarded as members of a Nuer tribe who concern our present discussion. Their status is relative to the social situation in which the question of status arises, and cannot be rigidly defined. (3) Nuer conquest has not led to a class or symbiotic system, but, by the custom of adoption, has absorbed the conquered Dinka into its kinship system, and through

the kinship system has admitted them into its political structure
on a basis of equality.

IX

A large number of Dinka who were not captured as children
are not adopted into Nuer lineages, and Nuer strangers cannot
be adopted into lineages of the dominant clan or into any other
Nuer lineages. Nevertheless, members of all local communities,
whilst they see themselves as distinct segments in relation to
other local segments, express their relations to one another in
terms of kinship. This is brought about by intermarriage.

We mention the rules of exogamy as briefly as possible and
only in so far as they have a direct bearing on the political
system. Nuer generally marry within their tribe, though they
sometimes marry women of other tribes, especially if they live
near the border. Sometimes, also, a man marries in one tribe
and then, taking his wife and family with him, goes to live in
another tribe. In recent times there have been occasional
marriages with the Ngok, and possibly with other Dinka tribes.
There are no exogamous rules based on locality. They are
determined by lineage and kinship values. A man may not marry
into his clan and, *a fortiori*, into his lineage. In most clans a
man may marry into his mother's clan, but not into her maximal
lineage, though this rule is less exact. A man may not marry
any woman to whom he is in any way closely related. A Dinka
adopted into a lineage may not marry into that lineage, but
may marry into collateral lineages of the same clan.

The rules of exogamy have been cursorily described. Nevertheless we consider them important, for the values which chiefly
regulate behaviour between one person and another in Nuer
society are kinship values. Nuer rules of exogamy break down
the exclusiveness of agnatic groups by compelling their members
to marry outside them, and thereby to create new kinship ties.
As the rules also forbid marriage between near cognates, a small
local community like a village rapidly becomes a network of
kinship ties and its members are compelled to find mates outside it. Any stranger who enters the village, if he is not already
related to most of its members, rapidly enters into affinal
relations with them and his children become their kinsmen.
Consequently the population of a Nuer village or cattle camp

can be placed on a single genealogical chart showing lines of descent and affinity, and, since affinity is fundamentally a relationship through kinship, we may say that all members of a village or camp are united by kinship ties and, therefore, are generally unable to marry into it. Consequently they are forced to take spouses from neighbouring villages of their district. Normally a man marries a girl who lives within visiting distance of his village. Hence a network of kinship ties stretches over a district and links in diverse ways the members of distinct political groups.

Looked at from the angle of a single village the circle of close kinship relations is limited to a small radius, and they tend to become fewer and more distant the nearer its periphery is approached. But the circumference of one such circle is intersected by other circles, so that there is no limit to the extension of a continuous series of kinship links. Exogamous rules, therefore, prevent the formation of autonomous agnatic groups and create extensive kinship ties within, and beyond, the tribal structure. Thus the kinship system bridges the gaps in political structure by a chain of links which unite members of opposed segments. They are like elastic bands which enable the political segments to fall apart and be in opposition and yet keep them together. This relation between kinship and political structure poses a set of complex problems. Here we wish to demonstrate only one point: the way in which dominant lineages serve as a political framework by the accretion of other lineages to them within local communities.

We have seen how every local community is associated with a lineage and that the members of this lineage who live in the community are numerically swamped by members of other lineages. We have also seen how all members of the community are in some way or other related by kinship. What gives a pattern to this complicated criss-crossing of cognatic threads is their relation to the dominant lineage of the community.

The Nuer have a category of *gaat nyiet*, children of girls, which includes all persons who are in the relationship of sister's son and daughter's son to a lineage. As a whole lineage can be spoken of as *gaat nyiet* to another if there is one such female link between them anywhere in the lines of their descent, and as there must be such a link if they live in the same community, owing to the rules of exogamy, it follows that people who live together are all *gaat nyiet* to one another. However, it is in relation to the dominant lineage of a community that the concept is mainly employed and is politically important. When people are not members of this lineage it is stressed that they are *gaat nyiet* to it. Nuer of other clans can never more closely identify themselves with the dominant lineage, because, for ritual reasons, they must remain autonomous units, but politically they accrete themselves to it through this kinship category. Moreover, outside ritual situations, being *gaat nyiet* to a dominant lineage gives people complete equality with it, and their accretion to it is often expressed in terms of lineage structure, so that a man will often give his ascent to the woman of the dominant lineage who bore one of his ancestors, and thus graft himself, through her, on to their tree of descent; though this is more usually done by Dinka than by Nuer. It is, however, the common practice for children of strangers who have been brought up at the home of their maternal kinsmen, who are aristocrats, to regard themselves as members of their mother's lineage, except in ceremonial situations, and to consider its members, rather than their father's lineage, as their true kinsmen.

Dinka who have not been adopted commonly trace their ascent to a female Nuer forebear and through her they graft themselves into a Nuer lineage and are accepted as members of it in ordinary social relations. Thus a Dinka often gives his ascent to the dominant lineage of his community through a woman, and sometimes through two or three female links, and though this is generally evident from female prefixes it cannot always be known. These Dinka individuals incorporate themselves into the structure of a Nuer lineage through their mothers, since they have no lineage structure of their own. This is different from the stressing of a female link (*gaat nyiet*) which unites a group of Nuer strangers or of Dinka to the dominant lineage of their tribal section and also from matrilineal modes of reckoning descent due to matrilocal conditions of residence, which may be temporary.

Owing to exogamous rules lineages are thus linked by

innumerable cognatic ties, so that however many lineages there may be in a local community their members are all related to one another by some kind of cognation and affinity. A lineage remains an exclusive agnatic group only in ritual situations. In other situations it is merged in the community, and cognation (*mar*) takes the place of lineage agnation (*buth*) as the value through which people living together express their relations to one another. The agnatic structure of the dominant lineage is not stressed in ordinary social relations, but only on a political plane where relations between territorial segments are concerned, for the assimilation of territorial segments to segments of the dominant lineage means that the interrelations of the one are expressed in terms of the other.

In every small tribal segment there is a lineage of the dominant clan of the tribe associated with it, and the members of the segment are joined to this lineage by adoption, cognatic kinship, or kinship fictions, in such a way that one may speak of them as an accretion around a lineage nucleus. As these different nuclei are lineages of the same clan, or, as we shall see in the next section, assimilated to it, the structure of the dominant clan is to the political system like the anatomical structure to the system of an organism.

X

We have seen how Dinka and strangers are linked to the framework of the dominant clan by adoption and cognation and how these links form an embracing kinship system which provides the non-political texture of the political system. Kinship values are the strongest sentiments and norms in Nuer society and all social interrelations tend to be expressed in a kinship idiom. Adoption and the assimilation of cognatic to agnatic ties are two ways in which community relations are translated into kinship relations: in which living together forces residential relations into a kinship pattern. A third way is by mythological creation of kinship fictions, and this way is appropriate to relations between dominant lineages and stranger and Dinka groups, living with them in the same tribal segments, which are too large and occupy too distinct a territory for incorporation by either of the other two methods. It is the way in which large pockets of strangers and Dinka are incorporated into the conceptual scheme of a tribe.

It has frequently been emphasized that political relations are often expressed in speech as lineage relations, in the sense that one talks of a local community as though it were a lineage, thereby assimilating to a dominant lineage those who share the same community life with it; and that lineage relations are often expressed as political relations, in the sense that one talks of a lineage as though it were identical with the local community in which it is only a nucleus, thereby depriving the lineage of its unique agnatic status and giving it a general residential value. In conformity with this way of describing community interrelations, they are personified in myths and derived from personal relationships of a kinship kind.

We do not propose to give a collection of Nuer myths. We have so far only mentioned one myth explaining group inter-relations: that which tells why the Nuer raid the Dinka. There are very few myths of this general kind. Most relate to clans and lineages in their corporate territorialized form and explain their association with one another as tribes and tribal segments, particularly the relations between dominant lineages and large stranger lineages living with them. We are not always able to explain mythological relations by the present-day political system, but this can often be done, and where we fail to do it we attribute our inability to ignorance, especially to ignorance of tribal history.

The two large Lou tribal sections, the Jimac and the Jaajoah which appear on the map on p. 56, but not on the clan tree of the JINACA, the dominant clan of the tribe, on p. 196, are divisions called after the JIMAC and JAAJOAH lineages. They are said to be *gaat nyiet*, children of daughters of the founder of the JINACA clan, and there is a myth accounting for this maternal link. Denac was said to have had, according to the Lou story, four sons, named Yin, Dak, Bal, and Bany, by one wife, and Nyang and two nameless brothers by a second wife. These wives are sometimes said to have been called Nyagun and Nyamor and the two primary sections of the tribe, Gun and Mor, to be named after them. Nyang's two brothers were eaten by an ogre. When, afterwards, the sons of Denac went fishing, the four sons of one mother went by themselves and Nyang by himself, for he would not accompany his half-brothers, but pined for the sons of his mother. When he caught a fish someone would come and steal it from him, for he was all by himself and only a boy. When he came home he would not sit with the other boys facing his father, but sat apart with his back to him, and when his father asked him why he was troubled he replied that he was thinking of his brothers whom the ogre had eaten. His father said to him, 'Never mind, take your two sisters and let them be your brothers.' So when Nyang went fishing he was accompanied by his sisters Nyabil and Fadwai. Nyang is the founder of the GAALIEK lineage, Nyabil of the JIMAC lineage, and Fadwai of the JAAJOAH lineage. These lineages together form the kinship framework of the Mor primary section of the Lou tribe and the myth explains their association. This maternal link has not prevented intermarriage between the GAALIEK and the JIMAC. Apart from questions of ritual and exogamy the descendants of Nyabil and Fadwai are treated as though these daughters had been sons, and they possess a mythological patent which gives them equal status in the tribe with the *diel*. In tracing their agnatic ascent members of these lineages do not go further back than their ancestress. From her they continue to her father, Denac.

In the Gaawar tribe there is an important JAKAR lineage which is mythologically attached to the GAAWAR, the aristocrats of the tribe, in the following manner. A man called Kar, or Jakar, descended from heaven by a rope that connected the sky with a tamarind tree, probably the tree in Lang country beneath which mankind is said to have been created. He was later followed by War, the founder of the GAAWAR clan, who was found sitting in the tree by Kar's sister who was gathering firewood accompanied by her dog. She returned to tell her brother that she had found a man whose head was covered in blood. Kar tried to persuade him to come to the village but he refused to do so. They then sacrificed an ox and roasted its flesh and the smell so attracted War, who was very greedy, that he climbed down the tree and entered the village. When he had eaten he wanted to return to heaven, but Kar cut the rope. Mr. B. A. Lewis has kindly furnished me with what he says is a less common version, found in the Gaawar tribe. War fell from heaven in a rainstorm and was discovered by a dog which belonged to Logh, but was with Kwec's wife when she was looking for wood in the forest and War was found. Kwec's wife took him home with her and a dispute arose between Kwec and Logh about the ownership of the foundling. Logh claimed War on the ground that it was his dog which had discovered him, and Kwec claimed him because his wife had found him. Then Kar joined in the discussion, saying that War was his brother.

This myth brings War and Kar and Logh into some kind of relationship to one another and is to be explained by the fact that the two main clans in the Gaawar tribe, next to the aristocratic clan of the GAAWAR, are the JAKAR and the JALOGH. The JALOGH are presumably the same clan as live to the south of Dok country where a small territory is named after them. Kwec was, doubtless, the founder of the KWEC lineage after whom a small territory, next to the Jalogh country, is named. We may surmise that, since both lineages are found in Gaawar country at the present day and in its present site to the east of the Nile, they also had close relations with the GAAWAR when all three clans lived in their homeland to the west of the Nile.

The richest clan mythology is that of the GAATGANKIIR, and it clearly illustrates the mythological integration of lineages of different origins to the dominant lineage system in a political structure, and shows how territorial relations are given a kinship value.

There are several versions of many of the incidents relating to Kir, the founder of the GAATGANKIIR clan, and we give an abridgement of one of these. A Dinka of the Ngok tribe, called Yul, saw a stalk of a gourd on a river bank and, having followed it a long way, arrived at a huge gourd. He cut this gourd open and out of it came Kir with various ritual objects. Yul's wife suckled the child as well as her own baby, Gying. When Kir grew up he turned out to be a witch and magician and the sons of Yul tried to kill him because his evil powers were destroying the cattle. Only Gying remained Kir's friend, and said to him, as he fled from Yul's home, that he would one day follow after him and join him.

In his flight Kir came to the Nile where he saw a man, called Tik, in the river and asked him for help. Tik struck the waters of the Nile and cut them in two and Kir crossed over to the west bank. Kir told Tik that when he had found a place to settle in Tik was to come after him. Tik accompanied Kir till they met a man of the Wot tribe who took them to his home where the JIDIET, the dominant clan of the Wot, sacrificed a black ox so that the lethal power of witchcraft might leave Kir's eyes and enable him to look at people and cattle without killing them. Kir then dug a hole for himself in a termite-mound near a cattle camp of the GAAWAR, where he performed many strange feats. Eventually the GAAWAR offered sacrifices and persuaded him to leave the mound and took him to their camp.

Kir was then given a wife, Nyakwini, who bore him Thiang before he killed her with his witchcraft. He then married Nyabor who bore him Kun. He likewise killed her. The people then gave him a lame woman, Duany, who bore him Jok. In Lou and Eastern Jikany versions the three wives were all daughters of Gee, the founder of the GAATGANGEEKA family of clans, and in versions to the west of the Nile the first two were GAAWAR and Duany a NYAPIR of the Bul tribe, but all accounts make Nyakwini and Nyabor more closely related to one another than either to Duany. After Duany had borne Jok she killed Kir with witchcraft, for she, also, was a witch. Later Thiang, her dead husband's eldest son, cohabited with her and begat Nyang.

In all the variants of the Kir myth the parts played by Gying and Tik are stressed. Gying was suckled with him and afterwards joined him and lived with him as a brother. When Kir died his eldest sons Thiang and Kun possessed cattle, but the youngest son, Jok, and Gying had no cattle. Thiang wanted to prevent Gying from acquiring cattle, but Kun gave him some, so Thiang said that Kun and Gying were to live together. Tik had saved Kir's life and had gone to live with him. There is a further story of how Gying and Tik were threatened by an ogre and shared a hut together and became like brothers, so that the lineages descended from these two men do not intermarry.

Without recording further details we may note how actual political relations are mythologically represented in the characters of these stories. The two largest segments of the Gaajak tribe which are named after nuclei of strangers are the Kong section, the stranger nucleus of which is a lineage descended from Tik, and the Dhilleak section, the stranger nucleus of which is a lineage descended from Gying, and these two sections live together as parts of the Reng primary section (see diagram on p. 140, and sketch-map on p. 58). The myth tells also how Jok and Nyang are sons of the same mother, Duany, Jok being begotten by Kir and Nyang by Thiang. This is a mythological representation of the structure of the Gaagwang tribe which has dominant lineage nuclei descended from both Nyang and Jok, and also of the political relations between the Gaagwang tribe and the Gaajok tribe, for these relations, especially to the west of the Nile, are of close alliance compared to the more distant relations between the Gaagwang tribe and the primary sections of the Gaajak tribe that also border them, the Thiang and the Reng. Thiang and Kun were begotten by Kir and borne by women who are generally represented as sisters, and the sections in which their descendants are dominant are the Thiang and Gaagwong primary sections of the Gaajak tribe, the third primary section of which, the Reng, has nuclei descended from Thiang, Gying, and Tik, whose relationships in the myth have already been noted.

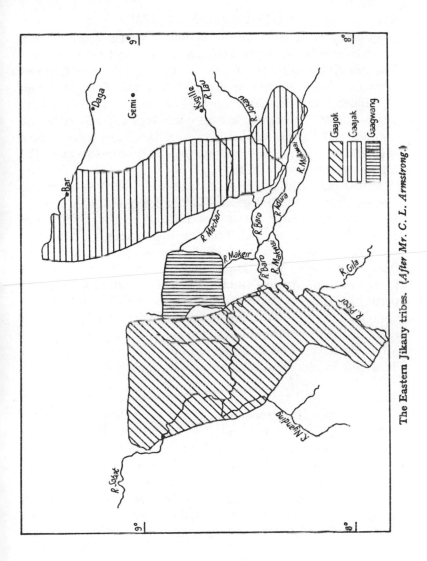

The Eastern Jikany tribes. (*After Mr. C. L. Armstrong.*)

In every Nuer tribe there are similar stories which explain the relations between the aristocratic clan and large stranger lineages living with it. Other myths explain the relations between these stranger lineages. Thus the lineages living at Nyueny and in neighbouring villages in Leek country, JUAK, NGWOL, JIKUL, &c., are all mythologically related to one another and to the dominant clan of the Leek tribe. These myths also explain the ritual symbols and observances of the lineages mentioned in them.

Actual interrelations of a political kind are thus explained and justified in mythological interrelations, and wherever, as far as we know, large lineages of different clans are politically associated there is a myth bringing their ancestors into some social relationship. This is especially the case between dominant lineages and stranger or Dinka lineages, and the mythological link gives them equality and fraternity in community life, while permitting ritual exclusiveness and intermarriage between them. Complete assimilation is impossible, for there must always be ritual distinction or the clan and lineage systems would collapse. Strangers have to be incorporated into the community of the dominant lineage and excluded from its agnatic structure.

XI

By adoption, the recognition of the equivalence of cognatic and agnatic ties in community life, and by mythological relationships, all persons in a tribal segment have kinship relationships of some kind to one another and the segments themselves are given a kinship relationship to each other within the political system. Although the categories of *diel*, *rul*, and *jaang* create social differentiation, it is on a ritual and domestic, rather than on a political, plane and is only indicated in certain situations of social life.

This is evident in the Nuer use of the three words denoting the three statuses. It is a common Nuer practice when addressing people and speaking publicly about them to use words which denote a closer relationship between them and the speaker than their actual relationship. This is commonly done with kinship terms and, also, in defining the status of a person in his tribe. Nuer do not emphasize that a man is a stranger or Dinka by alluding to him as such in ordinary social life, for it is in rare situations that his being other than an aristocrat is relevant: to some extent in payment of blood-cattle, in questions of exogamy, and at sacrifices and feasts. A stranger who has made his home with aristocrats is treated as a social equal and regards himself as such. People do not call him a *rul*, for he is a member of their community. They may even refer to him as a *dil* out of politeness. In the same way people do not refer to an adopted Dinka as '*Jaang*'; for he is by adoption a brother of aristocrats or of Nuer of other lineages. One would not ordinarily speak of unadopted Dinka residents as '*Jaang*', but as '*rul*'. Just as strangers tend to be linguistically assimilated to aristocrats, so Dinka tend to be assimilated to strangers, and people speak only of unconquered Dinka of Dinkaland by the contemptuous expression '*Jaang*'. Nuer do not make distinctions of status between people who live with them, share their fights, partake of their hospitality, and are members of their community against other communities. Community of living overrides differentiation of descent.

We again emphasize that the designations 'aristocrat', 'stranger', and 'Dinka' in a Nuer tribe are relative terms, being defined by the relations of persons in the social structure in specific situations of social life. A man is a stranger, or Dinka, in reference to a few, mainly ritual, situations, but is not indicated as such on other occasions; and a man is a stranger or Dinka in relation to members of a social group, but is not considered by them to have a differentiated status in relation to another group. A stranger is a stranger to you, your stranger, but is one of you *vis-à-vis* other people. A Dinka is a Dinka to you, your Dinka, but he is your brother *vis-à-vis* other people. In political structure all members of a segment are essentially undifferentiated in its relation to other segments.

How can it be explained that among a people so democratic in sentiment and so ready to express it in violence a clan is given superior status in each tribe? We believe that the facts we have recorded provide an answer in terms of tribal structure. Many Nuer tribes are large in area and population—some of them very large—and they are more than territorial expressions, for we have shown that they have a complex segmentary structure which the Nuer themselves see as a system. As there are no tribal chiefs and councils, or any other form of tribal government, we have to seek elsewhere for the organizing principle within the structure which gives it conceptual consistency and a certain measure of actual cohesion, and we find it in aristocratic status. In the absence of political institutions providing central administration in a tribe and co-ordinating its segments, it is the system of lineages of its dominant clan which gives it structural distinctness and unity by the association of lineage values, within a common agnatic structure, with the segments of a territorial system. In the absence of a chief or king, who might symbolize a tribe, its unity is expressed in the idiom of lineage and clan affiliation.

XII

In the Kir myth not only are the ancestors of important lineages, and, through them, the lineages and the territorial segments in which they are incorporated brought into relationship, but the ancestors of clans, and, through them, the clans and the tribes in which these clans are dominant, are linked together. Thus Kir, in various versions of the myth, is adopted by Gee, the founder of the GAATGANGEEKA family of clans; meets Wot, in whom the Wot tribe is personified; has relations with the GAAWAR; and so forth. The myth, thus, also mirrors intertribal relations and brings the whole of Nuerland into a single kinship structure, which we call the clan system as distinct from the lineage system of a clan.

The clan is the farthest range to which agnatic kinship is traced when the marriage of two persons is in question, but some clans have, nevertheless, an agnatic relationship to other clans, though Nuer do not regard it quite in the same way as relationship between lineages of a clan. They give the impression, when speaking of the ancestor of a clan, that they regard him as an historical figure, clearly delineated against a background of tradition, while, when speaking of the ancestor of a family of clans, they seem to regard him as a vaguer figure obscured in the dimness of myth.

We here note again that the dominant lineages in more than one tribe sometimes form part of the same clan structure. Thus, the lineages dominant in the Gaajok, Gaajak, and Gaagwang

PLATE XXVI

a. Youth (Eastern Gaajok) with ash hair-dressing

b. Youth (Eastern Gaajok) after removal of ash hair-dressing

PLATE XXVII

Initiation of boys (near Nasser, Eastern Gaajok)

tribes, to the east and to the west of the Nile, are all segments of the GAATGANKIIR clan. Also the dominant lineages of the Rengyan tribe, to the west of the Nile, and the Lou tribe, to the east of the Zeraf, are part of the JINACA clan. This distribution is easily accounted for, because we know that till recently

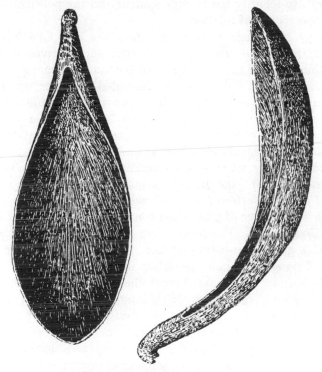

FIG. 14. Buffalo-horn spoons.

the Eastern GAATGANKIIR and the Eastern JINACA lineages lived with the other lineages of these clans in the Jikany and Rengyan areas to the west of the Nile.

There are also more general and mythological relationships between clans. In recounting these relationships Nuer personify the tribes and give them a kinship value by assimilating them to their dominant clans. Thus, they speak of Bor, Lang, Lou, Thiang, Lak, &c., as though they were persons and could have kinship relations between them like those between persons, and as though all the members of these tribes were of the same descent. By so doing they stress community relations and obscure clan differentiation in a political context. This habit often makes their statements appear confused, and even contradictory, but it accords with a strong tendency in social life, as we have seen in discussing the various meanings of the word '*cieng*', to identify the lineage system and the political system in a specific set of relations.

Many Nuer regard their ancestors Gee and Ghaak as the progenitors of all true Nuer, though one is given different classifications in different parts of Nuerland. Among the Lou it is said that all the tribes are descended from Gee, except the Jikany and Gaawar tribes. These two alone are differentiated because their proximity makes them significant for the Lou, whereas all the other tribes, which have no direct relations with the Lou, are vaguely classified as children of Gee. Among the Eastern Jikany all true Nuer tend to be classed as 'Gee' in contrast to 'Kir', the Jikany themselves. In the valley of the Zeraf and in Western Nuerland, where the tribes have a very much wider range of intertribal contacts, there is a wider range of differentiation. The Nuer tribes there fall into three classes: the Gee group, consisting of Bor, Lang, Rengyan, Bul, Wot, Ror, Thiang, and Lou, stretches in an unbroken line, from north-west to south-east, across the centre of Nuerland; the Ghaak group, consisting of Nuong, Dok, Jaloogh, Beegh, Gaankwac, and Rol, occupies the south-western part of Nuerland; and the Ril group, consisting of the Leek and Lak, occupies the lower reaches of the Zeraf and the Ghazal near their junction with the Nile. I have sometimes heard the Bul included in the Ril group. However, in Dok country and in adjacent tribal areas people further distinguish between the tribes elsewhere classed as sons of Ghaak and divide them into a Ghaak group, comprising Beegh, and Jaalogh, and a Gwea group, comprising Dok, Nuong, Gaankwac, and Rol.

In these classifications we note a further exemplification of what we have often observed elsewhere about Nuer classifications: their segmentary tendency and their relativity. Whilst, for example, other Nuer see the Dok and the Beegh as Ghaak they only see themselves as an undivided Ghaak group in opposition to the Gee fraternity and otherwise see themselves as parts of opposed segments, Gwea and Ghaak. It will be noted that these groups of tribes, often represented as families of clans, occupy distinct sections of Nuerland. Before the period of eastwards migration they ran from north to south, in three or four groups, to the west of the Nile. Territorial contiguity and a common clan structure, such as we find among the Jikany tribes, or close relationship within a clan system, such as we find among the Ghaak group of tribes, go together, and the values of the two systems may be assumed to interact. The segmentation of lineages within a tribe in relation to its political segmentation is thus repeated in the whole clan system of the Nuer, the segments of which are co-ordinated with the political segmentation of Nuerland. Those tribes which are adjacent to one another have a common opposition to other groups of tribes and this relation is reflected in the tendency for them to be represented, through their dominant lineages and clans, as closely related on a mythological and ritual plane.

Gee and Ghaak and Gwea are represented as brothers, sons of a mythological ancestor, sometimes called Ghau, the World, and sometimes Ran, Man, whose father is said to be Kwoth, God. Ril is often described as one of their brothers as well, though he is sometimes represented to be a son of a daughter of Gee, called Kar.

All sons of Gee have agnatic kinship (*buth*) which allows them to partake of one another's sacrifices. In these ritual situations only the true sons of Gee, the JINACA, the GAATHIANG, and JIDIET, and other clans descended from Gee, have *buth* interrelationship, but in other situations the tribes in which these clans have a dominant status are represented as brothers or first cousins. Thus Thiang is said to have been the eldest son of Gee, Nac (Rengyan and Lou) the second son, Ror and other tribes younger sons; and Rengyan (Nac) and Wot (Dit) are said to have been twins, as also Bor and Lang, sons of Meat.

Some tribes stand outside this big family. The Jikany tribes have dominant lineages of Dinka origin, descended from Kir, who was found in a gourd by a man of the Ngok Dinka, but, as was earlier explained, they are mythologically related to the Gee group, because Gee is variously represented as the protector or father-in-law of Kir. The GAATGANKIIR have a *buth* relationship with some lineage system of the Ngok Dinka, and therefore, in an unprecise political sense, the Jikany and Ngok Dinka tribes have, by analogy, a fraternal relationship. It may safely be assumed that at one time they had close intertribal relations. The GAAWAR clan have also an independent origin, their ancestor having descended from heaven. However, a number of mythological links unite him to the founders of various clans which are dominant in tribes of the Ghaak group (see pp. 230–1), and the Gaawar tribe therefore belongs to this group. Although the Nile now separates it from the other members of the group it was at one time their most northern extension on the west bank. Owing to *buth* relationship between GAAWAR and other clans of the family of clans descended from Kwook, Gaawar are said to go with the people of the Fadang section of the Bor tribe and the Atwot people, who are said to have lived at one time between the present Rengyan and Dok tribal areas.

Through the recognition of agnatic relationship between exogamous clans and of cognatic and mythological ties between clans not considered to be agnates, all the Nuer tribes are by assimilation of political to kinship values conceptualized as a single social system. A number of clans are not associated with tribes, but their lineages are included in this system by the affiliation of the clans to one or other of the large families of clans. Thus, the JIMEM, JIKUL, GAATLEAK, and JITHER are descended from Gee and belong to the Gee group; the JIKUL are mythologically attached to the Ril group and the JAKAR to the Ghaak group; and so on. The whole of the Nuer are brought into a single kinship or pseudo-kinship system and all the territorial segments of Nuerland are interconnected by that system.

XIII

In our view the unusual degree of genealogical segmentation in the Nuer lineage system is to be understood in terms of tribal structure, which is, as we have seen, characterized by its tendency towards segmentation. The association of the lineage system with the tribal system means that as the tribe splits into segments so will the clan split into segments, and that the lines of cleavage will tend to coincide, for lineages are not corporate groups but are embodied in local communities through which they function structurally. Just as a man is a member of a tribal segment opposed to other segments of the same order and yet also a member of the tribe which embraces all these segments, so also he is a member of a lineage opposed to other lineages of the same order and yet also a member of the clan which embraces all these lineages, and there is a definite correspondence between these two sets of affiliations, since the lineage is embodied in the segment and the clan in the tribe. Therefore, the distance in clan structure between two lineages of a dominant clan tends to correspond to the structural distance between the tribal segments with which they are associated. Hence the tribal system draws out and segments the dominant clans and gives them their characteristic lineage form. Evidence in support of this contention could be cited from any Nuer tribe; we propose to examine only a few typical examples.

We have observed that in the Lou tribe the Gaatbal and Rumjok secondary sections form the primary section of Gun in opposition to the Mor primary section, and how the dominant lineages of the Gaatbal and the Rumjok sections are descended from one wife of Denac and the dominant lineage of the Mor section is descended from a different wife, so that Gaatbal and Rumjok are to one another in a relation analogous to that of full brothers and the Gun stand to the Mor in a relation analogous to that of half-brothers. We have noted, likewise, how the dominant lineages of the Gaajak are descended from two closely related wives of Kir while the dominant lineages of the Gaajok and Gaagwang, which have a very close alliance, are descended from a third wife.

The GAATGANKIIR lineages in their relation to the segmentary structure of the Jikany tribes provide an excellent test of the hypothesis that lineage structure is twisted into the form of the political structure, for the same lineages are found at extremities of Nuerland where political conditions are not identical. Had I had more time in the Jikany countries, or had I formulated the problem more clearly in the little time I had to spend there, I might have been in a position to state my conclusions more dogmatically. We will briefly analyse the lineage system of the GAATGANKIIR in its relation to two of the Gaajak primary sections.

Thiang was the eldest son of Kir. He had two wives, Nyagaani and Baal. From these two wives spring the three main lineages of *cieng* Thiang, the Thiang primary tribal section, TAR, LONY (or GEK), and KANG. What is said to have happened is shown in the diagram on p. 242. Tar, being the only son of his mother, has founded an independent lineage and tribal section, that which lives in the extreme south of Eastern Gaajak country. The other four lineages are all sprung from Nyagaani and are collectively known as *cieng* Nyagaani. At first her four sons stuck together, but later Lony's family increased and became more powerful than those of his brothers and tried to lord it over them, especially over Lem, the eldest. Kang, son of Lual, took the lead against Lony, and compelled him to migrate. Owing to the prominent part played by Kang, the lineages descended from Lem, Leng, and Lual are collectively known as *cieng* KANG in contrast to *cieng* LONY. These two lineages live to the extreme north of Eastern Gaajak country.[1] When the brothers are spoken about, as quarrelling, migrating, and so forth, it must be understood that the lineages and the local communities of which they form part are being personified and dramatized.

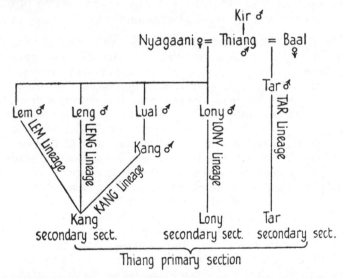

We see in this diagram how the splitting and merging of lineages, determined by the logic of lineage structure, follows the lines of tribal fission and fusion. Thus the descendants of Lem, Leng, and Lual, who live together, are merged in opposition to the LONY, and the LONY, who live adjacent to them, are merged with them in opposition to the TAR. The diagram does not show us the lines of descent which have become completely merged in those recorded,

[1] The distribution of the three divisions of the Thiang primary section of the Gaajak tribe contrasts with the unbroken territory of the segments of primary sections elsewhere in Nuerland. I have not visited the area, and cannot explain this unusual distribution by historical events nor state its structural consequences.

because such lines, having no localities specifically associated with them and therefore no community value, are not differentiated. That the diagram does not truly record historic lineage growth, but is a distortion of it, is further suggested by the fact that there are, on an average, five generations from the present day to Lem and Leng, six to Lual, and seven to Lony, who was the youngest of the four brothers.

The GAAGWONG lineage, which is the nucleus of the Gaagwong section, is called after Gung, son of Kun, son of Kir. The GAAG-WONG maximal lineage splits into several major lineages. To make illustration easier only those important among the Eastern Jikany are figured in the diagram: CANY, WAU, and TAIYANG (NYAYAN and NYAJAANI), the descendants of Buok, Wau, and Gee.

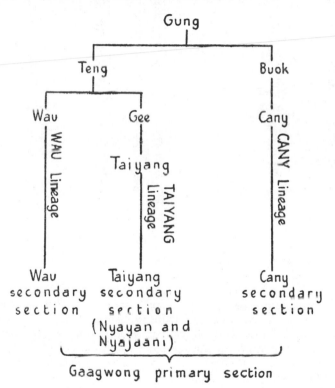

Gaagwong primary section

The CANY major lineage split up, as shown in the diagram on p. 244, into a number of smaller lineages of three to four generations in depth. In this diagram the traditional representation of cleavage between sons of the same father but of different mothers is shown in the lines which spring from Diu through his three wives: Mankwoth, Thul, and Mankang. The descendants of Dup are normally referred to as *cieng* MANKWOTH because they live with them. Common residence has reacted on the lineage structure, so that the DUP lineage has become very largely merged in the MANK-WOTH lineage. For this diagram I am indebted to the Government

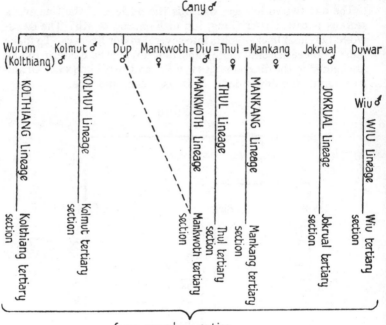

files of Nasser District. I have no record of the divisions of the WAU lineage.

In Western Nuerland WAU and CANY are politically unimportant lineages and are merged with *cieng* Taiyang, which is contrasted with *cieng* Jueny, called after Jueny, son of Teng, son of Gung, who founded a lineage politically unimportant among the Eastern Jikany. The TAIYANG lineage has two branches called after his wives Nyayan and Nyajaani. In Western Nuerland there is a third lineage springing from a third wife, Nyakoi.

It is interesting to observe that Jueny, whose line is politically unimportant among the Eastern Jikany, is there given as a son of Gee and merged in the TAIYANG line, while Duob is given as a son of Nyajaani and merged in her lineage. Here again we see how lineage structure is influenced by political relations.

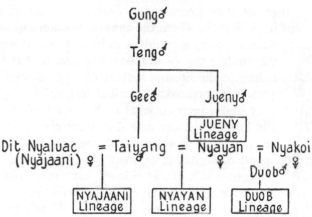

A wider and deeper analysis is required to prove the thesis we have put forward and of which we have given a few out of many examples. It is, however, supported by evidence of a different kind. We found that it was always easier to obtain a more complete record, and a longer line, of descent from members of dominant lineages in the larger tribes than in the smaller tribes, showing that greater attention is paid to the lineage system in the larger tribes and that the clan structure is broadened and deepened to serve its structural function. Also, we found it easy to obtain from any adult member of an aristocratic lineage an account of the other maximal and major lineages of his clan and a long list of ancestors, some nine or ten at least, giving a consistent length from the founder of the clan; whereas we found that we could not elicit the same information from members of clans which have no tribal associations. They were often able to trace their descent back for only some four to six generations, the time depth they gave was seldom consistent, and they were usually unable to give a coherent account of the other lineages of their clan. We attribute this fact to the absence of systemization through association with tribal structures. A lineage does not stand in territorial opposition to other lineages of its clan, but has with them only a vague ceremonial relationship, and this relationship may never be expressed in corporate action. Consequently there is generally a complete absence of any elaborate system of lineages like those of the dominant clans. There are many JIMEM clansmen and doubtless one could by putting together their genealogies construct some sort of tree of descent from Mem, in which the agnatic relationship between

various lineages could be indicated; but it would be very unlike the spontaneous statements that at once delineate the lineage system of large clans like the JINACA, associated with tribal territories.

It is also very noticeable that Nuer knowledge of the lineage system of a dominant clan tends to be restricted to those parts of the system that correspond to segments of their tribe. Thus the JINACA lineages which are associated with segments of the Lou tribe are well known to Lou tribesmen, but they have no, or very little, knowledge of the JINACA lineages of the Rengyan tribe. Likewise I experienced much difficulty in obtaining from Gaajok and Gaajak tribesmen a clear account of the lineages of the GAATGANKIIR clan which form the dominant nucleus of the Gaagwang tribe, though they were well informed about the lineages of the same clan which are associated with segments of their own tribes.

It follows from our account that, as we have suggested before, the lineage system of a clan can only to a very limited extent be considered a true record of descent. Not only does its time depth appear to be limited and fixed, but also the distance between collateral lineages appears to be determined by the political distance between the sections with which these lineages are associated, and it may be supposed that a lineage only persists as a distinct line of descent when it is significant politically. Ancestors above the founder of a minimal lineage are relevant only as points of departure for denoting lines of descent when these lines are rendered significant by the political role of the lineage system. We have

FIG. 15.
Leather
flail.

suggested that the depth of lineages is a function of the range of counting agnation on an existential plane, and we now further suggest that the range of counting agnation is largely determined by its organizing role in political structure.

Nuer consider that lineage cleavage arises from a fundamental cleavage in the family between *gaatgwan*, children of the father, and *gaatman*, children of the mother. Where there are two wives and each has sons, the lineage bifurcates from this point. A lineage bifurcation is a polygamous family writ large. *Thok dwiel*, lineage, means this; it is 'the entrance to the hut', the mother's hut. The tiny twigs we see in the *gol*, household, grow into the great branches of the lineages. It is for this reason that lineages are so often named after women, the mothers from whose wombs sprang the different lines of descent. As we understand the process, what happens is that certain lineage groups gain political importance and exclusiveness, becoming nuclei of tribal sections, and that only by so doing is their structural position stabilized and are the points of their bifurcation rendered fixed and permanent points of convergence in lineage structure. This explains how it is that in only a few out of a vast number of polygamous families is maternal descent structurally signifi-cant, and why the bifurcation occurs in the lineage where it occurs in the tribe.

This tendency towards co-ordination of territorial segmenta-tion and lineage segmentation can be seen in the various stages of territorial expansion between the household and the tribe. When brothers of an influential family live in different parts of a village and gather around them a cluster of relations and depen-dants, these hamlet-groups are named after them and they become the point at which the lineage is likely to bifurcate. Thus, if the brothers are called Bul and Nyang, people speak of the *gol* of Bul and the *gol* of Nyang, and if later the grand-children of one of them move to a different village site the lineage will split into two branches. Such minimal lineages as those pictured in the diagrams on pages 196–7 occupy adjacent villages, or widely separated divisions of the same large straggling village, and make separate camps along the same stretch of river or adjacent camps around a small lake. The points of divergence of lineages from clan trees are thus related to the size and distribution of inhabited sites in a tribal area.

The association of the tribal system with a clan may thus be supposed to influence the form of the lineage structure. We may further emphasize the morphological consistency between the two structures. There are always more villages than tertiary segments in a tribe and more tertiary segments than secondary segments, and so on, so that, since each territorial unit is associated with a lineage, the narrowing of such units from the multitude of villages to the single unit of the tribe must be reflected in the conceptual structure of the lineage system, there being a multitude of minimal lineages, fewer minor lineages, and so forth, till the single unit of the clan is reached. If this suggestion is accepted it is evident that the lineages are in number and structural position strictly limited and controlled by the system of territorial segmentation. The two systems may thus be represented diagrammatically by the same figure, though the correspondence is not exact.

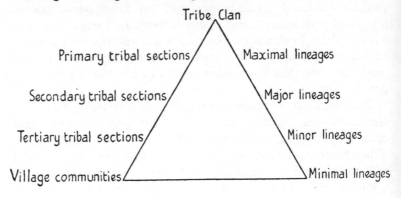

CHAPTER VI

THE AGE-SET SYSTEM

I

ALL male Nuer are initiated from boyhood to manhood by a very severe operation (*gar*). Their brows are cut to the bone with a small knife, in six long cuts from ear to ear. The scars remain for life, and it is said that marks can be detected on the skulls of dead men. They are particularly clear in Plates XXVI(*b*), XXVII, and XXVIII. The ceremonial of initiation is more complex, and the age-set system has greater social importance among the Nuer than among other Sudan Nilotes.

We have described, and others have described, elsewhere the ritual of initiation. Though we have since collected further information on the details of the rites, we consider that to transcribe it here would be out of accord with the plan of this book. The barest facts are related. Boys are now usually initiated between the ages of 14 and 16; in the old days at a somewhat later age, perhaps from 16 to 18. Whether a boy is initiated in one year or in another year may depend on the milk and millet supply. A boy must obtain his father's consent to the operation, but it cannot well be refused, for the boy would then run away to the home of a kinsman and the father would be humiliated. He afterwards goes to a member of his father's age-set who performs a rite to give him the blessing of the set. A member of the clan likewise gives him its blessing, and his father and maternal uncle bless him. The boys make their own arrangements with the operator and each presents him with a fishing spear. The operator is any man who has learnt the art.

Several boys are initiated at the same time, for it is thought that were a boy to be initiated by himself he would be lonely and might die. Also, it is easier to cater for the boys and to give them the care and attention they require during convalescence if they are initiated in batches. Usually some four to a dozen boys pass through the rites together. Initiation can take place at any season, but it almost invariably takes place at the end of the rains, when there is plenty of food and the north wind blows and cicatrizes the wounds. Each village acts independently in arranging for its boys to be initiated. After the operation the boys live in partial seclusion and are subject to various taboos. This is a time of mild licence and they pass out of it by a special rite. On the day of the cutting, and on the day of the passing out of seclusion, sacrifices are made and there is festivity, which includes licentious horseplay and the singing of lewd songs. Only age-mates of the father of the initiate in whose homestead the feasting takes place attend it: others keep at a distance lest they see the nakedness of their kinswomen and mothers-in-law.

II

All boys initiated during a number of successive years belong to a single age-set (*ric*). There has, till recently, been a four-year interval between the end of one such set and the commencement of the next. These four years are known as the time 'when the knife is hung up', and at the end of that period it is said 'the knife is brought out' and boys may then be initiated again. A certain *wut ghok*, 'Man of the Cattle', is, in each tribe, responsible for opening and closing the initiation periods and thereby dividing the sets. He performs the appropriate rite in his district, and when the news goes round other districts begin or cease initiation. He derives prestige from his functions, but they are ritual and give him no political authority. Sometimes, in Western Nuerland, they are performed by a prophet, but it is possible that in these cases the prophet is also a Man of the Cattle. The age-sets are organized independently in each tribe, at any rate in the larger tribes, but it often happens that when a new set has been started in one tribe an adjacent tribe will follow its lead, so that the names and periods of sets in neighbouring tribes are frequently the same. Also, though in different parts of Nuerland the names of the sets are different and the open and closed periods do not coincide, it is easy for a man who moves from one part to another to perceive in which set he would have been initiated had he been brought up in that part of the country.

To-day there are no closed periods and boys are initiated every year. The Man of the Cattle announces every few years that he s about to cut the sets and performs a ceremony by which all youths initiated up to that year fall into one set and all youths initiated after that year fall into a junior set. The number of years during which a set runs before being cut is variable, and this has probably always been the case. We conclude on the evidence that ten years may be regarded as an average period between the commencement of one set and the commencement of the next. It was found that generally two sets, but occasionally one, intervened between the set of a man and that of his eldest son. In the case of younger sons two or three sets usually intervene. It may be accepted that on an average the generations of grandfather—father—son cover six sets.

At the time of my inquiry into the age-set system there were members of six sets alive, but there were only a few survivors of the senior set and the members of the next senior were very infirm. Sets with no living members are not recorded in the lists below. Their names are irrelevant to an understanding of the system and their order is so ill-remembered that the statements of two informants on the matter are seldom in entire agreement. It should be noted, however, that as far back as Nuer recitation carries us the names are not uniform for the whole of Nuerland and that they are not repeated. There is no cycle of names such as we find in many parts of East Africa. The Lou and the Eastern Jikany tend to have common names; also the tribes of western Nuerland; while the tribes of the Zeraf have some names in common with the Sobat river tribes and some with the tribes to the west of the Nile.

Lou tribe	Eastern Jikany	Lak tribe	Western Jikany and Leek tribes
Thut	Thut	Thut	Lilnyang
Boiloc	Boiloc	Boiloc	Ruob
Maker	Maker	Ruob	Wangdel
Dangunga	Dangunga	Wangdel	Tangkwer
Luac	Carboc	Wooni	Rol
Lithgac	Lithgac	Kec	Juong
Rialmac	Rialmac	Pilual	Bildeang

Each age-set has two or three subdivisions. Each year in the initiation period may receive a separate name and constitute a division though probably two years often have the same name and the divisions are usually two-year periods. But though a set is thus stratified internally and the divisions are called by different names, all members of the set are known by the name of the first division, and this common name persists while the others eventually fall into disuse. Thus to-day one seldom hears of *Maker indit* and *Ngwak*, but only of *Maker*, under which title both divisions are included. Likewise one hears small mention of *Gwong indit*, *Carboc*, and *Nyamnyam*, and reference is normally to *Dangunga (Gwong)*, which term covers all three divisions. The senior division is called *indit*, the greater, and when the segmentary names are dropped the *indit* is dropped also, since its purpose is to distinguish the primary division from the later ones. Hence we have *Thut indit*, *Maker indit*, and *Boiloc indit*, the elder *Thut*, the elder *Maker*, and the elder *Boiloc*, but the *indit* ending in these names is eventually dropped and the complete sets become known as *Thut*, *Maker*, and *Boiloc*.

In recent years the matter has become somewhat complicated by the absence of well-defined closed and open initiation periods. Thus in my earlier visits to Lou and Eastern Gaajok I heard people speak of *Lieth indit*, *Lieth incar (Lieth intot)*, *Caiyat (Pilual)*, and *Rialmac (Rialdang)* as four divisions of the *Lithgac* age-set, but this was because there had been no declaration by the Man of the Cattle separating them into different age-sets. On a later expedition I found that the *Lieth indit*, the *Lieth incar*, and *Caiyat* had been declared to be a single age-set, and the *Rialmac* to start a new age-set, a second division of which, the *Kwekoryoamni*, has since been initiated. Similarly among the Western Jikany and Leek the *Bildeang* age-set has recently been declared separate from the *Juong*. At one time in Eastern Gaajok the *Lithgac* were cut off from the *Rialmac*, while in the adjacent country of the Eastern Gaajak they had not yet been separated and remained for the time being a single set. It may thus happen that, in modern times, a sub-division may for a time be regarded as the junior segment of one set and later become the senior segment of the next set. Below are given the sub-divisions of the age-sets in the Lou and Western Jikany tribes:

	Lou		Western Jikany	
Thut	{ *Thut indit* *Muothjaang* *Lilcoa*	*Lilnyang*	{ *Lilnyang* *Lilcoa* *Lilcuath*	
Boiloc	{ *Boiloc indit* *Golyangkakeat* *Laibwau*	*Ruob*	{ *Ruob* *Nomalith*	
Maker	{ *Maker indit* *Ngwak*	*Wangdel*	{ *Wangdel* *Wathcar*	

Gwong	Lou	Western Jikany	
Gwong	Gwong indit Carboc Nyamnyam	Tangkwer	Tangkwer Karam
Luac	Luac indit Karam Camthoari	Rol	Rol Pilual
Lithgac	Lieth indit (inbor) Lieth intot (incar) Caiyat (Pilual)	Juong	Juong Majaani
Rialmac	Rialmac (Rialdang) indit Kwekoryoam	Bildeang	Bildeang

III

In seeking to understand how membership of an age-set determines a man's behaviour we have first to realize that there is no
purposive education or moral training in the procedure of
initiation. Also, many of the characteristic features of the age-
set system in Kenya, where it is most highly developed, are
absent in the Nuer variation. There are not three distinct
age-grades of boys, warriors, and elders through which the sets
pass, for a boy who is initiated into manhood remains in this
grade for the rest of his life. Warriors are not prohibited from
marrying and they neither enjoy privileges nor suffer restric-
tions different from those of other male adults. The sets have
no administrative, juridical, or other specific political functions
and the country is not handed over to their care. The sets have
no definite military functions. Indeed, we are of the opinion
that the Nuer age-set system ought not to be described as
a military organization, though some writers give it this
character. Youths who have recently been initiated are anxious
for their first raid, and consider that they ought to earn for their
set a reputation for valour, and it is likely that raids were
generally conducted in the main by men of the most junior set.
However, there is no grade of warriorhood through which the
age-sets pass nor a grade of elderhood into which they enter.
Were boys and old men to take part in warfare against other
Nuer they would probably be killed, and it is understandable
that raids are the occupation of the strongest and fleetest,

though many middle-aged men accompany the expeditions and always have their share in inter-tribal fighting and local disputes.

The age-set system of a tribe is in no way its military organization. Men fight by villages and by tribal sections and not by sets. The war companies are local units and not age-set units, and within a company men of different sets fight side by side, though, especially in raids, most of the warriors would be members of the two most junior sets. Kinship and local ties determine a man's place in the ranks. Hence the age-sets are not regiments, though wars and raids are often spoken of as the actions of a certain set because they took place during the initiation period of this set and its members took the most prominent part in them, since skill in arms, love of adventure, and desire for booty are the privileges of youth.

It is in more general social relations, chiefly of a domestic and kinship order, and not in political relations that behaviour is specifically determined by the positions of persons in age-set structure. When a boy passes into the grade of manhood his domestic duties and privileges are radically altered. His change of status is epitomized in the taboo on milking which comes into force on the day of his initiation and continues for the rest of his life, but it is expressed also in other domestic tasks, in habits of eating, and so forth. At initiation a youth receives from his father or uncle a spear and becomes a warrior. He is also given an ox, from which he takes an ox-name, and becomes a herdsman. From now on, till he is a husband and father, his chief interests are dancing and love-making. Then he becomes 'a true man': 'he has fought in war and not run away; he has duelled with his age-mates; he has cultivated his gardens; he has married a wife'.

There is a sudden and great change in status from boyhood to manhood, but the modes of behaviour which differentiate these two grades do not distinguish one set from another, for the privileges of manhood are enjoyed by members of all the sets equally. Nevertheless, the sets are stratified by seniority and there are well-defined relationships between them. Before summarizing these patterns of inter-set behaviour we touch on some general characteristics of the whole system.

The age-set system is a further exemplification of the segmentary principle which we have seen to be so evident a quality of social structure. Tribes segment into sections and their sections further segment, so that any local group is a balanced relation between opposed segments. Clans segment into lineages and their lineages further segment, so that any lineage group is a balanced relation between opposed segments. Likewise the institution based on age is highly segmentary, being stratified into sets which are opposed groups, and these sets are further stratified into successive sections. We may therefore speak of structural distance in this new dimension. Just as the distance between political segments varies according to their positions in the political structure, and the distance between lineage segments varies according to their positions in the lineage structure, so the distance between age-set segments varies according to their positions in the age-set structure. The structural distance between any two sets is the social relation between those sets and the determinant of behaviour between their members.

The relativity of values which we noted in discussing the political and lineage systems may also be seen in the age-set system. We have noted that a set which is seen as an unsegmented whole by members of other sets is internally segmented, and that members of each of its segments see themselves as exclusive units in relation to the others, though these divisions close as the set becomes more senior and has a new position in relation to sets, since created, below it. Also, there is a tendency for members of two successive sets, adjacent segments of the structure, to fuse in relation to a third in feelings and in ceremonial actions. A *Rialmac* youth said: 'We and the *Lithgac* are about the same age and we can be free in speaking to them, but we must show respect to an older man, even if he is not of our fathers' age-set.' Although there are six sets with living members there are very few survivors of the two senior sets, and from the point of view of a young man they are merged with the one that follows them. Only four sets count, and, seen by individuals, they merge into two generation groups of equals and brothers, and seniors and fathers or juniors and sons. To a *Lithgac* son of a *Maker* father all members of the *Maker* age-set are his fathers, and the *Lithgac* and the *Luac* tend to see themselves as a single group in relation to the *Maker*, having a like attitude of respect towards them. But in relation to the *Dangunga* and to the *Lithgac*, the *Luac* identify themselves with the one or the other according to the direction of attention, and this is determined by the social situation. Any set tends to see the set senior to it as equals in relation to junior sets and the set junior to it as equals in relation to senior sets. It is possibly this contradiction which creates segmentation in any set. Thus, at sacrificial feasts men eat according to their position in the age-set structure, but which sets sit and eat together depends on the set of the owner of the feast and on the number of sets present at it. If a *Dangunga* kills an ox and there are *Maker* present, but not *Boiloc*, then *Dangunga* eat with *Maker* and *Luac* with *Lithgac* and the *Rialmac* by themselves; but if there are *Boiloc* present then the *Maker* eat with them and the *Dangunga* with the *Luac*, and the *Lithgac* with the *Rialmac*. The *Dangunga* would not eat with the *Boiloc* because they are the set of their fathers or fathers-in-law; and for the same reason the *Luac* must eat with the *Lithgac* if the *Dangunga* go with the *Maker*.

The age-set system differs from the territorial and lineage systems in one important respect. Whereas the people of a territorial segment remain, or most of them remain, in the same structural relation to other territorial segments for their whole lives, and whereas the members of a lineage have a fixed relationship to other lineages, an age-set group changes its position in relation to the whole system, passing through points of relative juniority and seniority. This mobility of age-set groups is peculiar to the system and is a necessary characteristic of it, for it is an institution based on the succession of generations. Probably, for oecological reasons, the actual political configuration remains very much the same from generation to generation. People pass through the political system without their structural position in it changing to any extent during their passage. It is the same with the lineage system. Nevertheless the mobility of groups through the age-set structure and their changing position in it should not be allowed to obscure the constancy of its structural form. There have pro-

PLATE XXVIII

a. Youth (Zeraf river)

b. Youth (Lou)

c. Man (Zeraf river)

PLATE XXIX

Man (Nasser Post)

bably always been the same number of sets in existence at any time and these sets always have the same relative positions to each other in the system, regardless of actual groups of men composing them.

It is significant that among the Nuer, as among other East African peoples, the age-set system is the first institution to undergo rapid and great modification under European rule and that the other social systems do not appear to be affected by the changes in its constitution. This tends to confirm the opinion we have earlier expressed, that whilst the age-set system is combined with the territorial and lineage systems in the same social cadre and is consistent with them, the consistency is not an interdependence.

IV

Within the age-set system the position of every male Nuer is structurally defined in relation to every other male Nuer and his status to them is one of seniority, equality, or juniority. It is difficult to describe these statuses in terms of behaviour, because the attitudes they impose are often of a very general nature. The following points may, however, be noted. (1) There are certain ritual observances and avoidances, chiefly between members of the same set, but also between sets. The most important of these are the segregation of the sets at sacrificial feasts, to which we have referred, and the stringent prohibition on members of a set burying an age-mate or partaking of the meat of beasts sacrificed at his mortuary ceremony; but there are a number of other ritual injunctions. (2) A man may not marry, or have sexual relations with, the daughter of an age-mate, for she is his 'daughter' and he is her 'father'. Also, while a man may always have sexual relations with the daughter of one of his father's age-mates he ought not to marry her unless either his father, or her father, is dead, and then only after the parties to the marriage have exchanged beasts in atonement to the age-set of the fathers. (3) Members of the same age-set are on terms of entire equality. A man does not stand on ceremony with his age-mates, but jokes, plays, and eats with them at his ease. Age-mates associate in work, war, and in all the pursuits of leisure. They are expected to offer one another hospitality and to share their possessions. Fighting is considered an appropriate mode of behaviour between age-mates, but a man ought not to fight a man of a senior set. The comradeship between age-mates springs from a recognition of a mystical union between them, linking their fortunes, which derives from an almost physical bond, analogous to that of true kinship, for they have shed their blood together. (4) Members of a set are expected to show respect to members of senior sets, and their deference to them can be seen in discussions, in etiquette, in division of food, and so forth. Whenever there is a question about the propriety of speech or action it is judged by reference to the relative positions of the persons concerned in the age-set structure, if kinship status is not also involved. Since every man has a known age-relationship to every other man in Nuerland with whom he is likely to come into contact, their social attitude to him, and his social attitude to them, is determined in advance by the distances between them in age-set structure, unless kinship takes precedence. Although it is possible for a man to avenge a breach of these patterns of behaviour by a curse, if it is a very serious breach, the ordinary sanctions of conduct are a man's conscience and desire for approval.

It will have been noted that the relations between the sets are defined in the idiom of family relationships. The members of a man's father's age-set are his 'fathers' and the members of his father's brothers' 'age-sets' are, in a less precise sense, also his 'fathers'. The sons of a man's set are his 'sons', and they may fall into several sets. The wives of members of a man's father's set are his 'mothers', and the wives of members of his sons' sets are his 'daughters'. All members of a man's own set are likewise 'brothers', though here the analogy is seldom expressed because the comradeship between age-mates is strongly affirmed in the idiom of the system, for they are all *ric*, age-mates, to one another. As, in any case, a man commonly addresses all persons much senior to himself as 'father' and 'mother', all persons much junior to himself as 'son' and 'daughter', and all persons of about the same age as himself as 'brother' and 'sister', the terminology of address between different sets is not a differentiating one and it cannot be said how far it is determined by specific age-set relationships. When speaking about sets senior to his own, but not that of his father or the set immediately senior to his own, a Nuer sometimes speaks about them collectively as though all their members were his fathers-in-law and their wives his mothers-in-law, for he is courting their daughters and is likely to marry one of them and so is circumspect in his dealings with their parents. Thus a *Lithgac* son of a *Maker* father regards members of the *Dangunga* set and their wives as potential fathers-in-law and mothers-in-law.

The age-set system thus influences persons through a kinship idiom and on the pattern of kinship. The sets never act corporately, but they function locally between individuals and, in ceremonial situations, between small aggregates of persons who live near to one another, for a man only has frequent contacts with those members of his set and of other sets who live in his district. No doubt relative positions in age-set structure to some extent determine behaviour between neighbours, and it can sometimes be observed that they determine it, but it is difficult to say to what extent, for men who live near one another are not only members of the same age-set or of different age-sets but are also kinsmen or affines. The age-set patterns of behaviour are, except in specific rites, of so general a nature that they cannot be isolated in a community where everyone is related in a number of different ways to everybody else. We have noted how persons who live together are always able to express their relations to one another in the language of kinship and how, when they are not actual kinsmen, they are recognized as equivalent to such by adoption or through some traditional, or mythological, connexion. The age-set stratification of all men, and by analogy all women, into groups whose inter-relations are on the pattern of family relationships is one of the ways by which community relations are expressed in kinship patterns and is comparable to the classificatory system of kinship nomenclature in its assimilation of social relations to a few elementary types. Age-relations are part of the general social ties of a kinship type which unite all persons living in a community. The members of a local group have group relations only with other groups of the same kind and it is these relations which we call political. They also have manifold contacts with one another—economic, ceremonial, food, play, and so forth—and political relations may be viewed as a specific organization of the texture of social ties, which control these contacts, in certain situations. It is this action of the age-set system, in establishing ties between members of local communities and in giving them a kinship value, that we chiefly stress in a political context rather than its indication of leadership, for outside small kinship and domestic groups the authority derived from seniority is negligible, and the sets lack leadership and administrative and judicial functions.

The age-set system has been briefly treated because of this action and also because, in the larger tribes at any rate, it is a tribal institution. It segments the male population of a tribe into stratified groups which stand in a definite relationship to one another and it cuts across territorial divisions, giving identity of status where there is political disparity and differentiating status where there is political identity. However, the political system and the age-set system do not seem to be interdependent. Both are consistent in themselves and to some extent overlap and influence one another, but it is easy to conceive of the political system existing without an age-set organization. There is evidence in East Africa that political development produces atrophy of the age-set organization. In conclusion we would again emphasize that adjacent tribes co-ordinate their sets and that the sets of any tribe are easily translated into the sets of another tribe. Initiation rites, more than anything save language, distinguish Nuer culture and give Nuer that sense of superiority which is so conspicuous a trait of their character. Only in the sense that age-sets are organized tribally and are common to all tribes can there be said to be a correspondence between the age-set system and the political system. There is no positive structural correspondence of the kind we have noted between the lineage system of dominant clans and tribal segmentation. It may be said, therefore, that whereas the political system and the lineage system of dominant clans are interdependent, the political system and the age-set systems are only a combination, in Nuer society. We may add that the common assumption that an age-set system merely by stratification integrates the members of a tribe has little to commend it.

V

In the way we have written this book we have in some measure broken away from the tradition of lengthy monographs on primitive peoples. These weighty volumes generally record observations in too haphazard a fashion to be either pleasant or profitable reading. This deficiency is due to absence of a body of scientific theory in Social Anthropology, for facts can only be selected and arranged in the light of theory. It is aggravated by the error of confusing documentation with illustration. We have also tried to describe Nuer social organization on a more abstract plane of analysis than is usual, for usually abstract terms are mistaken for abstractions. Whether we have succeeded in doing so is for the reader to judge, but in case it be said that we have only described the facts in relation to a theory of them and as exemplifications of it and have subordinated description to analysis, we reply that this was our intention.

It is difficult to know how far one is justified in pressing an abstraction. Once one has a theoretical point of view it is fairly simple to decide what facts are significant, since they are significant or otherwise to the theory, but it may be doubted whether it is wise, in discussing the political institutions of a primitive people, to give only the barest reference to their domestic and kinship life. Can this be done successfully? That is precisely the question we have asked ourselves, and we have concluded that an answer can only be given to it by making the attempt.

1. We first gave an account of Nuer absorption in their cattle and showed how this value in their system of oecological relations necessitates a certain mode of distribution and transhumance. We then described the concepts of time and space that arise very largely from ways of livelihood and disposition of settlements. We then examined the territorial sections which, through the values attached to them, form a political system. We further noted that structural distance in the lineage systems

of the dominant clans is a function of structural distance in the tribal systems and that there is no comparable interdependence between age-set structure and political structure.

2. By social structure we mean relations between groups which have a high degree of consistency and constancy. The groups remain the same irrespective of their specific content of individuals at any particular moment, so that generation after generation of people pass through them. Men are born into them, or enter into them later in life, and move out of them at death; the structure endures. In this definition of structure the family is not considered a structural group, because families have no consistent and constant interrelations as groups and they disappear at the death of their members. New families come into being, but the old for ever vanish. We do not suggest that the family is for this reason of less importance than structural groups; it is essential for the preservation of the structure, for it is the means by which new persons are born into its segments and the system is maintained. Nor do we suggest that the relations we consider structural are between groups that do not in any way vary. Territorial, lineage, and age-set systems change, but more slowly, and there is always the same kind of interrelationship between their segments. We do not, however, insist on this limiting definition of structure and our description and analysis do not depend on it.

3. Structural relations are relations between groups which form a system. By structure we therefore further mean an organized combination of groups. The territorial distribution of a Nuer tribe is not a haphazard aggregate of residential units, but every local group is segmented and the segments are fused in relation to other groups, so that each unit can only be defined in terms of the whole system. Similarly a lineage or age-set can only be defined in terms of the systems of which they form part. We have tried to show this in our account.

4. By structure we mean relations between groups of persons within a system of groups. We stress that it is a relation between groups, for relations between individuals may also be arranged on a regular plan, e.g., kinship relationships may be spoken of as a kinship system. By 'group' we mean persons who regard themselves as a distinct unit in relation to other

units, are so regarded by members of these other units, and who
all have reciprocal obligations in virtue of their membership of
it. In this sense a tribal segment, a lineage, and an age-set are
groups, but a man's kindred are not a group. A kinship relationship is a category and the kinship system a co-ordination of
categories in relation to an individual. In our opinion strangers
and Dinka ought to be described as persons of certain categories
rather than as members of social groups and that the relations
between them and aristocrats are not, strictly speaking, to be
described as structural relations.

5. The social structure of a people is a system of separate but
interrelated structures. This book deals mainly with the political
structure. Faced with the initial difficulty of defining what is
political we decided to regard the relations between territorial
groups as such, taking the village as our smallest unit, for
though a village is a network of kinship ties it is not a kinship
group, but a group definable only by common residence and
sentiment. We found that the complementary tendencies towards fission and fusion, which we have called the segmentary
principle, is a very evident characteristic of Nuer political structure. The lines of political cleavage are determined chiefly
by oecology and culture. Harsh environment together with
dominant pastoral interests cause low density and wide gaps in
the distribution of local communities. Cultural differences
between the Nuer and their neighbours also cause varying
degrees of political distance. Oecological and cultural relations
often combine to produce fission. In Nuerland itself culture is
homogeneous, and it is oecological relations that chiefly determine the size and distribution of segments.

6. These tendencies in, or principles of, political structure
control actual behaviour between persons through values. These
values appear contradictory. They are only seen to be consistent when we view structure as sets of relations defined by
reference to specific social situations. By political values we
mean the common feeling and acknowledgement of members of
local communities that they are an exclusive group distinct from,
and opposed to, other communities of the same order, and that
they ought to act together in certain circumstances and to observe
certain conventions among themselves. It does not follow that

behaviour always accords with values and it may often be found to be in conflict with them, but it always tends to conform to them.

7. Not only can we speak of the relations between territorial groups as a political system, the relations between lineages as a lineage system, the relations between age-sets as an age-set system, and so forth, but also in a society there is always some relationship between these systems in the whole social structure, though it is not easy to determine what this relationship is. We have shown that there is interdependence of a kind between the Nuer lineage system and their political system. This does not mean a functional relationship between clan groups and territorial groups, although they have a certain association, for clans, and even their lineages have no corporate life. Nor does it mean that when a man behaves in a certain way to a fellow clansman and in a different way to a fellow tribesman that there is a functional relationship between these two modes of behaviour. Nor, again, does it mean that there is a functional relationship between those members of a dominant clan who live in a tribe and the tribe of which they form part. But it means that there is structural consistency between the two systems—a consistency between abstractions. We are unable to show a similar interdependence between the age-set system and the political system.

8. Can we speak of political behaviour as a distinct type of social behaviour? We have assumed that certain activities, such as war and feuds, may be called political, but we do not consider that much is gained by so designating them. It is only on the more abstract plane of structural relations that a specific sphere of political relations can be demarcated. The behaviour of persons to one another is determined by a series of attachments, to family, joint family, lineage, clan, age-set, &c., and by kinship relationships, ritual ties, and so forth. These strands of relationships give to every man his sphere of social contacts. His field of actual contacts is limited; his field of potential contacts is unlimited. We distinguish a man's social sphere in this sense from structural space, the distance between social segments, which are groups of people who compose units in a system. We do not therefore say that a man is acting politically

or otherwise, but that between local groups there are relations of a structural order that can be called political.

9. We do not describe the different social ties which exist between persons living in the same district, but we may say that, in our view, the relations between this network of individual relationships, that together make up a community, and political structure, the relations that exist between territorial segments, present a problem of considerable importance, and we make some comments on it. (*a*) Social relationships are ordered by the political structure, so that a man's social sphere, and the joint social sphere of a number of persons living in the same village, tend always to be limited by the extension of their political groups. (*b*) Local communities, relations between which constitute the political structure, are only groups because of these many and varied relationships between the individuals who compose them. But it is the organization of these relationships into groups standing in a certain relation to one another within a system that interests us in our present discussion and we only study them in this organized form; just as one can, for certain purposes, study the relation between organs of the body without studying the interrelation of the cells that compose the organs. (*c*) In our view the territorial system of the Nuer is always the dominant variable in its relation to the other social systems. Among the Nuer, relationships are generally expressed in kinship terms, and these terms have great emotional content, but living together counts more than kinship and, as we have seen, community ties are always in one way or another turned into, or assimilated to, kinship ties, and the lineage system is twisted into the form of the territorial system within which it functions.

10. We have defined structure by what amounts to the presence of group segmentation and have discussed some Nuer systems from this point of view. We again emphasize that we do not insist on our definition and that we recognize that structure can be otherwise defined. But having so defined it, frequent allusion to a principle of contradiction in it was forced on us. To avoid misunderstanding, however, we would remark that the contradiction we have alluded to is on the abstract plane of structural relations and emerges from a systematization of

values by sociological analysis. It is not to be supposed that we mean that behaviour is contradictory or that groups stand in contradiction to one another. It is the relations of groups within a system that constitutes and exemplifies the principle. There may sometimes be conflict of values in the consciousness of an individual, but it is structural tension to which we refer. Likewise when we refer to the relativity of the structure we do not mean that a group is anything than an actual mass of people who can be seen and counted and plotted in space and time. We mean that on the plane of structural relations its position in a system is relative to the functioning of the system in changing situations.

11. Besides making a contribution to the ethnology of the Nilotes we have attempted in this book a short excursion into sociological theory, but we can only make a theoretical analysis up to a certain point, beyond which we perceive vaguely how further analysis might be made. Our experience in research and in writing this essay has intimated the lines of more extensive treatment. Social anthropology deals at present in crude concepts, tribe, clan, age-set, &c., representing social masses and a supposed relation between these masses. The science will make little progress on this low level of abstraction, if it be considered abstraction at all, and it is necessary for further advance to use the concepts to denote relations, defined in terms of social situations, and relations between these relations. The task of exploring new country is particularly difficult in the discipline of politics where so little work has been done and so little is known. We feel like an explorer in the desert whose supplies have run short. He sees vast stretches of country before him and perceives how he would try to traverse them; but he must return and console himself with the hope that perhaps the little knowledge he has gained will enable another to make a more successful journey.

INDEX